THE
GENIUS MYTH

ALSO BY HELEN LEWIS

Difficult Women
The Spark

THE GENIUS MYTH

A Curious History of a Dangerous Idea

HELEN LEWIS

THESIS

Thesis
An imprint of Penguin Random House LLC
1745 Broadway, New York, NY 10019
penguinrandomhouse.com

Copyright © 2025 by Helen Lewis

Penguin Random House values and supports copyright. Copyright fuels creativity, encourages diverse voices, promotes free speech, and creates a vibrant culture. Thank you for buying an authorized edition of this book and for complying with copyright laws by not reproducing, scanning, or distributing any part of it in any form without permission. You are supporting writers and allowing Penguin Random House to continue to publish books for every reader. Please note that no part of this book may be used or reproduced in any manner for the purpose of training artificial intelligence technologies or systems.

Thesis with colophon is a trademark of Penguin Random House LLC.

Most Thesis books are available at a discount when purchased in quantity for sales promotions or corporate use. Special editions, which include personalized covers, excerpts, and corporate imprints, can be created when purchased in large quantities. For more information, please call (212) 572-2232 or e-mail specialmarkets@penguinrandomhouse.com. Your local bookstore can also assist with discounted bulk purchases using the Penguin Random House corporate Business-to-Business program. For assistance in locating a participating retailer, e-mail B2B@penguinrandomhouse.com.

ISBN 9798217178575 (hardcover)
ISBN 9798217178582 (ebook)

Printed in the United States of America
1st Printing

The authorized representative in the EU for product safety and compliance is Penguin Random House Ireland, Morrison Chambers, 32 Nassau Street, Dublin D02 YH68, Ireland, https://eu-contact.penguin.ie.

For Rob and Alex

Contents

Introduction   1

PART ONE
Myth-making

Avonian Willy   11
Secular Saints   21
Galton's Good Breeding   37
Terman's Termites   51
Cyril and Hans: Twin Flames   63
William Shockley and the Genius Sperm Bank   83
Marilyn and Me   105

PART TWO
The Myths of Genius

So You Want to Be a Genius?   121
The Rebel   137
Monsters and Tortured Artists   151
Great Wives   169
Keepers of the Flame   187
A Cover Version   201
Alchemy   213
The Deficit Model   229

PART THREE
The Birth of the Modern Genius

Disruptors	243
Thomas Edison: The Lightbulb Moment	249
Elon Musk: Extremely Hardcore	261
Conclusion: An Idea That Won't Stay Dead	279
Acknowledgements	285
References	289
Sources and Further Reading	303

INTRODUCTION

'"Greatness" may be out of fashion, as is the transcendental, but it is hard to go on living without some hope of encountering the extraordinary.'

Harold Bloom, *Genius*

I apologize in advance. There is nowhere to start this book except with Elon Musk, perhaps the most overexposed man in human history – someone who might have gone down in history as a space pioneer who tried to get humanity to Mars, or as the innovator who made owning an electric car seem like an adventure rather than a penance. In other words, a genius.

Musk could have died a hero, toasted by environmentalists, entrepreneurs, and kids who dream of becoming astronauts. Instead, he has lived long enough to become a villain (at least to liberals). After he took over Twitter and turned it into his personal megaphone, Musk spent the next few years demolishing the mythology he had attracted during his early career. The man who bragged about his work ethic, including tales of how he used to sleep in the office because he was so 'hardcore', could be seen by the whole world blasting out jokes, memes and insults day and night. He sent a hundred posts a day on average during his first two weeks spearheading a government efficiency drive. (Ironically, any consultant brought in to make Musk's own companies more efficient might reasonably have suggested that their chief executive focus harder on his actual job, rather than procrastinating online.)

Once we began to see Musk's taste for conspiracy theories and cringeworthy memes, the headlines about him changed. The most obvious question used to be: *what made Elon Musk such a genius?* Now the question is this: *is Elon Musk a genius at all – or just a lucky idiot?* Online, you regularly see suggestions that he only became rich because he inherited an emerald mine (he didn't) or that he took over Tesla, booted out its founders and took the title for himself (he did). Perhaps, like the unbearable billionaire Miles Bron in the satirical film *Glass Onion*, all his previous successes were built on lies?

None of these arguments are entirely fair, but you can see the appeal of them. They are attempts to reconcile the inarguable evidence of Musk's early triumphs with our newfound knowledge of the gullible, easily distracted and emotionally dysregulated lover of lame jokes who posts from his X account. 'Of all the remarkable people I've met, Elon is probably the most likely to remain a world-historical figure – despite his best efforts to become a clown', wrote his former friend Sam Harris in early 2025.[1] 'He is also the most likely to squander his ample opportunities to live a happy life, ruin his reputation and most important relationships, and produce lasting harm across the globe.' Harris conceded that he could not understand what had happened to the Musk he knew – to the extent he wondered if he ever knew Musk at all.

For the right, however, there is no contradiction. They embrace Musk's belief that the federal government can be 'disrupted' – that is, run like a Silicon Valley start-up, with slashed funding, deliberately impossible deadlines and a macho work ethic. They applaud his lack of concern for the potential consequences if he's wrong. This is risk-taking, this is innovation. As for toting around his toddler X in press conferences, or leaping around MAGA rally stages like a spawning salmon, he is a genius, and geniuses are allowed to be a little bit eccentric. Here is the 'superman' imagined by the philosopher Friedrich Nietzsche, unbound by rules, propriety and perhaps even morality, utterly different from the passive, conformist herd of 'learned cattle' that makes up the universities, the media and the

INTRODUCTION

Deep State. The ubermensch is a being of pure action, a man who makes things happen. This is undeniably a true description of Musk.

To me, though, both approaches are flawed – and that's what this book is about. The argument over whether Elon Musk is a genius is really an argument about what our society *values*, and what it is prepared to *tolerate*. A suite of behaviours that would otherwise be inexcusable are forgiven when they are the price of greatness. The right wants to exaggerate his achievements for their own political ends. The left wants to denigrate them for the same reason. The final outcome of the referendum on Musk – eccentric and extraordinary, or overhyped and overindulged? – will also be a victory for the political tendency that promoted it.

My own view of Musk is closest to that of his biographer Walter Isaacson, who has said that his subject is 'a genius when it comes to material properties, when it comes to engineering' but 'not a genius' when it comes to 'human emotions'.[2] Personally, I would go further: Musk has qualities that made him perfectly suited for success in a particular place and time – the American tech scene in the early twenty-first century. An extreme tolerance for risk, a willingness to break the rules and an ability to master technical knowledge quickly, among others. Would he have been a world-changing figure in fifteenth-century Milan, or present-day Mali, or if he had been born among the Inca or Inuits? Probably not. (You can just as easily imagine him being the kind of advisor who assured the king his latest military innovation was ready to use when it wasn't, and got his head cut off as a result.) I'm happy to grant him *acts* of genius, but I am wary of describing any person as a 'genius.' That is, a member of a special and superior class of people. This is the genius myth, and it's what I want to demolish in this book.

So am I sharpening my axe to destroy the concept of individual achievement altogether? No, of course not. Because we all hunger to experience the transcendent, the extraordinary, the inexplicable. And that is what geniuses offer us. 'Once you saw phoenixes', writes

3

Ralph Waldo Emerson in his 1841 essay *Uses of Great Men*, 'they are gone; the world is not therefore disenchanted.'[3] Instead of animals that burst into flame, we have people who burn a little more brightly than those around them.

The ancient Greeks had a word, *deinos*, that meant both wonderful and terrible – awe-inspiring in its original sense. The conservative philosopher Edmund Burke, writing around the time of the French Revolution, echoed this by creating a division between the 'sublime' and the 'beautiful'. Anyone could appreciate the easy beauty of a waterfall or a watercolour, but he felt that we needed another category for objects or events that were 'productive of the strongest emotion which the mind is capable of feeling'. Encountering genius can feel like that – that vertiginous falling-away as you contemplate an artwork, or an equation, or a new concept . . . and have no idea how it was created by a human brain. Haven't you felt it, looking at van Gogh's almond blossom, or counting up the words Shakespeare gifted us, or listening to Mozart, or looking down at the earth from an aeroplane window, realising that tonnes of metal and flesh are resting on nothing but air? How did the Wright brothers do it – how did they *know* to do it?

I'm not such an iconoclast that I'm going to argue that talent doesn't matter – if you gave me a thousand years and the best teachers in the world I could still never paint like Monet or make a breakthrough in quantum physics. But something else is going on when an individual is anointed as a *genius*. For a start, that person is now assigned to a special category, somewhere between secular saint and superhero – and the reflected glow burnishes all their other achievements and opinions. (This is particularly troublesome when so many geniuses have also done and said extremely dumb, hurtful or discriminatory things.) As an onlooker, bestowing the word turns a subjective assessment – 'I like this' – into something that masquerades as objective fact. A natural phenomenon. An unavoidable, immutable truth.

INTRODUCTION

Oh, and one other thing – since so many talented people are weird, genius becomes a licensing scheme for their eccentricities. Genius transmutes *odd* into *special*.

This book focuses on the West, loosely defined, because this is where the double-edged concept of the individual genius was born. In Greek times, the word *genius* meant a visiting spirit – *you* weren't a genius, but one might speak through you. Socrates talked about the *daimonion* that guided him (a word that is the ancestor of our *demon*, but without the explicit connotation of evil). For Romans, inspiration might come from *furor divinus* (divine fury) or *furor poeticus* (possession by a poetic muse). They gave us the word *genius*, which means something between 'creator' and 'guardian spirit'. Roman authors argued that certain types of people were more likely to possess genius (unsurprisingly, these were men rather than women, and Roman citizens rather than slaves), but the word had not yet acquired its individualistic modern overtones. In the centuries following the collapse of the Roman Empire, the Jewish and then Christian traditions assigned the power of creation to God – and usurping his power was unwise.

In the Renaissance, however, the idea of 'great men' took hold, in the form of artists and sculptors. By the time of the Romantics in the eighteenth century, this new sense of the word had taken over: genius went from something a person *had* to something a person *was*. That switch matters, because it feeds the dark side of the genius myth: the idea of special people, a class above the rest. And it sets us up to be disappointed – how did *this thing* I love come from *this person* I deplore?

This book starts off by tracing this shift, through the first biographies of great men, on to the birth of the 'tortured genius' in the 1700s, and then into the IQ obsession of the late nineteenth century. If this book had an alternative title, it would be *Special People*. This is what I find poisonous about the idea of the genius – that people who succeed wildly in one domain stop thinking of themselves as any combination of talented, lucky and hardworking, and instead come to imagine that they are a superior sort of human. If you've ever watched a supposed 'public intellectual' express a political opinion so basic and uninformed it makes your teeth ache – perhaps one unknowingly formed in the crucible of their own limited personal experience – you will know what I mean.

On which point, a brief and uncharacteristic moment of personal humility by me. The focus in the following pages is undeniably eclectic, led by my own interests and knowledge (or rather, lack of knowledge). There are gaps in my brain, and this is an undoubtedly idiosyncratic book as a result. I'm more comfortable writing about artists and scientists than musicians and athletes, so my examples skew towards the former.

We will spend a lot of time on the development of IQ testing, and its effects and legacy, because this is the perfect distillation of the 'special people' thesis. Does someone with an IQ of 140 necessarily have better, more informed opinions on X or Y than someone with an IQ of 139? Clearly not. The precision is spurious and misleading. Can the social worth of human beings be neatly ranked by their ability to rotate shapes or find analogies? No. But something about IQ encourages these faulty ways of thinking. It can't be a coincidence that the political tendencies that most champion IQ online are full of people with the exact type of abilities that IQ tests reward.

The second section looks at some of the individual genius myths, and how they are sustained – whether by the estates of great artists or the biopic industry. I'll also take a step back from the portrait of the genius and see what's just outside the frame: the support staff, if you will. One of the shocks here will be that you don't even need to achieve great success to benefit from the genius myth – like the avant-garde British theatre director Chris Goode, it can be enough simply to fall into one of its pre-made patterns.

And finally, I want to look at the dominant model of genius today – the tech genius, the Prometheus, the innovator, the savant who can't make small talk but could dream in algorithms. I believe that Elon Musk is the reincarnation of Thomas Edison – not in a spooky way, but in the sense that their fame tells the same story about the culture that created it. Edison was called the Wizard of Menlo Park, and reporters besieged him to seek his views on God and the future of humanity. Musk talks grandly about dying on Mars (between endless posts on his own social media service) and believes that he can run a government better than any bureaucrat. Both have moved (or moved themselves) into that category of 'special person'.

But first, let's understand that geniuses do not just happen. No matter how talented a person is, to be accepted as a genius, they need a story to be woven around them. A genius myth. Consider, for example, the greatest English writer of them all: William Shakespeare.

PART ONE

Myth-making

Avonian Willy

'He thinks too much. Such men are dangerous.'

Julius Caesar, Act 1, Scene 2

How did Shakespeare become Shakespeare? It's not a trick question. When William Shakespeare died in 1616, at the age of fifty-two, he was a popular (and populist) playwright. But he was not an icon in the sense we would recognise – known to everyone, pored over by scholars, on the lips of every successor in his field. Today, there are specialised Shakespeare companies all over the world, including one – based at the Globe on London's South Bank – that tries to recreate the original performances as authentically as possible. The English town of Stratford-upon-Avon has become a shrine to his memory: you can visit two houses where he lived, as well as his wife's cottage, even though the man himself spent his working life in London.

All this acclaim is deserved, in my opinion. If anyone can be called a *genius*, it is William Shakespeare. He was a brilliant innovator, a fountain of creativity, a writer with an extraordinary gift for coining new words and phrases. I bet that in the last week you have heard or used a phrase that was gifted to us by Shakespeare. Perhaps you were 'eaten out of house and home' (*Henry IV, Part 2*), or fell victim to the 'green-eyed monster' (*Othello*). Shakespeare gave his characters an inner life that must have been awe-inspiring to audiences raised on passion plays and other religious pageants. In *Hamlet*, perhaps his greatest play, he gave us a puzzling protagonist and an ambiguous text that still prompts debate among directors and actors.

Shakespeare deserves his place in history, then. But still – how did he get there? Plenty of talented writers and artists are briefly fashionable without receiving the kind of veneration given to Shakespeare across the centuries. What separates Shakespeare from the rest is that a group of people *worked* to preserve his memory and celebrate his achievements. Seven years after his death, two of his fellow actors, John Heminges and Henry Condell, put together the 'first folio' of his plays. Both men were personal friends of Shakespeare, and he remembered them both in his will. In the Folio, they declared that they wanted to 'keepe the memory of so worthy a friend and fellow worker alive as was our Shakespeare'.

Their devotion is our great good luck: without the First Folio, eighteen of the plays – including *The Tempest* and *Macbeth* – would have been lost. That Shakespeare's legacy came so close to annihilation is revealing. Today, plays such as *King John* and *Double Falsehood* are scoured for any trace of the great man's input. Back then, it took two personal friends of Shakespeare to preserve his canon. For the first half of the seventeenth century, although Shakespeare was admired, he was not generally seen as the undisputed star among his contemporaries, let alone the greatest writer in the English language.

So what changed? The rise and fall of Puritanism helped. When theatres reopened in England after the Civil War and the reign of the Cromwells, the entrepreneurs who ran them had a problem. They didn't have enough newly commissioned plays to meet popular demand. So they turned to the old favourites – like Shakespeare – rewritten and restaged to suit the new mood. One of those impresarios was William Davenant, who liked to encourage speculation that he was Shakespeare's illegitimate son. Davenant loved spectacle, and he approached the texts with exactly zero reverence. He decided to have the witches in *Macbeth* 'whizzing through the air'.[1] He restructured the plots. He cut out the unfunny 'funny' bits. He renamed *Measure for Measure* to make it clear that romance was involved – it became *The Law Against Lovers* – and even rewrote lines that he felt needed punching up. (*Macbeth*'s 'screw your courage to the sticking place' became 'bring but your courage to the fatal place'.) Davenant also produced what one modern critic called 'a memorably ghastly Restoration version of *The Tempest*'.[2] Caliban got a sister. Ariel zipped around on a wire, and the whole thing was topped off with an orchestra and a ballet company.

Today, this sort of thing prompts strong letters to the newspapers about disrespecting a national icon. But the carefree Restoration attitude to Shakespeare kept his work alive – as did the later changes, such as the infamous seventeenth-century decision to give *King Lear* a happy ending. Shakespeare's plays survived precisely because they were not treated like the best china, brought out with kid gloves, to be admired on high days and holidays. They were raw clay, to be moulded into whatever audiences wanted to see.

But there was a problem. Who wrote all this great stuff, anyway? Audiences wanted to know. They weren't content with appreciating the work. They wanted to idolise the man, too.

In 1709, long after anyone who had known Shakespeare personally was dead, Nicholas Rowe produced a forty-page account of his life. This remained the standard text for a century, but it was sketchy and light on details. In the centuries since, more has been discovered, but nowhere near enough to satisfy demand. The absence of biographical data has driven some Shakespeare enthusiasts mad – they want the plays to have been written instead by a knowable aristocrat such as the Earl of Oxford, or a woman. The belief that Shakespeare didn't write Shakespeare's plays is surprisingly widespread, taking in everyone from the actor Derek Jacobi to the Supreme Court judge Sandra Day O'Connor, via Sigmund Freud and Malcolm X. The deaf-blind writer Helen Keller thought Francis Bacon wrote them. 'You think about a man basically with a second-grade education wrote some of the greatest poetry of all time?' joked the comedian Robin Williams to Johnny Carson in 1991. 'I think maybe not.'

At the other extreme, some Shakespeare fanatics have fallen prey to 'bardolatry', the practice of treating every object and place related to Shakespeare with the reverence of a medieval Catholic towards a fragment of the true Cross. If you want to mark the moment that Shakespeare had geniusdom thrust upon him, then look to a single year: 1769. That was when the actor David Garrick staged a Jubilee Festival in Stratford to celebrate the author's (presumed) birthday. The three-day extravaganza was completely absurd. There were verses addressed to 'Avonian Willy'. Stratford residents charged visitors to use their loos. And an extraordinary range of merch went on sale, from handkerchiefs to ribbons.[3] Relics from the mulberry tree in Shakespeare's garden were particularly popular; they were made into everything from toothpicks to inkhorns.

The only thing missing from all this was . . . Shakespeare. None of his plays were performed at the jubilee. Instead, attendees were treated to Garrick delivering an ode to the writer, set to music by the same composer who gave us 'Rule, Britannia!'. 'It is no wonder that he should endeavour to make a god of Shakespear since he has usurped the office of his High-priest; and has already gained money enough by it, to make a golden calf,' wrote Garrick's contemporary Charles Macklin.[4] That's one good reason to anoint a genius: you can siphon off some of the money and acclaim for yourself. At the same time, England gained a national poet – Shakespeare was the greatest writer of all time, and naturally, he wrote in English, the greatest language in the world.

And once established in England, bardolatry could be exported elsewhere. Shakespeare's works travelled to America and to the outposts of the British Empire. During Britain's imperial phase, the worship of Shakespeare carried an argument smuggled within it: how could a small, damp country in the North Sea claim such importance in the world? Because it was the land of Shakespeare. And Shakespeare himself knew England's worth: this 'jewel set in a silver sea'. Shakespeare might have started out writing for the groundlings, but he ended up working for the Warwickshire Tourist Board.

If Shakespeare has bardolatry, then Albert Einstein has 'priests' who guard his legacy – and who prevented the existence of his first child being revealed until 1986, nearly thirty years after his death. Pablo Picasso's heirs are still scrapping over the spoils of his estate. 'The word "genius", which experts on Picasso love to use, annoys me and makes me indignant,' his granddaughter Marina once wrote.[5] 'The Picasso name – the name I bear – has become a trademark. It's in the windows of perfume and jewellery shops, on ashtrays, ties and T-shirts. You can't turn on the television without seeing a robot airbrushing the signature Picasso on the side of a car.' (This is not an exaggeration: in the 1990s, the Picasso estate licensed his name to the French carmaker Citroën.) During his lifetime, Picasso was aware that everything he touched had value. Marina recalls him making paper animals for her as a child, but then refusing to let her take them home: 'They're the work of Picasso.'

A genius can be used to sell books, or cars, or toys, or really any kind of crap. When Einstein died in 1955, he left his copyright to Hebrew University in Jerusalem, and in the 1980s, the institution began to license his image rights, too; the university has now earned an estimated $250 million from doing so. Einstein was a genius, but he's also big business. In the 2000s, Disney licensed the name from the estate for $2.66 million to create 'Baby Einstein' toys designed to make your kid smarter. A programme to encourage African intellectuals is called the 'Next Einstein Forum'. An actor styled as Einstein recently popped up in a Super Bowl commercial to plug the telecom company Verizon. In Britain, Einstein's image is used to sell 'smart' electricity meters. Having a shorthand for 'clever person' is working out well for companies who want to flatter their customers or embellish their products.

Today, the word *genius* has been utterly devalued by its use as a branding tool. When my latest Apple purchase mysteriously ceases to work after three years, as it usually does, I take it to the Genius Bar, where an earnest hipster in a roll-neck can diagnose the problem. The web address Genius.com takes me to a lyrics site where I can find out whether Taylor Swift really is singing about being a sexy baby (she is). The Genius Brand is a supplements company, which sells 'nootropic supplements offer[ing] a safe, natural way to unlock the inner Genius each of us has.*' (The asterisk leads to a disclaimer noting that the products 'are not intended to diagnose, treat, cure, or prevent any disease'.)

So the idea of *genius* is ambient. But what about the individual cases? What is the process by which a playwright from the Midlands becomes England's national writer – or a stateless physicist becomes shorthand for 'smart'? Here's my argument. Because there is no objective definition of genius – and there never can be – societies anoint exceptional people as geniuses to demonstrate what *they* value. We call some people 'special' to demonstrate what *we* find special. And in turn, we give those special people latitude that is not extended to ordinary mortals. We have a set of stories about what geniuses are, and how they work, and how singular their achievements are – stories that are often entirely untrue.

This book is called *The Genius Myth* not to imply that genius doesn't exist, but to explore those stories as a form of myth-making. 'A person's right to be considered a "genius" by posterity is influenced by quite irrelevant factors,' wrote the psychologist Hans Eysenck, a troublesome character to whom we will return later, in his book *Genius*. 'He is more likely to be called a "genius" if he behaves oddly, dies young or very old, has episodes of madness, is psychopathic in his relations with others, disregards normal restrictions, and generally lives up to the stereotype of genius people have in their minds.'

To put it another way: *why is Elon Musk better known than Tim Berners-Lee?* As I am writing this, Elon Musk is unavoidable: he runs a dozen companies, and uses one of them, X, to blast his thoughts out into the world on an hourly basis. He is the subject of a biography by Walter Isaacson, who previously wrote about Leonardo da Vinci, Benjamin Franklin, Albert Einstein and Steve Jobs. (Isaacson convinced Jobs to grant him access by pointing out the company he would be in. You have to assume the same trick worked on Musk.) At every turn, Musk has sought out opportunities to self-mythologise, and he is now one of the leading candidates for our modern idea of a genius. Yet Tim Berners-Lee is the more original thinker, and his breakthrough in creating the World Wide Web has been more important. Every internet-era innovation, from smartphones to ChatGPT, rests on there being an internet at all. (There's a picture that does the rounds every so often, of Berners-Lee speaking on a news programme, where he is described as 'web developer'. The joke is that it makes him sound like a hobbyist reskinning WordPress templates, whereas he is literally the man who developed the concept of the World Wide Web.) Without Tim Berners-Lee, there would have been no Twitter for Elon Musk to ruin.

Now, Berners-Lee has no shortage of recognition – a knighthood, numerous advisory board positions, a fellowship at Oxford University – and he is widely celebrated within his own field. But he lives a quiet life, has not tried to make himself upsettingly rich and has never broken through into public consciousness in the way that Elon Musk has.

Here's one way to understand the difference between the two men, and it's key to the argument of this whole book. Berners-Lee describes his work like this:

> Most of the technology involved in the web, like the hypertext, like the Internet, multifont text objects, had all been designed already. I just had to put them together. It was a step of generalising, going to a higher level of abstraction, thinking about all the documentation systems out there as being possibly part of a larger imaginary documentation system.[6]

Did your eyes begin to skim that passage? Go on, admit it. They did. Berners-Lee is self-deprecating and technical, whereas Elon Musk does things like change the Twitter press office autoresponse to a poop emoji or insist that he will die on Mars. Elon Musk fires rockets into space, builds fast cars and tells people to leave his company if they are not 'extremely hardcore'. (More on that later.) He performs the cultural role of genius with apparent enthusiasm: saying odd and provocative things, espousing extreme work habits, maintaining an unusual personal life, drawing attention to himself with salty tweets. Love him or hate him, we can't stop talking about him.

Let me put it another way. Elon Musk has more than a dozen

children, with names like X Æ A-Xii and Exa Dark Sideræl. Tim Berners-Lee's children are called Alice and Ben.

We *want* great achievements to have been accomplished by unusual people – something about it feels cosmically just. And we hunger to know the details of their lives: their sleep patterns, their love lives, the moment that inspiration struck. We want to marvel at greatness, but we also want to wallow in gossip. And one man realised that long before everyone else. Let's meet him next.

Secular Saints

'Jealousy is the tribute mediocrity pays to genius.'
Fulton J. Sheen, attributed

Giorgio Vasari was a good artist. The Medicis employed him as a sculptor and architect. He designed the loggia for the Uffizi in Florence, part of his grand project of establishing the city as an artistic centre.* He designed cupolas and painted Madonnas, built corridors and sculpted saints. Had he lived in another age, he might be remembered as one of its most successful artists. But you have to feel a little bit sorry for Vasari, because he lived through one of the greatest flourishings of art and culture that the world has ever seen. The Renaissance.

As it happens, we have Vasari to thank for the word itself. He became the chronicler of this exceptional period of European history, which he called the *rinascita* (rebirth) of the classical tradition, after centuries of stagnation. This was the era of Michelangelo, Leonardo, Raphael, Donatello.† As these artists revived the arts of painting, sculpture and architecture, Vasari revived the Ancient Greek practice of hagiography, or 'writing about holy ones'. His lasting achievement is a book published in two editions,

---

* Perhaps you don't know, as I didn't, that 'Uffizi' translates as 'offices'.

† And other artists who weren't also Ninja Turtles, although those are always the ones who spring to mind.

which was called *The Lives of the Most Excellent Painters, Sculptors, and Architects*. You can trace many well-known stories about artists of the era to Vasari: Brunelleschi and the egg, Michelangelo's revolting boots, or the tale of how Verrocchio quit painting after being outstripped by his teenage pupil Leonardo da Vinci.

Vasari was born in 1511, in Arezzo, near Florence – and his work often tips into pro-Tuscan propaganda. His *Lives* promotes Leonardo and Michelangelo, and their work in the region, and deprecates Titian, born at the foot of the Alps and working in Venice. (Vasari did this even though he and Titian were friends.) The narratives created by Vasari, and the hierarchy he championed, persists today. 'The way you think of art is largely due to Vasari, whether or not you realise it, and whether or not you've actually read his book,' his biographers claim.[1] Until Vasari came along, most biographers recorded the lives of aristocrats. He broke with tradition by focusing on artists, who were 'manual workers with a spotty education and intensive technical training: by conventional standards, the meanness of their hardscrabble, hardworking lives could hold no interest for aristocratic writers and readers'.* Vasari wanted the project to be democratic: he wrote in the Tuscan dialect – an everyday language – rather than the more elite Latin. He wanted it to be comprehensive: its first word is 'Adam' and the last is 'death'. And he was always fascinated by innovation: we hear about Michelangelo designing his own scaffold to paint the Sistine Chapel, and the breakthrough that allowed sculptors to work in a dense stone called porphyry.

Surprisingly, given the exclusion of female artists from the

---

* Many of the artists themselves were illiterate. Even Leonardo da Vinci, one of the greatest polymaths of all time, owned only 116 books, according to the Codex he kept.

canon in the subsequent centuries, Vasari featured several women, including the Anguissola sisters and Properzia de' Rossi. Sofonisba Anguissola was one of the most successful artists of the era, serving as a tutor to the Spanish queen Elisabeth of Valois, and court painter to Philip II, before eventually dying at the age of ninety-three. But she is now largely forgotten.

The one female artist of the Renaissance who is remembered was born too late for Vasari to include: Artemisia Gentileschi, who has recently been the subject of exhibitions, plays and movies. Gentileschi's reputation has prospered in the twenty-first century because she comes with a readymade feminist legend: she was raped by her father's apprentice, and testified against him in court – risking her artist's hands under the thumbscrews to prove she was telling the truth. (Afterwards, she supposedly used her rapist's face as the model for Holofernes, whose head is cut off by the biblical heroine Judith.) I love Gentileschi's paintings, which have a sinuous softness to them and an exquisite use of light. Her Judith is also really hacking at Holofernes' neck – this is no delicate maiden afraid to get her hands bloody, but a steady-gripped butcher. But there is no denying that the story of her rape has become central to her mythology: she is now the heroine for every slighted woman. We love a bittersweet genius story, and hers is that she turned a sexual assault into great art. Sofonisba Anguissola's life and work cannot be reduced to a parable like this, and so she has not been reclaimed and promoted in the same way.

Vasari would have recognised this process, because he was an inveterate myth-maker. In fact, the whole project of acclaiming geniuses is rather like painting a portrait: an entire life and personality is honed down to key details. The idea that artists should be judged on their political appeal seems unfair, but it is an undeniable part of the story of genius. Biographies become morality tales. And *that* tendency is due in a large part to Vasari. He pioneered the idea of life-writing as a fable, following in the tradition of Aesop and Ovid, where the particulars of a story are employed to illustrate a theme.

Take the famous story of the Florentine architect Filippo Brunelleschi, which Vasari tells in his *Lives*. Artists have gathered from across Europe to discuss how to build a dome on the cathedral at the centre of Florence. There are many problems: the weight of the cupola, the lack of support from pillars at the side, the difficulty of building a framework. But Brunelleschi tells the city consuls that he has an answer to all these problems. They laugh at him.

Brunelleschi becomes angry, and rants about all the other problems the wardens haven't even considered, before being carried out by stewards. He doesn't even show them his plan. Then he proposes a test to demonstrate who has the ability to build the cupola: whoever can make an egg stand upright on the marble floor should get the job. All the other artists try to balance the egg on its end, and fail.

> Then they passed it to Filippo, who lightly took it, broke the end with a blow on the marble and made it stand. All the artists cried out that they could have done as much themselves, but Filippo answered laughing that they would also know how to vault the cupola after they had seen his model and design.[2]

This is a parable about trust – and about elitism. Brunelleschi was arrogant, unwilling to submit his designs to swine who couldn't appreciate them. His arrogance was justified, however, because he could hit a target others could not see. The mythological point of the story is that bureaucrats and second-raters shouldn't question a genius. Their job is to accept his superior knowledge, and acquiesce.

Vasari's *Lives* included serious artistic criticism and authoritative lists of great works. But from the start, what readers loved was the gossip and the personalities. Who wouldn't want to hear about impassioned rivalries and brave men arguing with the pope?

His great hero was Michelangelo, whom he describes as being of middle height, thin, with white-flecked black hair – and utterly devoted to art. Vasari's Michelangelo didn't care much about food or wine. He sometimes slept in his clothes. He wore his dog-leather boots for so long that when he eventually took them off, his skin came off, too. And he was a prodigy, once redrawing his tutor Domenico's outline of a woman: 'The difference between the two styles is as marvellous as the audacity of the youth whose good judgement led him to correct his master.'[3] (Remember: special allowances must be made for a genius, even if he is rude or arrogant.)

Vasari turns Michelangelo's life into a morality tale. He only gets to paint the Sistine Chapel ceiling because his rival Bramante knows that the Pope prefers sculptures to paintings. So Bramante recommends Michelangelo, a talented sculptor, for a job that will see him tied up for years holding a paintbrush. (The moral being that squalid motives rebound on you.) The bittersweetness regularly found in genius myths comes from the discomfort that Michelangelo suffers from painting above his head, tiring his muscles and injuring his eyesight. Vasari then adds, somewhat bathetically, 'I suffered similarly when doing the vaulting of four large rooms in the palace of Duke Cosimo.'[4] Nonetheless, the result is extraordinary – and Michelangelo is hailed as *il divino* – the divine one. The closeness of genius and God is evident to onlookers.

Michelangelo, then, is portrayed by Vasari as a single-minded art monk. What about his contemporary Leonardo da Vinci? In *Lives*, he becomes another archetype of genius: the scatter-brained polymath.

The young Leonardo was beautiful, 'marvellous and divine,' writes Vasari, and 'would have made great profit in learning had he not been so capricious and fickle, for he began to learn many things and then gave them up.'[5] Like Michelangelo, Leonardo is a prodigy who quickly outstrips his teacher, Andrea del Verrocchio. Soon after, Leonardo's father Piero asks him to paint something on wood to give to one of his tenant-farmers, and the young man studies 'lizards, newts, maggots, snakes, butterflies, locusts, bats and other animals of the kind, out of which he composed a horrible and terrible monster'. When his father asks to see the painting, still not knowing its subject, Leonardo arranges it on an easel and beckons his father into the room. 'Ser Piero, taken unaware, started back, not thinking of the round piece of wood, or that the face which he saw was painted.'[6] (The pupil who outdoes the master, and the painter whose talent creates freakishly realistic figures, are two of Vasari's favourite narratives.)

Recounting Leonardo's death, the biographer returns to his theme of wasted potential. When the King of France arrives to pay him a visit, Leonardo 'sat up in bed from respect, and related the circumstances of his sickness, showing how greatly he had offended God and man in not having worked in his art as he ought'.[7] He then suffers a 'paroxysm' and dies in the king's arms 'in the seventy-fifth year of his age'. The entire narrative is unlikely – there is no contemporary record of these events – but the point is to create a bittersweet legend of Leonardo's quicksilver brain. 'Thus, by his many surpassing gifts, even though he talked much more about his works than he actually achieved, his name and fame will never be extinguished.'

Why depict Leonardo like this? Michelangelo, who also worked across drawing, sculpture, anatomy, poetry, archaeology and museum curation, is not described as a scatter-brain. Because *the story is better this way*. It fits with our sense that Leonardo didn't leave much behind. The scrubby state of *The Last Supper*, caused by the artist's experimental decision to paint directly onto dry plaster, bolsters this argument: you can practically *feel* it crumbling off the wall.

One of the most human aspects of genius is that it is finite; it leaves us yearning for more. Take a step back, though, and it is strange to complain that a man who painted one *Mona Lisa* did not paint *two*.

Vasari's Leonardo demonstrates what I call the *deficit model of genius*, which suggests that exceptional talent extorts a price. (More on that later.) In the case of Leonardo, the price of his talent is a fatal lack of discipline. There will never be enough of him to satisfy us. Look what he did and then *imagine what he could have done*.* This mythology carries an emotional charge that a solid, thirty-year career in a single discipline could never replicate. This deficit model underpins the modern heirs of Vasari's *Lives*: Hollywood biopics. Today, we love to consume stories of tortured geniuses, thwarted geniuses, unfulfilled geniuses – geniuses who were too busy thinking about their work to change their socks.

One of the most enduring ideas we have inherited from Vasari's *Lives* is that genius shows itself early and decisively. There is some truth to this – research shows that mathematicians tend

---

* Terry Pratchett's satirical depiction of 'Leonard da Quirm' in the Discworld novels makes the mythology more obvious. His Leonard is tormented by the immense fertility of his own mind, waking up to sheets covered in scribbles. Sadly, most of his inventions are useless.

to do their best work before thirty – but the later careers of child prodigies are often tragically underwhelming. Scientists often do better in their mid-careers, with a 'hot streak' when they know enough about the discipline to have mastered it, but have not yet become bogged down in its shibboleths. Novelists can keep going for decades: witness Edna O'Brien, who published her first novel in 1960 and her final one in 2019. Some of the most creative and innovative people dart around in their early careers, 'sampling' different areas which interest them. Then they settle for a specialism, and drill deep into it, achieving success as late bloomers.

Yet Vasari's mythology of genius – of special people, not just inspired acts – is so compelling that his parade of prodigies is still the template for greatness. We instinctively feel that genius declares itself in childhood – that some people are marked from the start. We believe this so strongly, in fact, that the truth is sometimes subtly bent and twisted to fit the narrative. Take Carl Friedrich Gauss and the strange story of the school multiplication problem.

Gauss was born in 1777, to a working-class family which was perfectly normal in every way. His father Gebhard held various manual jobs, while his mother Dorothea could barely read. His brother George became a labourer. And yet Friedrich became one of the most brilliant mathematicians of his age. He invented the heliotrope, calculated the orbit of Ceres and developed an algorithm for determining the date of Easter.

Gauss is well-known inside mathematics, but he is not an A-list genius or obvious shorthand for cleverness like Newton or Einstein. Perhaps that's because he worked in several areas that are inaccessible to a lay audience – explaining his other breakthroughs would require mathematical notation and a facility for algebra, which is frankly beyond me. Or maybe the problem is that his childhood, while undoubtedly poor, lacks the kind of gothic details that make it appealing to genius-hunters. If you have heard of Gauss, it might be through a well-known story of his early brilliance. The tale runs roughly like this. At his schoolhouse, the teacher asked the boys to add up all the numbers from 1 to 100, write the answer on a slate and deliver it to the middle of the classroom. While the others struggled, the young Friedrich quickly deduced a formula which made it simple: 'fold' the numbers in the middle and add up each pair – 1 with 100, 2 with 99, 3 with 98. Each of these is 101, so the answer to the riddle is simply 50 x 101, or 5050. (The formula is $n(n + 1)/2$, where n is the highest number.) Friedrich wrote his answer down, took it to the middle of the class long before anyone else and astounded his teacher. Behold a wunderkind: talent hits the target; genius hits the target no one can see.

Stories like this are common in the literature of genius. They stick with us because they express something we believe to be true. Greatness is apparent early, and its possessors see things that the rest of us cannot. It feels nitpicking to ask the obvious question: did this actually happen? The answer is almost certainly no.

In 2006, the science journalist Brian Hayes hunted down the source of the Gauss tale, noting that 'I've been hearing about Gauss' schoolboy triumph since I was a schoolboy myself.'[8] Something about the story didn't make sense to him. Did the teacher already know the formula? If so, the story loses drama. Or was he adding up all the numbers individually, too? If so, he wasn't much of a maths teacher. Hayes tracked down a hundred examples of the Gauss narrative, in eight languages. All shared similarities – presumably because they all came from the same source – but were tweaked and padded out in different ways, as their authors filled in motivations and moral lessons. The story had undergone something like evolution by natural selection – twisting and turning to find the best form to survive.

Hayes traced the first appearance of the story back to 1856, the year after Gauss' death. It appeared in a memorial volume written by Wolfgang Sartorius, a fellow professor at the University of Göttingen. That version makes no mention of the idea of an arithmetical series, and merely has Gauss solving a problem as soon as the teacher states it, tossing his slate into the middle of the room. The idea of the 1–100 series first appears in a 1938 biography by Ludwig Bieberbach. Later versions make the numbers smaller, perhaps reasoning that adding up 1–100 was too big a task for seven-year-olds. The story really goes viral with its inclusion in Eric Temple Bell's 1937 work *Men of Mathematics* – a book almost as important to the mythology of maths as Vasari's *Lives* is to the arts. 'He turns the Braunschweig schoolhouse into a scene of gothic horror,' writes Hayes. Bell describes the teacher as a 'viral brute, one Büttner, whose idea of teaching the hundred or so boys in his charge was to thrash them into such a state of terrified stupidity that they forgot their own names.'[9] Modern versions of the story often follow this perfected version, adding an arrogant teacher getting his comeuppance – just like the disbelieving onlookers in the tale of Brunelleschi and the egg. *A child prodigy. His effortless dominance. The master overtaken by the apprentice. The sweet satisfaction of a bully meeting his match.*

Does it matter how this story has twisted and turned over the years? Hayes notes that in early versions, the teacher has a whip. But this detail peters out over the course of the twentieth century as readers get more squeamish. Later versions paint the task as 'busywork' to keep the pupils occupied. Every generation takes its own lessons from the story, and subtly alters the details to fit the spirit of the age. One constant remains, though: Gauss is always a prodigy, gifted from childhood with insights even his teacher cannot replicate. He solves the equation with a skill that is indistinguishable from magic.

That is a problem, though, because it reveals how the mythology of genius can be discouraging to anyone *not* anointed as brilliant. If talent is inborn rather than nurtured, how can a normal human compete with a genius? 'On first hearing this fable, most students surely want to imagine themselves in the role of Gauss,' writes Hayes. 'Sooner or later, however, most of us discover we are one of the less distinguished classmates.'

When you read Vasari, it takes a little while to notice what *isn't* there. His geniuses are strange, yes, and obsessive – but they are not *ill*. Nor do they lapse fully into madness. Those ideas were promoted heavily by members of a later movement, the Romantics. These writers and thinkers from the eighteenth century are responsible for the next development in our ideas of genius. They began to explore the notion that true inspiration could only be found in nature, and that a genius was therefore someone as close to nature as possible – a pure figure, with no one behind him, no context, no culture. Another related idea also emerged during this time: that libertine lifestyles, high-flown passions and the creation of great art all belonged together. 'We of the craft are all crazy,' wrote Lord Byron.

The Romans had noticed that great statesmen seemed prone to melancholy, and this idea was rediscovered by later writers. By 1681, John Dryden could write: 'Great wits are sure to madness near allied / And thin partitions do their bounds divide.' The birth of newspapers and journals in the next century allowed for real-time mythologising of famous artists. The reading public could now consume a poet's biography while he was still alive, bolstering the argument that these were special people, who could not be expected to endure bourgeois morality or mundane tasks.

They were free spirits, children of nature, and perhaps even sexually ambiguous.

Wider shifts in the culture helped to individualise the nature of genius. The mimetic art of the Renaissance – imitating the ancients – gave way to the idea of communing directly with nature. That increased the value of originality. The Industrial Revolution led to capitalism, and artists went from relying on patronage to competing in a marketplace. What we might now call 'branding' helped them stand out. The Enlightenment – an intellectual movement that emphasised reason and evidence – saw a decline in traditional religious beliefs which left a space for new secular saints. At the birth of America, the Founding Fathers asserted that 'all men are created equal'. That prompted the challenge: surely some men were more talented than others, more virtuous, more wise? 'Geniuses translated, decoded, and deciphered the mysteries of the universe . . . wonders themselves, they made the world wondrous again,' writes the American historian Darrin McMahon. 'Geniuses reassured that the universe was still a magical place'.[10]

Vasari's idea of innate talent was modified to promote the idea that the greatest geniuses were those people who were most uncorrupted by human society. They were somehow childlike. The French writer Jean-Jacques Rousseau's 1762 book *Emile, Or On Education* was incredibly influential. He argued that schooling ruined children's natural desire to explore, and turned them only into a mirror, reflecting back their teachers' and parents' words. 'Hold childhood in reverence, and do not be in any hurry to judge it for good or ill,' Rousseau wrote. 'Leave exceptional cases to show themselves, let their qualities be tested and confirmed, before special methods are adopted. Give nature time to work before you take over her business, lest you interfere with her dealings.'

Three decades later, this attitude bled through to Immanuel Kant's *The Critique of Judgement* (1790). He described genius as a 'natural gift' and added: 'Since talent, as the innate productive facility of the artist, belongs itself to nature, we may express the matter thus: Genius is the innate mental disposition through which nature gives the rule to art.' What Vasari would have called *God*, Kant calls *nature*; but these are two ways of expressing the same thought: that geniuses are set apart from the rest of humanity. Kant called them 'nature's elect'.

These European arguments were deeply influential in the new world, too. In 1854, the American writer Henry David Thoreau published *Walden*, an account of the two years he spent living in a self-built cabin in the Massachusetts woods. The Walden legend has been through three distinct phases: first, early readers lionised the author for going back to nature and living simply. This was the way for writers and thinkers to find profundity. Then, at the end of the twentieth century, feminist critics took to pointing out that Thoreau's return to nature did not stop him from having dinners with friends (the land was owned by his fellow writer Ralph Waldo Emerson) or getting someone else to do his washing. 'Quite a lot of people think that Thoreau was pretending to be a hermit in his cabin on Walden Pond,' wrote Rebecca Solnit. 'I did a quick online search and found a long parade of people who pretended to care who did Thoreau's laundry as a way of not having to care about Thoreau. They thought of Thoreau as a balloon and the laundry was their pin.'[11] Today, we are in a third phase, the backlash to the backlash, where people feel compelled to defend Thoreau from the charge of being a fraud. 'No other male American writer has been so discredited for enjoying a meal with loved ones or for not doing his own laundry,' wrote his biographer Laura Dassow Walls.[12] What all three eras share is a belief that the authenticity of Thoreau's solitude matters: the genius must return to nature.

The Romantics also developed the idea of *genius as an excuse*. In 1816, Lord Byron's outrageous behaviour – he had an affair with his half-sister – was so scandalous that it forced him to leave English society. But his misdemeanours soon became conscripted into the portrait of his genius, along with his mistress Caroline Lamb's pithy assessment that he was 'mad, bad and dangerous to know'. (He also helped out by dying young, at thirty-six – all those years of creativity lost.) Whatever Byron was, he wasn't *normal*. 'Certain life styles provide cover for deviant and bizarre behaviour,' writes the psychologist Kay Redfield Jamison.[13] 'The arts have long given latitude to extremes in behaviour and mood.' The Romantic poets used the idea of the mad genius to bolster their talent and status, and to claim an exemption from everyday morals.

We also have the Romantics to thank for the idea of the genius as a fey, otherworldly creature – thin to the point of insubstantial, feverish and delicate. Why might this be? Because those are all symptoms of tuberculosis, a lung disease which spread rapidly through the new, more densely populated towns and cities of the eighteenth century. Tuberculosis killed millions of people (and still does).* Also known as consumption, it came to be called 'the romantic disease'. While cancer became a metaphor for degeneration, Susan Sontag argued, tuberculosis was 'disintegration, febrilization, dematerialization'.[14] Lord Byron, who did not have TB, wanted to have it: 'How pale I look! – I should like, I think, to die of consumption.' His friend Tom Moore, who suffered

---

* Despite the discovery of antibiotics, TB killed around 1.3 million people worldwide in 2022, according to the World Health Organisation.

from the disease, asked him why. 'Because then the women would all say, "see that poor Byron – how interesting he looks in dying!"' (The poet John Keats, who *did* have TB, was under no illusions about what the blood in his handkerchief meant: 'I cannot be deceived in that colour; – that drop of blood is my death-warrant; – I must die.')

Tuberculosis is now rarer than it has ever been. But it was once unbearably common – and until the discovery of streptomycin in 1944, it was incurable. It was *the* Romantic disease, spread by modernity, through the air breathed by city dwellers living too close together, made worse by smog and industrial fumes. Once you understand how tuberculosis haunted the eighteenth and nineteenth centuries, you can see how it affected the Romantic idea of genius. The list of famous sufferers is extraordinary: the Brontës suffered from 'consumption'. So did the composer Frédéric Chopin, the eighteenth-century writers Laurence Sterne and Tobias Smollett, the illustrator Aubrey Beardsley, the muse and artist Elizabeth Siddal, the inventor Alexander Graham Bell, the scientist Anders Celsius, as well as Louis Braille, Schrödinger and Spinoza – even Immanuel Kant suffered from it as he tried to uncover the secrets of genius. The disease finished off George Orwell at forty-six, Anton Chekhov at forty-four, Franz Kafka at forty, Katherine Mansfield at thirty-four, and Elizabeth Barrett Browning at fifty-five. And those are just the cases that we are relatively sure about – until the TB bacillus was identified in 1882, the disease could be euphemised away as 'weak lungs' or 'wasting'.

This ubiquity is what made tuberculosis such a powerful Romantic metaphor for genius. It was a disease characterised by advance and relapse; it came and went with no clear pattern. The treatment was good air – a return to nature. It was also a disease of passion – 'afflicting the reckless and sensual,' Sontag writes – where flushed cheeks contrasted with snow-white skin. There was a gendered aspect to this, too: the illness separated male sufferers from the hearty, heterosexual ideal of manhood. A male TB patient was delicate like a woman. That fitted with the contemporary ideal of genius: a male body and brain fused with a female level of sensitivity. A genius was 'a male – full of "virile" energy – who transcended his biology'.[15] (Unsurprisingly, masculine women were not similarly lionised.)

The concept of a genius as strange, passionate, childlike and feminine (but not female) has never gone away. In June 1903, a twenty-three-year-old Austrian philosopher called Otto Weininger published *Sex and Character*, arguing that genius was confined to males. 'The man of genius possesses, like everything else, the complete female in himself; but women herself is only part of the Universe, and the part can never be the whole; femaleness can never include genius.'

No one lived their Romantic values quite like Otto Weininger. Four months after his book was published, he took a room in the Viennese guesthouse where Beethoven had died, asked the landlady not to disturb him until morning, and shot himself in the chest. His death was inexpressibly Romantic. His book, which had lukewarm reviews when first published, became a best-seller; Wittgenstein and Strindberg declared it a great influence on them; and several young men imitated his suicide. Madness, sexual ambiguity and an inability to live on this corrupted earth: Otto Weininger had fully internalised the Romantic conception of the genius.

But when he died, right at the start of the twentieth century, another set of ideas were gaining force, and the poets and philosophers were no longer in control of the conversation. Genius was about to encounter the new obsession with data.

Galton's Good Breeding

'Men who leave their mark on the world are very often those who, being gifted and full of nervous power, are at the same time haunted and driven by a dominant idea, and are therefore within a measurable distance of insanity.'

Francis Galton, *Hereditary Genius*

As the eighteenth century yielded to the nineteenth, Europe and America moved into the great age of classification – an era when it seemed as if the whole world could be itemised and pinned to a cork board like a rare beetle. The genius would be no exception.

The pioneer of this new approach was a brilliant and strange man called Francis Galton. Like many gentleman scholars of the age, he was obsessed with taxonomy. He wanted the world to be orderly and comprehensible – not messy like humans, whom he had trouble understanding.

Galton came from an intellectual, upper-middle-class family – his half-cousin was Charles Darwin. Both his grandfathers, Samuel Galton and Erasmus Darwin, were members of the 'Lunar Society of Birmingham', a club devoted to invention and innovation, alongside the engineer James Watt, the potter Josiah Wedgwood, and the chemist Joseph Priestley. (The Lunar Society met every month on the night of the full moon – when it was easiest to drive home.) But his own early years were unpromising.

His father wanted him to become a doctor, so he was sent to study at Cambridge, where he achieved only a second-class mark in his exams, and then had a mental breakdown. As soon as his father died in 1844, the young Francis abandoned medicine.

Galton seems to have combined a restless scientific curiosity with an almost total absence of human feeling. As a young man, he attended a slave market in Constantinople, writing home: 'If I had 50 pounds at my disposal I could have invested in an excessively beautiful one, a Georgian . . . most of the black ones were fettered, but they seemed very happy dancing and singing.'[1] By contrast, when his cousin Charles Darwin observed the slave trade up close, the experience drew him to the abolitionist cause. 'I was told before leaving England, that after living in Slave countries: all my opinions would be altered,' Darwin wrote to his sister Catherine in 1833. 'The only alteration I am aware of is forming a much higher estimate of the Negro's character.'[2]

The animal researcher Temple Grandin, who has autism, has an exquisite sense of animal moods but once confessed to looking at humanity like 'an anthropologist on Mars'.[3] Galton's memoirs have the same tone. Travelling through Europe, Asia and Africa, the scientist saw captivating sights, yet *nowhere* is there a hint of human connection. His African travels are almost laughably colonial. He ate rhino (delicious) and rejected a king's niece as 'I presume, a temporary wife' because she was covered in red ochre and he was wearing a white linen suit. Galton's time in Africa convinced him more than ever of European superiority.

On his return to Britain, he lived the life of a gentleman amateur, investigating any subject he found interesting. He has one of the most eclectic CVs of any human in history. He popularised the use of fingerprints in police work. He designed a pocket register to count crowd sizes, which used a fine needle to prick paper kept in compartments. He created a 'beauty map' of the British Isles, which gave top marks to London and bottom ones to Aberdeen. He outlined the concept of 'correlation', one of the building blocks of modern statistical analysis, writing in 1888: 'Two variable organs are said to be co-related when the variation of the one is accompanied on the average by more or less variation of the other, and in the same direction.'[4] (One example: when the weather gets hotter, ice-cream sales go up.) He studied weather, and described the anti-cyclone – the opposite of a cyclone, where air rotates around a central area of high pressure – in a letter to the Royal Meteorological Society. He even identified the best way to cut a round cake to keep the inside edges moist (take out slices from the middle, like the leaves of an extendable dining table, and smoosh the two ends back together). In light of his enthusiastic racism, it is somewhat ironic that he also invented the dog whistle.

As Galton approached middle age, all this dilettante energy began to be focused on a single subject: bloodlines. In 1859, his cousin Darwin had published *On the Origin of Species*, laying out the theory of evolution by natural selection. Darwin believed that animal life was ruled by 'survival of the fittest'. Galton wondered how far his theory applied to humans. 'If a twentieth part of the cost and pains were spent in measures for the improvement of the human race that is spent on the improvement of the breed of horses and cattle, what a galaxy of genius might we not create!' he wrote.

The result of his thinking was an academic paper called 'Hereditary Talent and Character', published in 1865, which he developed into a book four years later with a slight change of title. It was now called *Hereditary Genius*. The book was his attempt to quantify and classify greatness, drawing on a monumental amount of research and the latest discoveries in science. Galton rejected the Romantic ideal of geniuses as eccentric, iconoclastic, unworldly figures – sensitive souls who were too good for the world, who might have to retire to nature, who might die young of a wasting disease, who might compose their great poems under the influence of opium, or awe-inspiring waterfalls, or all-consuming passion. No. For Galton, this would not do. From now on, genius would not be a random lightning strike, or a visitation from the gods: it would be dissected, exposed, explained. It was a grand undertaking – and it opened one of the darkest chapters in human history. The preface to the second edition of *Hereditary Genius*, published in 1892, sets out Galton's concerns about the previous model of greatness. 'If genius means a sense of inspiration, or of rushes of ideas from apparently supernatural sources, or of an inordinate and burning desire to accomplish any particular end, it is perilously near to the voices heard by the insane, to their delirious tendencies, or to their monomanias,' he wrote. 'It cannot in such cases be a healthy faculty, nor can it be desirable to perpetuate it by inheritance. The natural ability of which this book mainly treats, is such as a modern European possesses in a much greater average share than men of the lower races.'

From the start, then, Galton's great scientific project was marked by his own prejudices. His study of hereditary genius led him to coin the term *eugenics*, from the Ancient Greek for 'good' and 'birth' – the improvement of the human race through selective breeding. He even wrote a novel, *Kantsaywhere*, about a eugenic utopia which gave out breeding licences to the most deserving. Those who failed their intelligence exams were forbidden from reproducing, and sent to labour colonies – 'under conditions that were not onerous' – or encouraged to emigrate by 'surveillance and annoyance'. Those who obtained a second-class certificate could have children 'with reservations'. Those who passed with flying colours, like his heroine Augusta Allfancy, were encouraged to start breeding young: the ideal first-time parents were a twentysomething woman and an older man.

In his book, Galton drew up a list of English judges in order to see how many of their close relatives were also 'eminent' men. The results were 'striking', he discovered, and Galton followed up by accounting for the 'most illustrious statesmen, commanders, literary men, men of science, poets, musicians, and painters, of whom history makes mention'. Next came a list of prominent members of the clergy, followed by 'the Senior Classics of Cambridge . . . then the north country oarsmen and wrestlers'. Add to that more than twenty 'eminent' musicians in the Bach family, a galaxy of talented Cassinis, a hat trick of Herschels, and many distinguished members of the Darwin family, from Erasmus to Charles. (Galton modestly excluded himself.) He paused to consider whether reputation is really a proxy for innate talent but only briefly: 'If a man is gifted with vast intellectual ability, eagerness to work, and power of working, I cannot comprehend how such a man should be repressed.' (A small reminder that this was a man who had seen human beings bought and sold at a market.)

Like the good scientist he aspired to be, Galton set out his criteria for inclusion. He was looking for the top fraction of a per cent of humanity. He estimated the frequency with which genius occurs by comparing lists of eminent men in a popular textbook with the overall size of the male population over fifty. (He reasoned that an early death prevented a man from reaching his full potential.) He took it for granted that the textbook would be objective, remarking that 'its intention, which is very fairly and honestly carried out, is to include none but those whom the world honours for their ability'. These calculations allowed him to conclude that one person in every 4,000 was 'eminent' and one man in every million was 'illustrious'. This latter 'X' category contained 'men whom the whole intelligent part of the nation mourns when they die; who have, or deserve to have, a public funeral; and who rank in future ages as historical characters'. To assist readers in understanding these big denominators, Galton compares them with the number of horse chestnut trees in 'Bushey Park', or an individual's chances of securing a place in the Oxford vs Cambridge university boat race, an event which 'excites almost a national enthusiasm'.

Everyone outside these high bounds, meanwhile, was classified into lettered groups: A–G for the bands above the average, and a–g for those below it. Those in the highest normal group, G, almost did not need education, because their natural talents were so great. 'The best care that a master can take of such a boy is to leave him alone, just directing a little here and there, and checking desultory tendencies,' he wrote. The 'mediocre classes', meanwhile, contained 95 per cent of the population. They were fine but unmemorable. He defined mediocrity as 'the standard of intellectual power found in most provincial gatherings, because the attractions of a more stirring life in the metropolis and elsewhere, are apt to draw away the abler classes of men, and the silly and the imbecile do not take a part in the gatherings'. As for the lowest groups, Galton considered them less intelligent than the smartest dogs: 'Certainly the class G of such animals is far superior to the g of humankind.'

A great irony pervades Galton's work. Despite his belief that superior men had a duty to reproduce, improving the racial stock, he had no children himself.

In Galton's words, we can see the foundation stones of the modern idea of genius. It is a rare gift, possessed by individuals, which allows them to achieve greatness. 'I acknowledge freely the great power of education and social influences in developing the active powers of the mind, just as I acknowledge the effect of use in developing the muscles of a blacksmith's arm, and no further,' he wrote. Look, Galton was saying – it was simply a fact that some people were better than others. Accepting this truth was the key to happiness, according to Galton, and by middle age a man ought to be 'no longer tormented into hopeless efforts by the fallacious promptings of overweening vanity,' instead ensuring that he 'limits his undertakings to matters below the level of his reach, and finds true moral repose in an honest conviction that he is engaged in as much good work as his nature has rendered him capable of performing'. (These are not generic uses of 'he' and 'him', incidentally: Galton believed that although genius was carried in the female line, it did not show itself in women. Just as well, really. Even women at the upper levels of the mediocre classes might have trouble marrying, he thought, since 'one portion of them would certainly be of a dogmatic and self-asserting type, and therefore unattractive to men'.)

Galton's thesis provided the perfect intellectual cover for the Victorian belief of a natural order, where the poor regrettably, but inevitably, lacked the ability to rise above their circumstances; where women did not appear in collections of the illustrious because their natural tendency was towards the emotional and domestic; and where intellectual differences between 'the highest Caucasian and the lowest savage' were taken for granted. This is the most extreme form of genius as a right-wing idea.

Galton's whole enterprise reeks of complacency, the same sentiment which produced this now-forgotten verse of *All Things Bright and Beautiful*: 'The rich man in his castle / The poor man at his gate / God made them high and lowly / And ordered their estate'. Galton might have lost his religious faith in the 1860s, but he still subscribed to a belief in just deserts. Once, God ordained a human hierarchy. Now, genetics did the same.

In its focus on singular individuals, Galton's work echoed the other great Victorian development of the mythology of genius: Great Man theory. The name comes from the historian Thomas Carlyle's 'On Heroes, Hero-Worship, and the Heroic in History', a series of lectures which contained the assertion that 'the history of the world is but the biography of Great Men'.

It's important to remember now that Carlyle was writing from a defensive position. He aimed to redeem the concept of hero worship at a time when it had fallen out of fashion. 'This, for reasons which it will be worth while some time to inquire into, is an age that as it were denies the existence of great men; denies the desirableness of great men. Show our critics a great man, a [Martin] Luther for example, they begin to what they call "account" for him; not to worship him, but take the dimensions of him, – and bring him out to be a little kind of man!' Update the language, and these sentiments could be the rallying cry of the MeToo movement, or #RhodesMustFall, a campaign to remove public statues of the cruel Victorian colonialist Cecil Rhodes. Carlyle argued that such movements ought to fail, because we crave heroes, great men, geniuses, no matter how often we are told they are compromised or simply don't exist. 'Hero-worship endures forever while man endures,' he observed.

Carlyle's argument – that history is decided by great men – neatly laced together with Francis Galton's belief that greatness is innate and inherited. You are born a Caesar, and you conquer the world.

Yet it isn't hard to find flaws in the reasoning of *Hereditary Genius*, and readers did so from the start. The criteria for 'excellence' were deeply subjective – reputation and obituary size, among others. One of the neatest challenges to the book is that it depends on statistical methods developed by the German mathematician Carl Friedrich Gauss, whom we have already met. Galton's work cannot exist without Gauss. Yet there is no suggestion in Gauss' family tree that he would become a mathematical genius, rather than a labourer like his brother. Incidentally, Gauss also did not share Galton's belief about female intellectual inferiority. He declared himself full of 'astonishment and admiration' when he discovered that one of his correspondents, who sent him letters about number theory under the pseudonym 'Monsieur Le Blanc', was a talented female mathematician called Sophie Germain. Unlike complacent Galton, who believed everyone got what they deserved, Gauss understood that when 'a woman, because of her sex, our customs and prejudices, encounters infinitely more obstacles than men in familiarising herself with knotty problems, yet overcomes these fetters and penetrates that which is most hidden, she doubtless has the noblest courage, extraordinary talent, and superior genius'. The history of scientific genius studies might have been very different had its founder been a self-made man, rather than the odd, entitled, oblivious Galton.

There are other obvious challenges to Galton's reasoning. The psychologist Dean Keith Simonton, who has devoted most of his career to studying 'greatness', points out that Galton does not account for the effect of environment, the existence of nepotism and the transfer of material resources. It is hard to make a scientific breakthrough while crippled by rickets or handicapped by lead poisoning. It is hard to paint a masterpiece when you are forbidden from formal artistic training because of your sex. It is hard to conduct experimental research as a Jew, at a time when Jews are excluded from university posts. It is hard to launch a new literary movement when you are pregnant with your fifth child in five years. It is hard to succeed as an eminent lawyer when you are black in nineteenth-century America, and the profession has a colour bar. As early as 1873, the botanist Alphonse de Candolle identified eighteen factors that correlated with scientific flourishing, aside from a person's innate gifts. These included independent wealth, favourable public opinion, a lack of religious repression and a temperate climate in which to work.

For me, it's the inability to separate the effects of genetics and nepotism that is the real killer. Reviewing *Hereditary Genius* in 1870, the historian Herman Merivale noted the inclusion of the Atkyns family of judges, writing that 'the whole list has the unmistakeable character of a snug little party of jobbers, rather than that of a galaxy of genius'. His words neatly anticipate the modern debate about 'nepo babies' in creative professions. Now, it is possible that, say, Gracie Abrams would have supported Taylor Swift on tour without being the daughter of the film director J. J. Abrams. Or that Eve Hewson would have been cast in so many television shows without being the daughter of Bono. Or that Romeo Beckham would have modelled for Burberry regardless of his parents. Or that the careers of Honor Swinton Byrne (daughter of Tilda Swinton and John Byrne), Deacon Phillippe (Reese Witherspoon and Ryan Phillippe), Lily-Rose Depp (Johnny Depp and Vanessa Paradis), Lily Collins (Phil) and Bryce Dallas Howard (Ron) would have taken off without their family connections. Some of those named above are genuinely talented, but the sheer number of second-generation Hollywood princelings should make us wonder.

Perhaps acting ability is inherited, in the manner Galton described. (The Redgrave family would have made him cry with delight, or at least smile quizzically.) Or perhaps growing up around film sets, and soaking up the lessons of the business from an early age, is an enormous advantage – quite aside from having parents to pull strings for you. Or maybe there's an even more radical explanation: a sizeable percentage of the population could be actors if they tried, but most don't get the chance. (This is the favoured explanation of people waiting tables in Beverly Hills.) Galton did attempt to control for the difference between genetics and family connections by comparing the achievements of nephews and sons of great men. But he admitted that the calculation was beyond him.

Galton's orderly, explicable world in *Hereditary Genius* aligned with his own neat, tidy mind and his obsession with taxonomy. But the real world is messier – many great careers and creative achievements depend on a single moment of luck. Even readers at the time sensed this; the contemporary reaction to Galton's book among non-scientific readers was cool.[5]

Nonetheless, *Hereditary Genius* was an influential book – one of those works that fires up a tightknit intellectual crowd. The year after Galton died in 1911, a eugenics conference was held in London, attended by Winston Churchill, Alexander Graham Bell, Arthur Balfour and Charles Darwin's son Leonard. The year after that, a woman known as Mrs Bolce was so taken with Galton's ideas that she called her baby 'Eugenette'.[6]

Because he died childless, Galton donated his estate to University College London. The first Galton Chair of Eugenics was a disciple of his called Karl Pearson, who repaid the favour by writing a thoroughly celebratory biography of his hero. (Three buildings at UCL named after Galton and Pearson were renamed in 2020 because of their association with eugenics.) Like his master, Pearson was intellectually dazzling. He created the discipline of mathematical statistics, and his book *The Grammar of Science* was the first text selected by a young Albert Einstein for his 'Olympia Academy' study group with friends. The next holder of the Galton Chair was Ronald (R. A.) Fisher, a man so brilliant he is known as the 'father of modern statistics'. You could not teach an undergraduate statistics course now without relying on Fisher's work, and thus Galton's patronage. (Fisher's name has also recently been removed from several university buildings and awards, because he was also an enthusiastic proponent of eugenics.) To us, Galton's odd ideas make him seem a crank. But to the generation of geneticists and statisticians that came up in his shadow, he was an intellectual giant.

Hereditary Genius inspired other attempts to classify high achievers into groups and draw lessons from their lives. 'In the past the phenomena of genius have mostly been approached from two distinct standpoints,' the sexologist Havelock Ellis wrote in the preface to his 1904 book *A Study of British Genius*. The first was by 'alienists' (psychiatrists) who noticed that 'certain men of eminent genius had presented symptoms which may properly be termed insane'. The second group of genius hunters were the anthropologists. Ellis identified himself with the second group, a reflection of the prevailing trend in genius studies.

Reading the book made me feel sorry for Ellis, a curious, open-minded scientist confronted with an impossible dataset which entirely resists statistical analysis. Early on, he says that he will not use graphs, because it is 'undesirable to give an air of precision to data' that is so incomplete. He defines genius as 'high intellectual ability', and sources his list from the *Oxford Dictionary of National Biography*, whittling down its 30,000 entries by excluding royalty and nobles who inherited their positions. He excludes 'villains' like the would-be regicide Titus Oates, and women who slept their way to the top. (Sorry, Lady Hamilton.) Then he removes anyone whose entry receives fewer than three pages in the *ODNB*, reasoning that this shows their contributions to the world are minor. He ends up with 700 names, and then realises that he has a problem: his list excludes Jane Austen. Her life was uneventful – she was born, she lived quietly, she wrote books, she died – and so she did not merit three pages in the *ODNB*. We might call this the Austen Problem, and it shows once again the way 'genius' functions as a mythology rather than an objective category. A genius needs a story as well as achievements. Despite Austen's inclusion breaking his own rules, Ellis adds her, plus some other boringly vanilla high achievers, back in to his list, finally coming up with 1,030 individuals. Then he notes that J. McKeen Cattell's list of 1,000 'eminent men' published in 1903's *Popular Science Monthly* contains sixty British entries who are not on his list. A sense of despair emanates from the page. If this is science, why have he and McKeen Cattell come up with such different lists?

In the end, Ellis produces a final list of 975 men and 55 women. He details their parentage, social class, childhood and youth, longevity, pathology and pigmentation. (I held my breath, but he was only talking about eye colour.) He concludes that East Anglia 'has no aptitude for abstract thinking', while people in the south-west of England are 'sailors rather than scholars'. The Welsh are poetic, while Scottish genius is concentrated in 'the tract between the Cheviots and the Grampians'. Sligo has produced no geniuses, while Dublin claims fifteen.

Sweeping judgements. Questionable statistics. An impressive, if doomed, hope that humans can be reduced to numbers and understood. This was Francis Galton's intellectual inheritance, and even a social scientist as accomplished as Havelock Ellis could not escape it. Perhaps it would have been better to stick with Vasari's approach of merely describing high achievers without attempting to quantify their lives in such minute detail – to treat the whole enterprise as a storytelling project rather than a scientific one.

Unfortunately, though, the work of Galton and others inspired researchers to double down on their search for an identifiable source of genius. Because they had a new weapon – the IQ test – and a new myth. That geniuses were people with a 'genius-level IQ'.

Terman's Termites

'The purpose of Genetic Studies of Genius *is to throw light on the factors which make for superior achievement, particularly achievement in the realm of intellect.'*

Lewis Terman, Genetic Studies of Genius

Oddly enough, IQ tests were developed as a way to identify underachieving children, not high-flyers. At the turn of the twentieth century, the French psychologists Alfred Binet and Théodore Simon were asked by the French ministry of education to develop a scale to identify less able children, so that they could be helped at school.

The result was the Binet-Simon test, which included a series of graded tasks, such as following a beam of light, repeating back a series of digits and constructing sentences from three given words. Other tasks would prove more controversial, such as identifying the prettiest face from a set of drawings. Binet always stressed the limitations of the test. He believed that children developed at different rates and in different ways, and worried about the 'brutal pessimism' of thinking that intelligence could not be improved. When the German psychologist William Stern proposed presenting the results as a single number, a 'mental age', Simon called it a *trahison* (betrayal) of his aims.

One of the strange quirks of average IQ is that it has risen quite noticeably since the measurement first came into use. The

Flynn Effect is named after the researcher James Flynn, and it states that IQ scores rose by 3.3 points every decade over the twentieth century. (As a result of this, the average '100' score has been systematically made harder to attain.) In 2012, Flynn speculated on why this was.[1] If asked what dogs and rabbits have in common, a person today would answer that both are mammals, he said. A child in 1900, by contrast, would reply: 'You use dogs to hunt rabbits.' The average person from the 1900s 'would get the question wrong because, before people had lots of formal schooling, they had a utilitarian mentality, and they were fixated on the concrete world and using it to advantage'. Modern teaching methods have taught children the importance of taxonomy – and of abstract thinking – and that has improved IQ test scores. As a result, modern researchers are cautious about the comparisons they make between different groups and their IQ test scores, particularly across time.

Early IQ researchers were much more cavalier about making bold statements – which often reflected their personal prejudices. The entire field is now tainted by the work of people such as Henry Herbert Goddard, who studied 'feeble-mindedness' in a family he called the Kallikaks. The name came from the Greek words for 'good' (*kalós*) and 'bad' (*kakós*), and his contention was that the family had two branches, the 'good' one descended from Martin Kallikak's legitimate marriage and a 'bad' one from his affair with a 'feeble-minded' barmaid. The book was an instant success when it came out in 1912 – the same year that Winston Churchill attended that Galtonian eugenics conference – and it bolstered support for the idea of selective breeding. But Goddard's premise was later debunked: the supposedly 'illegitimate' child of Martin Kallikak that started the bad side of the family wasn't illegitimate – wasn't even Martin's child – and the boy grew up to be a successful landowner. Even Goddard came to accept its flaws. Yet this was the man who translated the Binet-Simon test into English and brought it to America – bringing IQ mania to a new continent, and a fresh set of enthusiasts.

It was in America that the science of IQ attracted the attention of a young psychologist called Lewis Terman.

Born in 1877, the young Lewis had been a shy boy, the twelfth of fourteen children born in Johnson County in rural Indiana. His family were prosperous enough to own 150 books, including the *Encyclopedia Britannica*, but his schooling was frequently interrupted by the need to work on the family farm. He planned to become a teacher, but when he was ten, a 'book peddler' stopped by the Terman family home, selling a book on phrenology – the wildly popular (but unfortunately completely worthless) theory that the shape of the skull indicated a person's aptitude and personality. The peddler 'felt the bumps' of the whole family. 'When it came my turn to be examined he predicted great things of me,' recalled Terman, years later. 'I think the prediction probably added a little to my self-confidence and caused me to strive for a more ambitious goal than I might otherwise have set . . . As my older brother bought a copy of the book, I finally became familiar with its contents and believed in phrenology until I was fourteen or fifteen years old. This was my introduction to the science of individual differences and the diagnosis of personality.'[2]

At university, Terman decided his thesis would be on mental tests. His mentor G. Stanley Hall was unimpressed, warning prophetically about 'the danger of being misled by the quasi-exactness of quantitative methods'. But Terman believed in the possibilities offered by IQ measurements to divide up humanity in useful ways. In 1916, while at Stanford University, he revised Binet's test – hence its modern name, the Stanford-Binet test. That same year, he wrote a book called *The Measurement of Intelligence* which argued that among 'laboring men and servant girls' there were thousands of people of 'sub-normal' intelligence. 'They are the world's "hewers of wood and drawers of water" . . . The fact that one meets this type with such extraordinary frequency among Indians, Mexicans, and negroes suggests quite forcibly that the whole question of racial differences in mental traits will have to be taken up anew and by experimental methods.'

These hewers of wood, he thought, should be segregated into special classes and taught practical skills. 'There is no possibility at present of convincing society that they should not be allowed to reproduce, although from a eugenic point of view they constitute a grave problem because of their unusually prolific breeding.' These were not unusual ideas for the time. In 1924, the US passed the Immigration Act, limiting the number of arrivals from 'inferior' countries. It was signed into law by President Calvin Coolidge, who had earlier claimed that 'Biological laws show . . . that Nordics deteriorate when mixed with other races.' In 1927, the US Supreme Court confirmed that the sterilisation of those with low IQs was constitutional, with Oliver Wendell Holmes' infamous judgement in the 1927 *Buck v. Bell* case: 'Three generations of imbeciles are enough.' That language now seems offensive, but to Holmes it was scientific. In 1910, Henry Herbert Goddard had proposed a classification system based on IQ tests: 'moron' was for those with IQs between 70 and 51, 'imbecile' for 50 to 26, and 'idiot' for 25 and below. Goddard proposed that morons, imbeciles and idiots should be removed from society.*

---

* The ideas of Galton, Goddard and others found their most extreme expression in Nazi Germany, which made 'feeblemindedness' one of its criteria for sterilisation in 1933. Cases were judged by a panel. An estimated 400,000 people were sterilised under this law.

What is striking now about the pronouncements of Francis Galton, Henry Herbert Goddard and Lewis Terman is not just their callousness but their self-assurance. *This is how the world is, and science can prove it.* For empirically minded researchers engaged in the study of a new field of knowledge, there was a remarkable narrowness to the worldview of the early genius hunters. They truly seem to have had no concept of a self-fulfilling prophecy. Terman believed that men were more intelligent than women, for example, and this was reflected in his parenting: he never urged his daughter Helen to achieve academically in the way he did with his son Frederick, even though IQ tests revealed that *both* of his children were gifted. Frederick became a Stanford professor. Helen became a housewife.[3] Later, when Terman's granddaughter Doris was poised to win a family Easter egg hunt, his wife Anna intervened to ensure she did not beat his grandson.

In 1922, Terman published a paper called *A New Approach to the Study of Genius*, describing how he planned to use the new science of IQ to uncover future geniuses in childhood, and then track them, mining their lives for insights. His dataset was huge: 1,000 children would be recruited from across California, mostly nominated by their teachers.

The first volume of observations, published in 1925, was called *Genetic Studies of Genius*, and is today known as the Terman Study of the Gifted. It is an extraordinary document, although not for the reasons its creator intended. Terman had sent out researchers (usually female) to identify and interview the 'gifted' children – which he defined initially as having an IQ over 140, before dropping his sights to 135 – and they returned with reams of data. After the initial interviews, the researchers continued to collect data for decades afterwards, tracking the children throughout their lives.

The Terman Study is a fascinating landmark in the social sciences, thanks to its breadth, duration and quirkiness. He was open to the possibility that all kinds of traits and circumstances might show some correlation with genius, and so he enquired not just into the obvious possibilities such as parental occupation but also physical characteristics, maternal temperaments and sexual orientation. His researchers spelunked through data which turned out to be useless for identifying genius, but nonetheless gives us intriguing glimpses of life in twentieth-century California. The mean number of teeth at the age of eight was eleven for boys and twelve for girls,[4] and 0.5 per cent had symptoms of active tuberculosis. Terman's team checked his 'Termites' for dental cavities and high blood pressure, felt their necks for enlarged glands, and proclaimed that 'abnormalities of the genitals were rare'.

Most of the data Terman recorded is still anonymised, but in the 1990s the journalist Joel N. Shurkin was given access to it, and he obtained the consent of some Termites to identify them. The creator of the sitcom *I Love Lucy*, Jess Oppenheimer, was a Termite. So was Shelley Smith Mydans, who reported on the Second World War and wrote a novel based on her experiences in a Japanese camp. So was Ancel Keys, a pioneering physiologist who studied diet and starvation, and created the standard 'K' ration given to US troops. So was Lilith James, who wrote the play on which the Broadway musical *Bloomer Girl* was based. And so was the film director Edward Dmytryk, nominated for an Oscar for 1947's *Crossfire*. All these people had interesting lives and unusual careers. What they were not, however, were geniuses – in Francis Galton's definition, they were eminent but not illustrious.

Terman's researchers *did* administer their IQ tests to two boys who went on to win Nobel Prizes for physics – William Shockley and Luis Alvarez. They were both rejected from the study. Their IQs were too low.

We should thank Terman's study for debunking one persistent myth. He concluded that, far from the Romantic stereotype of weak and wasted geniuses, the children he studied were 'physically superior' to the general population. (This makes sense: further research has shown that higher IQ is correlated with better health outcomes.) Some of his other results were equally unsurprising: the Termites earned more than the average over their lives, and were much more likely to go to college. By 1947, 90 per cent had done so, with 70 per cent graduating – ten times the usual rate in California at the time. The group had also published ninety books and monographs, as well as 1,500 academic articles, and held more than a hundred patents.

By 1947, though, Terman had to concede that his 'genius' children were merely very, very gifted:

> That the group contains no one who shows promise of matching the eminence of Shakespeare, Goethe, Tolstoy, da Vinci, Newton, Galileo, Darwin or Napoleon is not surprising in view of the fact that the entire population of America since the Jamestown settlement has not produced the like of one of these. Such eminence in a given field is usually possible only at a given stage of cultural progress, and can never be very closely paralleled in a different era. For one thing, science and scholarship are growing so highly specialised that eminence is becoming progressively more difficult to obtain. Conceivably, if Darwin were living today he might just be another specialist in a restricted field of biology.[5]

Terman's plea sounds defensive – perhaps he regretted the initial title of his project – but it raises a point that has always bothered me, too. So many of our pantheon of geniuses, even now, date back to the late nineteenth and early twentieth century. The same forty-year period gives us Thomas Edison's phonograph and electric lightbulb, Vincent van Gogh's *Sunflowers*, Albert Einstein's theory of relativity, Marie Curie's work on radiation and Pablo Picasso's *Les Demoiselles d'Avignon*. (The last forty years have given us Damien Hirst's shark, Ozempic and Facebook. It's hard not to feel we've gone wrong somewhere.) Perhaps that fin de siècle was the last moment before high specialisation took over in the sciences, and before modernism splintered our idea of what art should be. Or the late nineteenth century created so many international superstars because it marked the beginning of truly mass media, with illustrated newspapers and magazines allowing the whole world to gaze in one direction? Think about the comparison with now, when many of our most bankable movie stars are in their fifties – i.e. they became famous before smartphones and social media shattered the idea of a shared celebrity culture. It is also possible that this is pure temporal bias – a delay in recognition.

Terman might have had his doubts about genius hunting, but that did not stop his researcher Catharine Cox Miles from trying to squash the concept of genius into the IQ model. She embarked on a doomed Galtonian project – trying to estimate the intelligence of the geniuses of the past. Shurkin calls this 'one of the silliest experiments in the colourful history of social science.'[6] Like Havelock Ellis, she turned to a biographical dictionary for help, measuring the length of entries with a ruler. Terman was sceptical. 'Although possessing the merit of objectivity, this criterion, admittedly, is far from ideal in that eminence is influenced by circumstances other than intellectual achievement,' he wrote. 'The genius who survives as such has successfully run the gauntlet of premature death, the stupidities of formal education, the social and ethical pressures of his immediate environment, and the more general cultural influences that have given direction and content to the civilisation in which he was born . . . Genius in the sense of eminence is not a biological concept, though it does have biological prerequisites in ancestral genes, nutrition, and escape from mortal disease.'[7]

She immediately ran into the Austen Problem, too. The ruler method was bad news for Cervantes and Copernicus – with so little known about them, they were assigned IQs of 105 – but much better for the German writer Goethe, who scored 210. Thanks to the work of Cox Miles, we can finally settle the quarrel for dominance between Newton (190) and Leibniz (205). Galileo beats Leonardo; a victory for the sciences. The booby prize went to Napoleonic general André Masséna, who came last. His IQ was deemed to be exactly average. As for William Shakespeare, that mysterious genius flickering in the biographical half-light, he did not make the list at all.

One recurrent theme of Terman's study was how difficult it was to predict the path a person's life might take from observing them as a child. Jess Oppenheimer, who became one of America's most successful comedy writers, was initially described by the researchers as a 'conceited, egocentric boy' who was 'ruined by his mother'. Terman's assistant Melissa Oden added: 'I could detect no signs of a sense of humour.'

But to call the research a failure would be unfair. Not only did it disprove Terman's hypothesis that genius could be spotted in childhood – an interesting and valid scientific result – but it demonstrated quite how savagely a person's life can be affected by factors outside their control. And that's because one great, world-shaking event happened right in the middle of the Termites' lives: the Second World War.

Terman never explicitly studied the effect of the conflict on his subjects, but later researchers did. They discovered that the older Termites were less successful in career and economic terms, because their prime family-making and career-building years coincided with the early 1940s. For some Termites, such as physicist Norris Bradbury, the war brought unique opportunities. He supervised the production of 'Fat Man', the atomic bomb dropped on the Japanese city of Nagasaki, and succeeded Robert Oppenheimer as director of the atomic weapon research programme at Los Alamos. For others, though, the war brought only disruption and discrimination. One family in the study was half-Japanese, with five children who all scored highly enough to be recruited as Termites. After Japan's attack on Pearl Harbor led to America declaring war, one of the half-Japanese Termites changed his surname and retreated to a remote farm for the duration of the war to avoid being sent to an internment camp.

For some of those in the study, the war brought tragedy. One Termite, whose identity is not public, died after being exposed to fatal radiation while working on an atomic bomb.[8] Another Termite, the psychiatrist Douglas McGlashan Kelley, administered inkblot tests to twenty-two Nazi defendants before the war-crimes trials at Nuremberg, declaring them fit to be prosecuted. The experience never left him, even after he returned to America. On New Year's Day in 1958, he was cooking a meal for his family when something went wrong – he either accidentally burned himself or got into a fight with his wife. According to his son, something broke in Kelley in that moment, and he retreated upstairs and took a cyanide capsule – the same method of suicide used by Nuremberg defendant Hermann Göring. He died within seconds, at the age of just forty-five. The war left a deep scar across the lives of so many Termites.

Terman's female subjects were particularly affected by the limited opportunities available to them. He noticed that his gifted girls had masculine leanings in terms of interests and ambitions, which he attributed to 'being due chiefly to the tendency of gifted women to vary from the norm towards masculinity'.* The 1957 study found that many were badly adjusted, felt they had not reached their potential and would have liked to devote more energy to their careers. Terman struggled to reconcile his data, which showed the existence of so many clever girls, with the male dominance of the professions at the time. When he retested his subjects' IQs in 1927, he found that some of their scores had dropped – which should not have been possible, according to his model. Those drops were larger in girls. He was puzzled.

Even without overt sexism, economic conditions limited the lives of the female Termites. One woman, nicknamed 'Sara Ann' by Shurkin, took a physics degree and married a fellow scientist. She and her husband realised that if she got pregnant, he could get a draft deferment from military service. However, they appear to have got somewhat carried away with the plan. She had eight children in ten years, and never worked as a physicist. When Sara Ann felt her children were old enough not to be badly affected, she got divorced. In her fifties, she lived for a time in a commune. 'I think I was made, as a child, to be far too self-conscious of my status as a "Termite," and of being smart and

---

* In 1925, Terman and Catharine Cox Miles gave his subjects a test to see how masculine or feminine they were. One question asked children to complete the sentence, 'Eggs are best for us when . . . ' The masculine answer was fried or hard-boiled. Even in the 1920s, other scientists were able to point out that this was hardly objective.

young for my grade (all passive),' she wrote later, 'and given far too little to actually do with this mental endowment (so I'd stop thinking about myself).'

Ultimately, that special status was the biggest problem with Terman's study. His presence represented a thumb on the scales of each child's life; a big dose of royal jelly turning worker bees into potential queens. Their parents got to brag about their little Termite, and the kids themselves were aware from an early age that they were special. Allowing teachers to recommend participants introduced all kinds of bias: were they more likely to see boys as clever, which might explain the male dominance of the sample? Did teachers prize precocity, which never translated to adult success? Intelligence has a narrow definition, and – particularly in children – is often inferred from confidence and eloquence. (Terman also recruited a sample of creative children, who excelled in art or music, which suggests that he was wrestling – as I find myself doing regularly – with the difference between scientific and artistic genius. That group had an average IQ of 114.) Terman's researchers also under-sampled schools in California that served poor and minority communities, perhaps because they assumed such places would not harbour future geniuses.

His study was fascinating, eccentric, conscientious, biased and brilliant. And just like Francis Galton, he found that genius was resistant to scientific study. But at least Terman's researchers were honest. Not every genius hunter was.

Cyril and Hans: Twin Flames

'The arrogance of excellence.'

Vintage car advert

On 16 October 1976, a small, strange advert appeared in the personal columns of *The Times*. 'Sir Cyril Burt. Could Margaret Howard or J. Conway who helped Sir Cyril in studies of the intelligence of twins or anyone else who knows them tel. (Reverse charges) Oliver Gillie, 01-485 8953.'[1] Those two sentences were enough to destroy the reputation of one of Galton's most avid disciples, and discredit his search for the origins of genius.

Cyril Burt, even his friends and admirers would have conceded, was an odd man. He was born in the late Victorian era, a decade and a half after the publication of *Hereditary Genius*, and grew up in London and the village of Snitterfield in the West Midlands. He always had poor balance, was late to start walking and talking, and was, according to his sister, struck with 'virtual horror of the school gymnasium'. He was always clever, though. His father was a doctor, and the family socialised widely. One of the local families, in nearby Claverdon, were the Galtons – the sister and brother of Francis – and the young Cyril soon heard about the work of the ageing eugenicist. He was particularly interested in Galton's application of statistics to the study of talent and character.

In part thanks to Galton's influence, Burt decided to pursue psychology at Oxford University, starting in 1902, when the subject was then very new. There were only two psychological labs in the whole country; one at Cambridge University and the other at University College London. 'For psychologists, the decade in which Burt was fortunate enough to commence his serious study of the subject was perhaps the most exciting decade since the death of Aristotle,' writes his biographer Leslie Hearnshaw.[2] In 1900, Gregor Mendel's work on heredity had been rediscovered – the friar studying peas was finally given his due – opening up new areas in the research of genetics. Around that time, Freud's *The Interpretation of Dreams* was first published, Pavlov was working with his dogs, and Charles Spearman championed the idea of 'factor analysis', a statistical technique he used to search for 'g', the mysterious concept of 'general intelligence'. In 1905, Binet and Simon launched the first intelligence scale. In 1907, the Eugenics Society was formed, with the express aim of studying how the human population could be improved by selective breeding.

Cyril Burt wanted to follow in Galton's footsteps and study individual differences. After finishing his degree, he secured a job at University of Liverpool, which he combined with a part-time post at the London County Council fine-tuning the 'anthropometric observation of children in schools'. This was a great Galtonian project. Burt hoped to identify (in the language of the day) delinquents, morons, imbeciles and, of course, 'the gifted child'. He was London's official psychologist for nearly twenty years, from 1913 to 1931.

In 1925, he published *The Young Delinquent*, his most popular work, which did pretty much what it said on the tin – outlining 'the main forms of mental subnormality to be met with among the young'. The book made him a public figure, and he gave radio talks on psychology. This was a productive period of Burt's life, and he seems to have enjoyed his work. He sometimes lived with the families he studied in the East End, and from the start – as a good Galtonian – he was interested in twins. Working-class mothers with little money sometimes sent one twin to an institution or foster home to ease their financial burden. The council kept records of both twins; so did Burt. However, as Hearnshaw notes, this data was collected 'fairly casually and without any clear-cut research design'. This would prove troublesome later on.

From the start, Burt believed that 'cognitive efficiency' was innate and largely heritable. He was obsessed with general intelligence, which was the subject of his first paper in 1909, and the subject of a 1972 article published after his death. In that 1909 article, he argued – with echoes of Galton – that bishops were more intelligent than butchers, and therefore bishops' sons did better on tests than the sons of butchers. Intelligence must be hereditary, and social position followed.

Now, Burt was not reflexively bigoted in the way that Galton was. In 1912, he investigated sex differences in intelligence and found them 'astonishingly small – far smaller than common belief and common practice would lead us to expect'. And although he casually referred to 'savage races', he was not a scientific racist like Galton. Writing in the *Eugenics Review* in 1912, Burt noted: 'In the case of the individual we found the influence of heredity large and indisputable; in the case of the race, small and controversial.' Most modern researchers would agree.

But there *was* a political edge to his views: Burt's research made him a strong supporter of grammar schools – selective institutions which admitted the brightest students on the basis of a test known as the 'eleven-plus'. Selective education claimed to filter children by academic ability – but too often stratified them instead by class and economic background. Research showed then, and still shows now, that middle-class children dominate grammar schools and that there is no such thing as a 'tutor-proof' test for entry to selective education.

The whole ethos of the eleven-plus exam was also a small-scale echo of Terman's hunt for baby geniuses. It depended on the idea that it is possible to pick winners early, and that it was in society's best interests to separate them from the common herd and nurture them appropriately. (My father passed the eleven-plus in the 1950s and went to a grammar school. As a result, he became the first person in our family to go to university – and that created the conditions in which I was raised. You could say that my entire career depends on the genius myth.)

In 1946, Burt became the first psychologist to receive a knighthood. In 1960, he was made the honorary president of the new high IQ society, Mensa, whose creation he had proposed on the radio a decade and a half earlier; his introduction to Mensa's official history, published in 1966, bills him as 'Professor Sir Cyril Burt, F.B.A, D.Litt, Ll.D., D.Sc.'[3] Here, Burt proclaims that 'most people readily admit that a few exceptional individuals, like Newton and Shakespeare, are born geniuses, and that at the other end of the scale a small number of unfortunates are born mentally deficient. But between these two extremes they commonly suppose that all the rest of us are, in the famous phrase, "created equal" . . . Such a view flies in the face of all we know of human genetics.' Burt's evidence for this model of intelligence was 'studies of children with different heredity but similar environments' and 'studies of children with different environments but identical heredity'. In other words, studies of unrelated children raised together in orphanages and his own research on identical twins separated at birth. One group had identical genes but different environments; the other had the same environment but different genes. Burt claimed to have studied fifty cases of separated identical twins through his work at the London County

Council, leaving him with 'no reasonable doubt that children vary widely in their innate ability'.

By the mid 1960s, when this introduction was written, Burt was long past his days as a data collector. He might have had a knighthood and many other professional honours, but he had moved away from active research in the 1930s, when he was appointed to the psychology department at University College London. He had also just survived a difficult decade in his personal life: his wife left him in 1952, and he spent the rest of his life being attended by a secretary-housekeeper. He had been diagnosed with Ménière's disease, which affected his hearing, and made him reluctant to appear in public. He never went abroad again after the symptoms developed in 1941. The nasty streak in his personality begin to grow. Although he could be generous with his time, particularly to students, he badmouthed colleagues and blocked rivals from job opportunities. In 1950, he retired from University College, waved off with flowers, a toast from his grateful pupils and a collection of £130 to buy him a typewriter. His successor, Roger Russell, was convinced he was a 'great man'. He asked Burt to continue lecturing, but the relationship soon dissolved into acrimony. 'In my experience he was intolerant of those who held different views than his own and of those he thought might be challenging his pre-eminence,' wrote Russell in 1976.[4]

Burt's Galtonian methods – his psychometric tests and his insistence on innate talent – fell out of favour in his old department. He spent his long retirement defending his positions and attacking anyone who questioned his status. In 1963, he lost control of the journal he had edited since 1947, even though it had only survived because of financial support given directly to him by a rich admirer. Nonetheless, when he died in October 1971, at the grand age of eighty-eight, childless like Galton, his place in history seemed secure. The golden era of his work had attracted admirers among younger generations of psychologists, like his future biographer Leslie Hearnshaw. A year after Burt's death, the American psychologist Arthur Jensen could write: 'Everything about the man – his fine, sturdy appearance; his aura of vitality; his urbane manner; his unflagging enthusiasm for research, analysis and criticism; even such a detail as his firm, meticulous handwriting; and, of course, especially his notably sharp intellect and vast erudition – all together leave a total impression of immense quality, a born nobleman.'[5]

A born nobleman. Exactly the tribute that a good Galtonian would have wanted.

After delivering Burt's eulogy, though, Hearnshaw accepted a grant of £300 from Burt's sister Marion to write a full-length biography of him. 'I knew from my contacts with Burt as examiner and committee member that he could be difficult and prickly in business matters, but I regarded this as the justifiable prerogative of a great man in his dealings with lesser mortals,' Hearnshaw wrote later. In other words: *he was a star, so let him do it.*

But even as he was working on the book, the intellectual tide turned. The American psychologist Leon Kamin published *The Science and Politics of IQ* in 1974, which argued against the hereditarian model . . . and then suggested that Burt's twin studies might be fraudulent. That explosive claim led, eventually, to that newspaper advertisement looking for the mysterious research assistants, Margaret Howard and 'J. Conway'.

The advert had been placed by *The Sunday Times*' science correspondent, Oliver Gillie, who had developed suspicions about Burt's work. On 24 October 1976, he published the results of his investigation, under the unambiguous headline: 'Crucial data was faked by eminent psychologist.' The charge was that Burt's twin studies were fabricated – or at least the later data was false. The evidence lay in the correlations Burt had drawn between heredity, environment and intelligence. These are measurements of how interlinked two variables are, expressed as a number between zero (no relationship) and one (completely correlated). Burt had found that identical twins reared together had almost identical IQs, scored as 0.944, and those raised apart had a correlation of 0.771. The problem with these figures is that they remained the same between 1955 and 1966, when his sample size expanded dramatically (from 21 to 53 pairs of identical twins raised apart, and from 83 to 95 pairs raised together). For any correlation to remain precisely the same, to three decimal places, when the sample sizes changed is . . . *unusual*. Burt's twin research contained twenty such identical correlations. That had to be fraud.*

Perhaps the matter could have been settled by interviewing Burt's research assistants, Misses Howard and Conway? 'Miss Howard' had collaborated with Burt on several articles in the *British Journal of Statistical Psychology* in the 1950s, while 'Miss Conway' had written for the same publication between 1958 and 1962. Therefore they might well still be alive. Sadly not. Oliver Gillie placed the newspaper advert just in case the women could be found, but his bald conclusion was that Cyril Burt had made them up. He knew that another sleuth, Jack Tizard at the University of London Institute of Education, had tried to contact them the previous year, with no success. These accusations bolstered an earlier claim by two fellow psychologists, Alan and Ann Clarke, who said that after they had submitted their PhD theses to Burt, they were surprised to see their papers appear in the *British Journal of Educational Psychology*. Even more remarkably,

---

* One irony worth noting is that later research has suggested that Burt's figures, however they were obtained, were broadly correct.

the text had been altered to attack one of Burt's professional rivals.[6]

In his biography, which eventually appeared three years after the newspaper advert, Leslie Hearnshaw tries to be scrupulously fair. But he finds no evidence that Burt conducted any field work after 1955, and he may not have done *any* research after his retirement in 1950. He acknowledges that Burt's own story of the data collection changed over time. Then he runs through various defences, including the argument that if Burt had decided to fake his data, he was clever enough to have done it more carefully. Perhaps, Hearnshaw suggests, the *original* twin studies were valid – if a little sloppy in their data collection – but the records were lost in the Second World War. And maybe Cyril Burt, retired, lonely and unwell, embittered by the unhappy exit from his university department, was unable to tell the many researchers who contacted him that his most interesting data had disappeared.

At a distance of fifty years, this good faith is striking; but Hearnshaw had once respected Burt enough to deliver a eulogy at his memorial service. He also understood the politics of taking down his former hero – dealing a blow to those who believed strongly that intelligence was largely inherited, and to the grammar school system that Burt had championed so strongly. At the time, Burt still had plenty of defenders, who thought that the comprehensive movement was full of hippies who didn't care about the evidence. The Burt defenders claimed that the progressives found the 'truth' about the innate, inherited nature of IQ was inconvenient to their deluded ideas of equality, and so unfairly denied its existence. (An omen here of the current discourse around 'wokery' and the 'communism' of diversity initiatives.) Both sides knew that discrediting Burt was an appealing way of discrediting his ideas – even in science, evidence rarely stands or falls on its own merits, but by the reputation of its champions. A genius therefore becomes the human embodiment of a political argument – and smashing the genius' reputation is a more compelling way of demolishing that argument than a tedious, footnoted appeal to the facts.

What about the missing Misses, Howard and Conway? Hearnshaw found one of Burt's twins who remembered being tested for intelligence by a Margaret Howard in Aberystwyth. One of Burt's former pupils, Professor John Cohen of Manchester University, also recollected meeting her in the 1930s, noting her 'roundish face, her brown eyes and bobbed auburn hair, her slightly tinted spectacles, and her competence in mathematics'. Of Miss Conway, however, there was no trace. The most generous suggestion is that they were casual staff at the London County Council – social workers. (The lack of paper trail around the names of Burt's many research assistants – often female, always less well-paid and recognised than the great man – tells its own story, of course.) There was no record of correspondence with the pair, and Burt's careful diary records no meetings with them.*

One clue to Miss Howard's true identity is that when Burt stopped editing the *British Journal of Statistical Psychology*, her contributions abruptly stopped. The same was true of Miss Conway, who had never written for any other journal. The conclusion surely must be that even if the names were both taken from real women, they ended up as alter egos of one man. Cyril Burt. And these were not the only helpful shadows surrounding

---

* After Hearnshaw's book, two independent researchers, Robert Joynson and Ronald Fletcher, each wrote books defending Burt. Their central contention was that the odd results were explained by Burt losing some of his twin data in the war, and having to reconstruct it. They also found no evidence of the research assistants, but concluded that Howard and Conway were pseudonyms, and that this was eccentric but not unethical.

Burt. 'Of the more than forty "persons" who contributed reviews, notes and letters to the journal during the period of Burt's editorship,' writes Hearnshaw, 'well over half are unidentifiable, and judging from the style and content of their contributions were pseudonyms for Burt.'

This is a story of status, hierarchy and privilege: Cyril Burt was both a leader in his field and personal patron of its next generation. Like Galton before him, he had become woven into the academy and into an intellectual tradition. People owed him, both morally and materially. There was every reason to defend him and little reward for a demolition, and so his reputation stayed intact until after he was dead.

As honorary president of Mensa, Burt had argued that 'when a pioneer has hewn a route through the jungle the rest can follow in his track'.[7] The great psychologist had believed himself a genius, and he had constructed a hall of mirrors to prove himself right.

The name of Hans Eysenck is little remembered now, but when he died in 1997, he was the third-most-cited social scientist, behind Marx and Freud. (He had published seventy-five books and 1,600 journal articles.) In 2002, the American Psychological Association named him the thirteenth most eminent psychologist of the twentieth century, ahead of Carl Jung, Solomon Asch and Ivan Pavlov. Throughout the second half of the twentieth century, Eysenck was the leading light of personality studies, arguing that our inner selves can be graded on introversion, neuroticism and (later) psychopathy. Because he died just a few days after Diana, Princess of Wales, the *Guardian* obituary described him as the People's Psychologist. His autobiography is called *Rebel with a Cause*.

As an undergraduate, Hans Eysenck studied under Cyril Burt.

And after Burt died, Eysenck defended his mentor. 'Scientists have extremely high motivation to succeed in discovering the truth; their finest and most original discoveries are rejected by the vulgar mediocrities filling the ranks of orthodoxy,' he wrote. 'They are convinced that they have found the right answer . . . The figures do not quite fit, so why not fudge them a little but to confound the infidels and unbelievers? Usually the genius is right, of course (if he were not, we should not regard him as a genius) and we may in retrospect excuse his childish games, but clearly this cannot be regarded as license for non-geniuses who foist their absurd beliefs on us.'[8]

I am oddly grateful to Eysenck for this passage, a phenomenal example of 'saying the quiet part out loud'. A genius does not have to play by the rules in pursuit of a great discovery. Hang on though. What if his great discovery turns out to be garbage, perhaps *because* he bent the rules? Ah, then he wasn't a genius after all. This kind of circular logic ought to disqualify a scientist from being taken seriously. Yet in 1995, Eysenck published a book called *Genius*, which makes an astonishing series of claims, all supposedly backed by scientific research. Again, he was blasé about outright fraud, arguing that 'many famous scientists . . . deviated significantly from the paths of righteousness, including Ptolemy, Galileo, Newton, Dalton, Mendel . . . ideology may cause fraud, and it also seems to influence how the accusation is treated'.[9]

Eysenck believed that geniuses needed a particular combination of psychological traits, scoring high on both psychoticism ('an inclination not to limit one's associations to *relevant* ideas, memories, images etc') and ego strength. He made airy, assured judgements: the physicist Stephen Hawking was 'first-rate, but no genius'. And he dismissed the idea that women are just as brilliant as men: 'Creativity, particularly at the highest level, is closely related to gender; almost without exception, genius is only found in males (for whatever reason!). Illustrations abound. There are no women among Roe's eminent scientists, and very few in *American Men of Science*, or among members of the Royal Society; none on a list of the leading mathematicians, and none would be found among the 100 best-known sculptors, painters or dramatists.'[10]

Did you inhale sharply at this? I did. Why *are* there no women in the 1906 compendium called *American Men of Science*? It's a three-pipe problem. As for Eysenck claiming he could find no notable women in the Royal Academy – well, *give them a chance*. The great scientific club was founded in 1660 but refused to grant women membership until 1945. Men had a three-century head start. Hertha Ayrton, the great electrical engineer, won the Hughes Medal from the Royal Academy in 1906 for her work on arc lights, but was still barred from becoming a Fellow. Other great female physicists had to work outside the system, too. The Austrian-American actress Hedy Lamarr had an intelligence every bit as eclectic as that of Francis Galton, and was similarly self-taught. She tinkered with a tablet that would carbonate drinks, and suggested improvements to traffic lights, before inventing a frequency-hopping system to prevent torpedoes being jammed. (It was eventually adopted by the US Navy.) *And* she played Delilah for Louis B. Mayer, never mind marrying six times. Say what you like about Francis Galton, but no one praises his acting abilities or seductive power.

Reading Hans Eysenck's *Genius*, the uncomfortable questions only become more pressing. On page 162, noting clusters of scientific innovation throughout history, Eysenck speculated that perhaps role models acted as mentors and inspirations to an entire generation that followed them, causing a flowering of discovery. 'An alternative, or possibly additional cause, is the postulation of extraterrestrial factors,' he added. *Sorry?* There follow six pages on sunspots, and the possible correlation of solar activity and fertile intellectual periods like the Renaissance in Europe and the Middle Ages in China. Eysenck wonders if magnetic storms and their 'very energetic emissions may have some influence on biological organisms, although we would of course demand exceptionally cogent evidence'.

He concludes the chapter by suggesting that there is enough data for a 'rough portrait' of the genius. 'Clearly, he should be male, of middle or upper-middle parentage, and preferably come from a Jewish background,' Eysenck writes. 'He should receive intellectual stimulation at home, but ought to lose one parent before the age of 10. He should be born in February, and die at 30 or 90, but on no account at 60! He should so arrange it that at the time of his maximum creative powers (between 35 and 45, or even younger for mathematicians and poets) there should be a minimum of solar activity.' Oh, and he should have gout – a painful condition which affects the joints, caused by a build-up of uric acid. After all, 'uric acid has been found to be quite highly correlated with achievement and productivity, although only slightly with IQ'.

There's no hint in Eysenck's taxonomy that genius might be an arbitrary, manmade category, and therefore immune to this kind of scientific precision. Nor that correlation and causation are tricky beasts. Gout might well be correlated with professional achievement, but only because the condition is more common in middle-aged men with enough money to eat a lot of rich food. The kind of people with gout are also the kind of people who are most likely to have done well in their careers. However, you can't scoff pints of beer and buckets of shellfish and expect it to *cause* a rise in your productivity. If you're hunting for genius, you should look elsewhere.

What is this guy smoking, I thought to myself. And then it got worse, because then I heard about his cancer research.

Anthony Pelosi is a cheerful soul, and he has spent thirty years trying to destroy Hans Eysenck's reputation. When I read Eysenck's verdict on Cyril Burt out loud to him, about how geniuses were allowed to make stuff up, he laughed. 'I don't think he was talking about Burt there at the time, really. He was really talking about himself.'

In the early 1990s, Pelosi was a young psychiatrist, and he read Eysenck's famous research on the links between personality and heart disease. The older man was claiming that different personality types were more likely to suffer from particular ailments: there was a 'heart disease-prone' personality and a 'cancer-prone' personality. (The latter led him to question the scientific consensus that smoking caused lung cancer. He concluded that smoking 'does not kill'.) In one paper, Eysenck and his collaborator Ronald Grossarth-Maticek claimed to have treated extreme high blood pressure successfully with psychotherapy. They claimed the trial worked but, Pelosi told me, 'you look at the tables, you're having huge death rates down the line'. Feeling that such experiments were unethical – it seemed that the subjects had been exposed to unproven treatments for their conditions, instead of being given safe, tested alternatives – Pelosi read on. As he did so, he came to a more startling conclusion. He no longer believed the research was unethical. He believed the data was impossible.

In 1992, while Eysenck was still alive, Pelosi and his co-author Louis Appleby published their first article in the *British Medical Journal* on the psychologist's claims about heart disease and cancer. These were very carefully worded, he says, because the lawyers 'wouldn't allow us to say this is fraudulent'.[11] ('These long awaited papers contain some of the most remarkable claims ever to appear in a refereed scientific journal,' they write; a sentence which can very much be read two ways.)

Pelosi made formal complaints to professional bodies, and tried to interest the British Psychological Society in the issue. When they showed little interest, he says that he told them: 'Someday this will come back and bite the British Psychological Society in the bottom. It will bite lots of people in the bum.' He spoke to a journal editor, who worried that academic disputes were common, and that such serious accusations would require intensive legal support. Throughout the 1990s, however, other scientists came forward to question Eysenck's data on personality types. In 1995, the year Eysenck published his book on genius, at least twenty papers questioned his findings.[12] But neither his university nor the professional bodies acted.* Nothing happened, either, when leaked documents revealed a year later that he had received £800,000 in research funding from tobacco companies.†

Eysenck died the following year, in 1997. At his death he was an eminent but controversial man: there are five portraits of him held in the collection of the National Portrait Gallery. In 2001, an exhibition on the last one hundred years in psychology

---

* Eysenck's university, King's College London, investigated in 2019. That year, the British Psychological Society printed a call to investigate Eysenck's work in its in-house magazine, but countered it with an official statement that concluded: 'The conduct of research lies with the academic institution which oversees the work carried out by its academics and we welcomed the investigation into this research carried out by King's College, London.' Found at www.bps.org.uk/psychologist/role-auditing-hans-eysenck

† When asked about this by *Channel 4 News* in a documentary, Eysenck said: 'I'm not sure of any of this . . . we get a lot of research money. As long as somebody pays for the research I don't care who it is.' Quoted in Peter Pringle, 'Eysenck took £800,000 tobacco funds', *Independent*, 31 October 1996.

at London's Science Museum staged a replica of his personality testing lab. As an example, a single one of his articles – a 1985 paper titled 'Personality and Individual Differences', offering a modified version of the Eysenck Personality Test – has been cited more than 3,000 times. Others have more.[13]

But like many other self-styled geniuses in this book, he was also an attention-seeker and a hate figure. He was interviewed in *Penthouse*. He dabbled in research on astrology. He was assaulted on stage by a student for his views on IQ and race. (He believed that the environment was not solely to blame for racial differences in IQ.) His work on IQ gave succour to the National Front and other racist groups – although he always denied holding racist views himself, and even his most critical biographer Rod Buchanan states that 'he was too self-absorbed, too preoccupied with his own aspirations as a great scientist to harbor specific political aims.'[14] He accused anyone who complained about his work of being politically motivated; 'the scattered troops' of the left, trying to censor a maverick thinker. Hans Eysenck was deeply invested in all the mythology of genius. He was Galileo uttering forbidden truths; he was Cyril Burt pursuing unorthodox methods in pursuit of nobler goals; he was an intellectual titan among lesser mortals with middling IQs. In 2016, long after the first questions had been raised over Eysenck's work, a psychologist called Philip Corr wrote a defence of him for the *Times Higher Education* magazine. It was headlined: 'Sometimes you need a pariah.'[15]

Reading it is an unearthly experience: Corr defends Eysenck in the same terms that Eysenck had defended his own mentor, Cyril Burt. 'If Eysenck had been muted in his early days, he would not have gone on to inspire several generations of academics to change the world of psychology and psychiatry,' writes Corr, praising the older man for his debunking of Freudian ideas. But even he struggles with the kooky stuff – and he doesn't mention the problems with the data. 'Eysenck's later years were characterised by largely unproductive forays into astrology and parapsychology, as well as his battles over IQ and smoking, which generated much heat but little light. However, the contrarian, defiant and oppositional attitude that led him down these apparent culs-de-sac is exactly the same one that drove him to make such remarkable progress in his earlier career.'

Corr regrets that if Eysenck were working today, he would be consumed by Twitterstorms and cancelled for wrongthink. 'Even if he had managed to secure an academic position in the first place, he certainly wouldn't have landed a chair. That would have saved a few feathers from being ruffled, but would it really have been in the long-term interests of science?' It's a question worth pondering, since it posits the genius – Eysenck, in this case – as unique and irreplaceable.

But is that really the bargain – that peddling questionable data and supplying ammunition for the far right is a price worth paying for the furtherance of psychology as an academic discipline? Must we say: you want Freudian psychoanalysis debunked? Then you have to sign off on all that guff about cancer-prone personalities, too.

In 2019, Pelosi finally got an article published, alongside an open letter to King's College, London, saying 'there is clearly evidence that this must be investigated'. The letter listed sixty-one questionable articles – twenty-six jointly published by Eysenck and his collaborator Ronald Grossarth-Maticek, 'and the rest single-authored by this man who considers himself a genius.' In a rebuttal – on a website that has since been deleted – Grossarth-Maticek denied any allegations of unethical conduct or that he had engaged in research fraud, saying that he was open about his approach to data collection, which used 'the most effective method of evidence in the history of psychology and epidemiology'. He characterized the requests for retractions as a witch-hunt, writing: 'Doesn't this procedure remind us of the fascist book burning? The Nazis wanted to make disagreeable authors disappear from literature so that they could no longer be quoted.'* When King's College agreed to investigate, Grossarth-Maticek sent a letter to its president, arguing that the university was 'a powerful representative of British and Jewish psychology. All of them don't want the little German Grossarth to dominate the scientific world stage.'[16]

When King's College eventually published its conclusions on its divisive star, the university declared Eysenck's twenty-six co-authored papers 'unsafe'. One of them is the paper that started Anthony Pelosi on his quest, published in *Behaviour Research and Therapy* – a journal Eysenck himself founded. More than a dozen further papers have since been retracted by the journals involved, going back to 1946, and more than seventy have 'expressions of concern' attached to them. The corrections and retractions relate to Eysenck's observational work on the factors which lead to cancer, and his interventions to curb the disease.

But where does that leave Eysenck's work on IQ, and on genius – his implicit contention that white men held the best jobs and made the biggest breakthroughs because of their superior intellect and personalities? There has been no inquiry into this portion of Eysenck's work, and there is no suggestion of one. The 'IQ wars', as they have come to be known, are now one of the

---

* The rebuttal also insisted that the younger man had not been manipulated by Eysenck, and their relationship was 'equal and very creative'. Archived here: https://web.archive.org/web/20191103050120/https://www.krebs-chancen.de/referenzen-und-gutachten/denunziation-englisch/

fiercest and most toxic debates in science. Because those who argued for the inherited nature of IQ came to be associated with theories of European racial superiority, the entire discipline became tainted, and their opponents – the environmentalists – gained the upper hand. This has led to widespread assumptions that only racists believe intelligence is heritable, and that 'IQ tests only measure how good you are at IQ tests'. Neither of these is true: the current scientific consensus is that there is *some* relationship between genes and intelligence, and that performance in IQ tests is correlated with wider educational performance and career success. The mistake is to think that this numerical figure is some inerrant and absolute ranking of intelligence.

That said, I do find the political reaction against the hereditarians understandable. The grand coincidence that Eysenck's work is 'unsafe', while that of his mentor Cyril Burt contained falsified data, ought to give us pause. What viewpoint were both men trying to promote with their work? What mythology allowed them to fiddle the figures and still consider themselves scientific heroes?

Pelosi believes that Eysenck had a 'quasi-religious' belief in his findings, and he lays some of the blame on the milieu that surrounded the celebrated academic. 'We have a self selection of these guys as they gather around each other,' he told me. 'A lot of his own pupils were egging him on: "*You are a genius, Hans.*"' As an academic superstar, Eysenck was able to dictate papers to his secretary and send them out to be published. He ranged far beyond a narrow specialism where an individual researcher might be able to be confident about their findings, becoming a universal smart person, a public intellectual. He wasn't visited by genius; he was a genius. His view of IQ fed into a particular mythology, which justified a particular view of the world, and encouraged him to adopt a particular view of himself. He played a genius on television. Even his wife Sybil bought into the mythology. Her unpublished and unfinished autobiography has an astonishing title: *I Married a Genius*.

Telling me this, Pelosi breaks into laughter again, a full-throated Scottish roar. 'I think my wife would like to write something... *I Married a Daftie*.'

William Shockley and the Genius Sperm Bank

'In terms of my own capacities, my children represent a very significant regression.
My wife – their mother – had not as high an academic achievement standing as I had.'

William Shockley

At five months, baby Billy could say his own name, according to his father's diary. Billy was a precocious kid, but he had a terrible temper, screaming and biting visitors. But his parents, May and William Sr, seem to have surrendered to their son. William Sr had become a father late in life – he was in his mid fifties when Billy was born – and May hated being pregnant. One baby was enough. Billy would be an only child.

There were a few early clues to the man that Bill (his eventual nickname) would become. William Sr was a proud descendant of John Alden and Priscilla Mullins, who had arrived in the US on the *Mayflower* in 1620. As Bill was growing up, he would have heard these pilgrims mythologised as 'true Americans' – a casual insult to the many tribes who already lived on those lands before the white settlers arrived. Bill's parents kept him out of school until he was eight, and two years later sent him to the Palo Alto Military Academy, in what is now Silicon Valley. Then, in 1916, the most consequential event of young Bill's life happened, although he didn't realise it at the time: Lewis Terman came to town.

That's right – we have already met young Bill, who grew up to be the Nobel Prize-winning physicist William Shockley. He failed to make the cut for Terman's 'study of genius', which required an IQ of 135 or higher. Bill was tested at eight: he scored 129. He was tested again at nine: 125. *Sorry, kid, but you didn't make the cut.* (Three years later, Terman tested Bill's mother May, who scored 161.) How did Bill take this news? In later life, he claimed to find it funny. But maybe his wisecracks covered something more serious, because Bill also grew up to be a fervent advocate of eugenics. He argued for the genetic inferiority of black people, and proposed that those with IQs under 100 be offered cash payments in return for being sterilised. 'Later in life, Bill joked often about how he could not qualify for Terman's gifted study, yet could still win a Nobel Prize in physics,' writes Shockley's biographer Joel N. Shurkin.[1] 'That he subsequently used the same IQ tests as the basis for his unpopular beliefs about race and intelligence never seemed to vex him, nor did the fact he was living proof the tests should not be taken too seriously.' The persecuted became the persecutor.

Shockley's story is one of extraordinary success – not just his role in the invention of the transistor, for which he won the Nobel Prize, but for his work during the Second World War on bomb targeting. But then, at the height of his fame, he torched his reputation. He went, in the words of his obituary in the *Los Angeles Times*, 'from being a physicist with impeccable academic credentials to amateur geneticist, becoming a lightning rod whose views sparked campus demonstrations and a cascade of calumny'.[2] His eugenic beliefs were not just thought experiments indulged by an out-of-touch academic. In an episode of near-unbelievable crankiness, Shockley became involved with a project known as the 'Genius Sperm Bank'.

So what happened? Why was William Shockley so tormented by the question of intelligence – and the question of genius? Why did he destroy himself over an illusion?

His biography provides some answers. Shockley's failure to excel at Lewis Terman's IQ test was not a fluke. On 18 May 1925, he took a college entrance exam and scored in the 69th percentile in the sciences – good but not astounding. He was in the lower half for English and French, and the 45th percentile on quadratics. The teenage Shockley was not marked for greatness any more than baby Billy had been. But he did have one enormous advantage – he grew up in California in the first half of the twentieth century.

That proto-Silicon Valley was a site of *scenius*, that alchemical space of collective achievement. After the Second World War, the area around San Francisco had an animating idea: progress came through *technology*. (At the end of the twentieth century, this 'California ideology' mutated into the idea that progress comes through *disruption*. More on that later.) The investor Paul Graham, whose start-up incubator Y Combinator has invested in many tech businesses – giving them not just money but mentors and a network – has argued that 'nothing is more powerful than a community of talented people working on related problems'.[3] He cites the example of Florence during the Italian Renaissance, which produced Brunelleschi, Ghiberti, Donatello, Masaccio, Filippo Lippi, Fra Angelico, Verrocchio, Botticelli, Leonardo and Michelangelo. Only 300 kilometers north of Florence lies Milan, which was a similar size, and yet Milan produced nothing like that list – there is no Milanese Leonardo da Vinci. 'Something was happening in Florence in the fifteenth century,' Graham writes, adding 'to make Leonardo you need more than his innate ability. You also need Florence in 1450.'

Graham concludes that talented and ambitious young people should ask where the most exciting place in the world is right now – and then move there. William Shockley didn't have to do that. He was there already. First, he attended the University of California, now known as UCLA, and then, in 1928, he transferred to the California Institute of Technology, widely known as Caltech. That was the place to be in the late 1920s – what Shurkin describes as 'a relatively small school just beginning its march toward one of the great centres for science in the world'. Caltech actively recruited researchers from other institutions, promising them their own labs, and their independence. As a result, the university 'attracted not only some of the brightest researchers, but the most iconoclastic, giving the school an edge of excitement, an atmosphere tinged with adrenaline'.[4] It even had a faculty club, the Athenaeum, a 'hostel for the world's greatest scientific minds', which hosted guest speakers. This atmosphere suited Shockley, who was known for his intensely competitive nature and his love of magic and practical jokes.

Being at Caltech in the late 1920s placed Shockley in the middle of a paradigm shift in physics.* Throughout the preceding decades, physicists had struggled to reconcile their theoretical model of the atom with the results of their practical experiments. The answer came from no longer imagining the atom as a tiny solar system, with the regularity of clockwork and the stability of a circle. Electrons were now vibrations. Or maybe they weren't anywhere, really. This was quantum mechanics, a mind-bending set of ideas so counter-intuitive that the venerable Albert

---

* This is Thomas Kuhn's theory that innovation happens in bursts, when an old model, or paradigm, is overturned. More on that later.

Einstein struggled to accept them. But William Shockley was young enough to find the new model exciting.

When he finished at Caltech, Shockley moved to the east coast, to the Massachusetts Institute of Technology for his PhD. He drove across the country with a fellow student called Frederick Seitz, who was headed for Princeton. On their arrival in New Jersey, police pulled over the car and, seeing the unshaven Shockley, decided to search it. They found a loaded gun in the glove compartment. Shockley suffered no consequences from this. He got the gun back. It was a brief moment of danger, a mere footnote in this story, but it is also a sobering reminder of the insulation provided by race, class and academic connections. Would a black version of Shockley – equally talented, or perhaps even with a higher IQ – have been jailed and thrown off his course? Very possibly. Would a black Shockley have got the place at MIT at all? Very unlikely. Leonardo da Vinci couldn't have been Leonardo if he started out in Renaissance Milan, and in the same way, Shockley didn't just need to be Shockley. He needed to be white, and male, and American – and attending the best American universities at a time when physics was undergoing a revolution. By this point in time, however, Shockley was already beginning to see himself as a special type of person. 'He was inclined to believe that society should be governed by a vaguely defined intellectually elite group, rather than by majority rule as in a democratic society,' his driving buddy Seitz wrote in a 1994 memoir.[5]

Shockley got married in August 1933, to a woman called Jean Alberta Bailey, about whom his friends and family knew nothing. She was well-read, and he used to explain physics problems to her in order to get them clear in his own mind. Their daughter Alison quickly arrived. Three years later, with his PhD completed, he left MIT to work for Bell Labs. Here, he became part of another site of *scenius*. Bell Labs, a research and development organisation now located in Murray Hill, New Jersey, has become a staple of textbooks on innovation. Nine Nobel Prizes were awarded for work done there, including the one awarded to Shockley. Claude Shannon, the founder of modern cryptography, worked there. Researchers at Bell invented the laser, the solar cell and the UNIX operating system. Patents on innovations developed there earned *millions*. Every so often, one of today's entrepreneurs will suggest that we need a new Bell Labs, but that is, sadly, impossible – the original was owned by the telephone company AT&T, which had an effective monopoly in the United States. That made it rich, and gave it expansive ambitions. Researchers could follow their interests, as long as those interests might be profitable for AT&T. Often, one breakthrough unlocked another. When Shockley arrived at Bell, the great challenge it faced was extending the distances over which phone calls could be made. He addressed himself to the problem, between practical jokes – such as unleashing a mechanical duck on the stage while a visiting speaker was present – and demonstrating his athletic fitness. (He liked to backflip into rooms at work.) He filed his first patent application within a year of arrival. He was not yet thirty.

His uncomfortable views on race were already beginning to emerge, however. His wife Jean wrote in September 1939 about inviting 'one of the stenographers here – a colored girl with a wonderful name, Pocahontas Foster' to lunch with Bill and another friend, who was also 'half-convinced that the Negro really is an inferior race'. Shockley told his wife that Foster was more impressive than the average white stenographer, which pleased her. Perhaps because of his childhood experiences, he was already interested in IQ as a measurement, too. When he asked Jean to take their daughter for an IQ test, she refused, saying she didn't want to place any burden on Alison.

The Second World War then intruded on Shockley's world. Like other American physicists, he immediately spotted the significance of Lise Meitner and Otto Hahn's work on nuclear fission – the research that would make the atom bomb possible. But he wasn't exceptional enough to be invited to Los Alamos to join the team assembled by J. Robert Oppenheimer. Shockley started work on chain reactions in his own lab, but when he applied for a patent, the government shut down his work – the subject was too sensitive to allow dabblers into the field. Instead, he was assigned to work on more mundane military problems, such as getting depth charges to explode correctly when dropped from planes. In August 1942, Jean had another baby, William Alden (another 'Billy'), although Shockley's work meant he rarely saw his family. A third child, Richard, would follow in 1947.

During this intense period of military research, nothing seemed out of the ordinary in the Shockley household. But on 6 November 1943, Bill wrote his wife a note which stated bluntly: 'Dear Jean: I am sorry that I feel I can no longer go on. . . . I hope you have better luck in the future.'[6]

Then he loaded his revolver with a single bullet and fired it at his temple. The chamber was empty. He survived. Shockley then wrote another note, observing that there was only a one in six chance of the suicide attempt succeeding, and therefore he was 'sorry that I was not sufficiently ingenious or painstaking and [sic] find a more practical and suitable means of solving our problems'. He never gave his wife either of the letters.

The story behind the invention of the transistor is a complicated one – and it does not reflect well on Shockley. After the war, he returned to Bell Labs, where he now held a management role. He began to supervise two other men, Walter Brattain and John Bardeen, who were trying to find something better than vacuum tubes to amplify the electric current in telephone lines. Vacuum tubes made long-distance calls much smoother, but their range was limited. Shockley suggested a device that used an electrical field instead, but it didn't work. Brattain and Bardeen then went off on their own and developed what became known as the point-contact transistor, which used two dots of gold on a germanium crystal to amplify the electrical signal.

The executives at Bell Labs were delighted with the discovery, but Shockley wasn't. He began researching his own variation, the sandwich transistor, and when the lab came to file patents, he was furious that his name was not included. Patents were vital for establishing precedence, and for being able to exploit the commercial potential of a discovery. In retaliation, Shockley appears to have threatened management with an insurrection. To mollify him, Bell Labs placed him at the centre of all publicity, and included him in all the official photographs. When the announcement of the discovery was made in June 1948, Shockley was the one who answered journalists' questions. He quickly wrote a textbook, *Electrons and Holes in Semiconductors*, which further cemented his reputation as the inventor of the transistor. The electronic age was here, and Shockley was its father.

Unsurprisingly, the team at Bell Labs never recovered from this. Although Brattain and Bardeen were initially relaxed about the framing of their discovery, they grew disillusioned with Shockley as a manager. When Brattain asked him to overhaul the team, Shockley wrote a memo noting that he was 'overwhelmed by an irresistible temptation to do my climbing by moonlight and unroped'. (This was more than a metaphor; Shockley was an accomplished climber.) This was Cyril Burt's model of genius – untameable, irreplaceable, in need of perpetual indulgence. How could such a man be expected to play by the rules of corporate life?

Shockley's team felt differently. In 1950, Brattain and Bardeen refused to report to him any longer. In July 1951, Bardeen left Bell Labs, saying Shockley 'used the group largely to exploit his own ideas'. (He ended up at the University of Illinois, where he won a second Nobel in 1972 for research on superconductivity – work that Shockley had blocked him from doing at Bell.)

Shockley's sandwich transistor wasn't a bust. It led to the more successful junction transistor, which was mass-produced by Bell from 1953. But he had begun to chafe at his lack of promotion, and that fostered his growing obsession with psychological testing. He first took over the system for merit-based raises at Bell, and when he founded his own company, the Shockley Semiconductor Laboratory, he forced his employees to take strange psychometric tests. At home, things were changing, too: Jean was diagnosed with cancer, and when she recovered, he announced that the marriage was over. The next year, he met a young woman called Emmy at a friend's house, where he read out a paper on creativity in laboratories. She critiqued it. He fell in love. After his divorce, he became a lecturer at Stanford University – where, in a neat piece of irony, the provost was Lewis Terman's son Frederick.

Although Shockley didn't know it, the most productive years of his life were already over. His company folded within a year after a group of his senior staff, nicknamed the 'Traitorous Eight' by journalists, decided they could not bear to work with him. Shockley would not listen to their ideas, and was becoming paranoid, insulting and confrontational. He subjected his staff to lie detector tests. The rebels went on to found Fairchild Semiconductor, which itself splintered, and two of its alumni then founded a firm called Intel. One of their researchers created the microprocessor, making everyone involved extremely rich. Fairchild is now seen as one of the companies that created Silicon

Valley – so you could also attribute its birth indirectly to Shockley's terrible personality. In 1961, his car was hit by a drunk driver, and it took him months to recover. Emmy was hurt even more badly.

The Nobel laureate was now in his fifties, out of ideas and left behind by his former protégés. And that's when he started to talk publicly about IQ.

What exactly made Shockley immolate his career is hard to guess. Was it the lingering pain of the car accident? Was it his long-held principles finally becoming the sole focus of his life? Was he hungry for attention, and found a surefire method of obtaining it? Did he consider himself special – the genius who launched the electronic age – and so he decided to make his life all about that special quality?

Shurkin's biography leaves the question open. But his account of the second half of Shockley's life demonstrates a pattern of intellectual degradation which the internet – thanks to polarisation and the attention economy – has since made ubiquitous. Shockley saw himself as a 360-degree public intellectual, whose views on every subject were worth hearing. Anyone who demurred must be motivated by ideology and could therefore be ignored.

Shockley's first speech on IQ and eugenics came at a press conference for Nobel scientists in Minnesota. When asked what the chances were of nuclear war, he answered, 'Fifty-fifty, I think,' before adding: 'But if there is nuclear war man would at least have to begin to control his own genetics.' He followed this with a speech to a Nobel-branded conference on genetics. Why the hell was he there, as a physicist with no relevant expertise in biology? Because he was a Nobel laureate, of course. A 'genius'.

Then, as now, there is an assumption that superior knowledge and expertise in one domain confers authority in others. It is one of the worst outcomes of the mythology of genius, because it encourages exceptional people to stray far outside their competence – to see themselves as omni-experts, superior minds who have much to contribute on any issue. (Once, when a house guest contradicted him, Shockley snapped back: 'What law of nature have *you* discovered?') Over the next three decades, his views on IQ would bring him into contact with many geneticists who believed that his questions, though provocative, were legitimate. What the real experts could not stand was his unscientific bull-in-a-china-shop approach to the subject – and his dismissal of all criticism as politically motivated. (A modern version of this might be a successful entrepreneur who succumbs to paranoia about the 'woke mind virus' and declining birthrates endangering the West.)

And there was another way in which Shockley's story foreshadowed today's media landscape. His views became more and more extreme as he expounded them in public, and faced a backlash for doing so. His initial speech to the Nobel-branded conference began in humane terms, talking of his wartime visit to India, and the terrible toll of famine. Then he moved into the story of a robbery in San Francisco – an acid attack on a shopkeeper, carried out by a man who was one of a dozen children, all raised on welfare benefits. The eugenic subtext was obvious. He acknowledged that a purely genetic explanation for genius could not account for Leonardo da Vinci, the brilliant son of ordinary people, but suggested that the painter was merely an expected genetic fluke. (There was no acknowledgement of the importance of *scenius*.) His prescription for improving humanity was a Galtonian one: the mentally backward should be discouraged from having children.

Complaints followed, but nothing serious, and Shockley carried on riding his new hobby-horse. He expanded on the acid attack story in an interview to *U.S. News and World Report* in 1965: the perpetrator was now identified as black, and the victim as white. The attacker was one of seventeen children whose mother had an IQ of 55. Were black Americans less intelligent than whites, he wondered out loud. Someone should study the problem: 'There are eminent Negroes whom we are proud of in every way, but are they the ones who come from and have large families? What is happening to the total numbers? This we do not know.' Like Oliver Wendell Holmes declaring that 'three generations of imbeciles are enough', Shockley now favoured enforced sterilisation for those with low IQs.

The interview brought condemnation from his fellow academics at Stanford, in unhelpfully vague terms. He was causing 'mischief' and spreading 'pseudoscience', they said. Over the next years, Shockley's statements kept getting more extreme, and the reaction became more and more outraged. But rather than refuting him as a scientist, critics focused on the moral implications of his words. That allowed him to pose as an empiricist – just asking questions – under siege from hysterical leftists. The best rebuttals explained not that he was evil, but that he was wrong. As the criticism mounted, Shockley gravitated towards the most controversial part of his thesis – differences in racial IQ – and became obsessed. He approached a delicate subject with all the tact and sensitivity of a rhinoceros. He declared he would not accept invitations to talk about physics unless he could also talk about eugenics. He attracted support from avowed racists and white supremacists (although he did not accept funding from overtly racist groups). He alienated his friends with his relentless crusade, talking of little else.

Like Cyril Burt and Hans Eysenck, Shockley became swept

into the 'IQ Wars' of the twentieth century. In America, these became synonymous with two extreme positions: far-right arguments about innate racial superiority, and hard-left advocacy for pure blank slatism. Because the subject is so controversial, it attracts dogmatists, cranks and the occasional researcher trying to chart a moderate course, who is then shouted at by everyone else. In 2018, the geneticist Kathryn Paige Harden argued for 'a middle ground between "let's never talk about genes and pretend cognitive ability doesn't exist" and "let's just ask some questions that pander to a virulent on-line community populated by racists with swastikas in their Twitter bios".'[7]*

William Shockley was a master of the second type of scholarship – the 'just asking questions' model. He used the Stanford press office to promote his public statements. He sought out black academics to debate, because these events attracted more coverage. He got friendly local newspaper editors to request coverage of his speeches from news wires. His statements were simultaneously extreme and spuriously precise, which gave them an aura of authority. In 1972, he claimed that 'for each 1 percent of Caucasian ancestry, the average IQ of American black populations goes up approximately one IQ point'.

Something about the subject of intelligence has a warping effect on its most furious proponents. Francis Galton had an incredible intellect but little humanity. Shockley's obsession fed the same tendency within him, and turned another great scientist into a cold, cruel observer who saw people as little more than

---

* When Harden began to advance the arguments she would later turn into her 2021 book *The Genetic Lottery*, which argued for social equality – but conceded that genetic differences in IQ exist – the *New Yorker* reported that she was subjected to 'parades of arguments and counterarguments, leaked personal emails, and levels of sustained podcasting that were, by anyone's standards, extreme'.

collections of statistics. He insisted that he was only ever talking about group intelligence – there were talented, exceptional black people, he said – but one incident shows how this ideology played out in practice. By the 1970s, he had taken to asking reporters who wanted to interview him to sit through a presentation on the heritability of IQ. When a medical writer called Syl Jones phoned to request an interview, Shockley and his wife recorded the phone call, as had become their habit. They reviewed the tape of their conversation and agreed that the journalist understood the scientific basis of Shockley's work. Nonetheless, they made Jones take more tests on statistics. He passed them. And so they granted him an interview.

In October 1974, a black man and a white man turned up at Shockley's house – Jones and his photographer. Shockley offered a handshake to the white man: 'Hello, Mr Jones.' But Syl Jones was the *black* man. 'It was a wrong guess that seemed to stagger him,' Jones wrote six years later. 'Obviously stunned by my blackness, he insisted that I submit to one final test, concocted on the spur of the moment, concerning the application of the Pythagorean theory to some now long-forgotten part of his dysgenic thesis. I came up with a satisfactory explanation and Shockley had no choice but to grant me the interview. Since that day, he has viewed me as "the exception that proves the rule".'[8] Jones had not told Shockley he was black before he arrived at the house, he wrote, because 'I was hoping for a confrontation.'

Despite this inauspicious beginning to the interview, Jones made every effort to represent Shockley fairly – and to explain Shockley's views to his readers. His reward was another interview, this time published in *Playboy* in 1980. It is a perfect, strange artifact of its time: thousands of words on IQ printed between adverts for cigarettes and razors, and pictures of OJ

Simpson selling leather cowboy boots. Two pages in a row carry similar taglines: Benchmark bourbon – 'Sip it with arrogance' – and one for vintage cars: 'The arrogance of excellence'. Shockley's ideas flourished at a time when elitism was not yet a dirty word. (That has now changed: today's elites like to pretend they are regular, everyday people. The sociologists Sam Friedman and Aaron Reeves studied entries in the biographical dictionary *Who's Who* and found that in recent decades, hobbies such as 'drinking beer' had replaced frank declarations of love for the opera and skiing.)[9]

In the article, Syl Jones comes across as a sympathetic but stringent interviewer. When Shockley mentions the idea of a 'bonus' being given to those with 'defective' genes if they agree to be sterilised, he asks dryly: 'That sounds vaguely familiar to us. Does it remind you of any particular mass movement within the last forty years?' Shockley replies that his plan is a 'thinking exercise' and voluntary sterilisation would 'not require Hitler's concentration camps'. He certainly had given the idea a lot of thought: he proposed $1,000 per IQ point below 100, because '$30,000 put into a trust for a 70 IQ-moron, who might otherwise produce 20 children, might make the plan very profitable to the taxpayer'.

Shockley gave many more quotes like this – musings which anyone with common sense could have seen would be inflammatory. Perhaps this is part of the paradox of genius: the same analytical intelligence which allowed him to see the flaw in a statistical table, or solve a mathematical problem in an unexpected way, also made him reject limits on his political thinking. What was so wrong with taking an idea for a walk? But that practice has different implications in an engineering lab and when you are talking about other human beings. Asked why anyone should listen to a physicist talk about genetics,

Shockley answered: 'Out of the mouths of babes.' Jones pressed him, saying that a man nearing seventy was hardly a 'babe'. Shockley replied that 'occasionally, truth can come from an unlikely source . . . why should anyone have listened to Einstein when there were no relativists at the time?' Then he was asked about himself.

PLAYBOY: That's not the first time you've mentioned Einstein in comparison to yourself. Einstein is considered a genius. Are you a genius, in your opinion?

SHOCKLEY: Insofar as genius may be sweat and effort, perhaps. I would not like to try to define exactly what genius is or to say that I necessarily belong to that class. Certainly, there have been very great technological developments that have followed from very simple observations that anyone might have made had he been there at the time. My track record is definitely somewhat better than that. But in terms of people such as Newton, Einstein and Maxwell, I would say that they belong to a higher level of genius. The contributions I have made are largely technological.

Maxwell here is James Clerk Maxwell, a Victorian physicist who was the first to describe electromagnetic radiation – a paradigm shift as significant as Newtonian physics or Einstein's theory of relativity, but one without an accompanying mythology. Shockley might have been reluctant to bracket himself with the great physicists of the past, but the label of *genius* still hung around his neck anyway. Who knows how that affected him – did it encourage him to think, as Hans Eysenck did, that he deserved particular latitude? In any case, he confessed that his own superior mind resulted in him rejecting evidence which contradicted his beliefs.

PLAYBOY: Geneticist Cyril Burt is a name you know quite well, since you used some of his data on identical twin studies in your own work. That data has now been shown to be falsified, or at least tampered with by Burt himself. Why did he deliberately skew the data?

SHOCKLEY: I'm not sure, and in any case, it is rather pointless speculation now. There seems to be little doubt that Burt's data did have a great deal of fakery in it.

PLAYBOY: Don't you think his fakery reflects on your own credibility? Here is a man who was a scientist, and evidently had no qualms about tampering with the truth. Whether or not his motives were political, we can't say. But doesn't that hurt your case?

SHOCKLEY: Certainly. It's only human nature to make that kind of connection. That is why it is so important to have a better study on identical twins – one that is scrupulously objective – so as to refute all these sorts of criticisms.

PLAYBOY: Are you now denouncing Burt's data?

SHOCKLEY: I would not use the word denounce. I would regard it as deplorable and sad, but it happened and it is unfortunate.

PLAYBOY: We're asking because Burt's data was central to at least part of your thesis.

SHOCKLEY: As well as other data.

A statistician as good as Shockley could hardly deny the obvious conclusion to be drawn from Cyril Burt's too-perfect twin data: *Burt was a fraud.* But that didn't make him reflect on whether his own political views might compromise his scientific objectivity. The most compelling moments of the interview were its human ones. At one point, Jones asked about Shockley's own offspring – two of whom were college graduates, and one of whom even had a PhD in physics. 'In terms of my own capacities, my children represent a very significant regression,' he said. 'My wife – their mother – had not as high an academic achievement standing as I had.' He was making a well-evidenced point: that exceptional success is rare, and his children were closer to the average than he was. But again, it sounded heartless and dehumanising; a snub to his first wife and a dismissal of his children, whom he rarely saw. His eldest son was dismissed as a 'college dropout'.

Shockley also said that he wanted to found the field of 'raceology' – the study of races – and that he bore no personal prejudice against black Americans. In fact, he added, his nurses after the car accident had been largely black, and had provided excellent care. 'What was it that impressed you so highly?' asked Jones. 'They gave us the best care and were the most natural and comforting that I had,' replied Shockley. 'In fact, while my cast prevented me from doing so, they were the ones who cleaned my rear end properly.'

Why did Shockley give this interview, when his views were already so well-known and well-rehearsed? Because he wanted publicity for a new venture: masturbation. Despite his claims to

Syl Jones that he was no genius, Shockley had allowed himself to be recruited to a madcap scheme called the Repository for Germinal Choice, better known as the 'Nobel sperm bank'. He was one of three Nobel laureates who signed up for the scheme.

The project was the brainchild of an eccentric millionaire, Robert K. Graham, who made his fortune by selling scratch-proof lenses for spectacles. He had been mulling the idea since the 1960s, and by the late 1970s he had started to seek donations. Graham was clear about the need for the sperm bank – the American population was getting lazy and degenerate – and clear about the answer. He would collect the sperm of great scientists and distribute it to (high IQ, married) women, who would have superior babies. 'Graham valued, by miraculous coincidence, exactly the same kind of analytical talent he himself possessed,' writes David Plotz in his account of the venture.[10] 'Like Graham, Shockley started to fear the genetic decline of the US population at the moment that Americans decided to stop listening to men like him.'

Shockley made his first donation on a visit to Southern California in 1977 – when he was close to seventy years old. Graham and his assistant returned for more sperm the next year, flying to San Francisco to wait while Shockley delivered a sample in a room at a Travelodge. The trip nearly ended in disaster: Graham didn't want to put the sperm through the X-ray machine at the airport, because radiation can cause genetic abnormalities. Instead, he smuggled it on board and was foiled by stewards who noticed the plumes of liquid nitrogen curling out of the container. He eventually persuaded a pilot to let him fly with the sample in the cabin the next day. Graham was delighted with Shockley's contribution, writing to him to say he would be back soon: 'We don't want such a superb asset to go unutilized.'[11]

In 1980, when the *Los Angeles Times* reporter Edwin Chen first heard about this odd millionaire and his underground bunker of genius sperm, he worried that the story sounded too fantastical to be true. So he started phoning round all the Nobel laureates he could find. They denied any knowledge of such a scheme – until he got to Shockley, who cheerfully confessed his involvement.

Chen published a story on 29 February that year, detailing the sperm bank's existence and Shockley's donation. The reaction was so overwhelming that Robert K. Graham held a press conference on 2 March. 'We aren't thinking of a super race,' he insisted. 'We are thinking in terms of a few more creative, intelligent people who otherwise might not be born.' Unfortunately for him, the involvement of Shockley brought eugenics – and racism – into the story from the start. The plans were roundly mocked everywhere from newspaper columns to *Saturday Night Live*, and Shockley made things worse by revelling in the publicity. The backlash spooked the two other (anonymous) Nobel laureates who had been involved, and they never donated again. Their donations did not produce a single baby, and neither did Shockley's – he told *Playboy* he had no idea that men's sperm declines in quality with age, a great example of a scientific blind spot.

Although the Repository for Germinal Choice became a laughingstock, the publicity brought customers: after Graham's press conference, the sperm bank received more applications than it could handle. By 1985, Graham had dropped his demographic sights to sports stars and self-made businessmen, one of whom said that the pursuit was so intense he 'started to feel like the dog at the dog breeders' meeting'. When David Plotz tracked down other donors, he found that the 'Nobel sperm bank' branding was a lie. The closest the bank came to fulfilling that promise was the *son* of a Nobel laureate, who saw his donations as 'work' – the only real work he appeared to have done in life. 'I am helping the human race because I have good genes,' the man said. 'I have studied evolutionary biology and this is what evolution is all about. Winning is passing on your genes, and losing is failing to do so.' He had no children with his wife.

The mothers who sought out genius sperm were often equally unusual people. One was obsessive about her children's IQs, and claimed they were such perfect specimens that people *volunteered* to babysit them. The first couple to reveal they had borne a Nobel sperm bank baby were Jack and Joyce Kowalski, who had Victoria in April 1982. After they went public about their hopes for Victoria, whom they planned to raise as a 'female Thomas Edison or Einstein', it emerged that the couple had just been released from prison. They had been using the identities of dead children to obtain loans. They had also lost custody of Joyce's children from her first marriage, after allegedly punishing them for poor academic performance.[12]

The golden child of the Nobel sperm bank was Doron Blake, born in August 1982. His name means 'gift' and his mother Afton doted on Doron, breastfeeding him until he was six and boasting about his IQ of 180. A psychologist who investigated her patients' past lives, Afton Blake had Doron relatively late in life and raised him alone. She thrived on publicity: Doron was photographed for magazine covers and gave unbearably precocious quotes to reporters about how he read *Hamlet* aged three. (He was also bullied at school for being a donor baby.) After a while, Afton began to charge reporters for interviews with her son, building up a fund for him to attend Reed College in Portland, Oregon. In adulthood, he continued the practice, but as he got older, it became wearisome to repeat the same answers to the same questions and he has recently dropped out of view. His Facebook page records him teaching Buddhist and Chinese philosophy at a school in Connecticut, and there are two kids in his profile picture. 'It was a screwed-up idea, making genius people,' he told

Plotz. 'The fact that I have a huge IQ does not make me a person who is good or happy . . . I don't think you can breed for good people.'

William Shockley died in 1989 of prostate cancer which had spread to his bones. He did not allow Emmy to tell his estranged children he was dying; in fact, they discovered his death from newspaper reports. His obituary in the *Los Angeles Times* captures his triumphs – his wartime service, the transistor, the Nobel – and his later turn to eugenics. It ends like this: 'In addition to his wife, Emmy, Shockley is survived by two sons, William and Richard; a daughter, Alison Ianeli, and a granddaughter. No services are planned.'

William Shockley thought himself a genius, and the idea poisoned him from the inside. Instead of being commemorated as a great innovator, he is now treated as an embarrassing footnote to the history of Silicon Valley. No one will be building a Shockley Lab, or endowing a Shockley Prize. Like Cyril Burt, he went hunting for genius and found himself instead in a hall of mirrors.

Marilyn and Me

'I do get disappointed that so many members spend so much time solving puzzles.'

Lancelot Ware, Mensa co-founder

Who has the highest IQ in history? One answer would be: a little girl from Missouri. In 1956, she took a version of the Stanford-Binet test and recorded a mental age of 22 years and 10 months, equivalent to an IQ of 228. (The score needed to get into Mensa is 140, and the average IQ in the general population is 100.) Her score lay unnoticed for decades, until it was uncovered and sent in to the *Guinness Book of World Records*, which declared her to be the smartest person who ever lived. A genius, in other words. Her name, appropriately enough, was Marilyn vos Savant.

But vos Savant didn't make any scientific breakthroughs, or create a masterpiece. For most of her life, in fact, she was utterly unremarkable. She graduated high school 178th in a class of 613, according to a 1989 profile in *New York* magazine. She married at sixteen, had two children by nineteen, became a stay-at-home mother, and was divorced at twenty-six. She briefly studied philosophy at Washington University, but her parents made her quit. She married again and was divorced again at thirty-five. She became a puzzle enthusiast, joined a high IQ society, and occasionally wrote an essay or a satirical piece under a false name for the local newspaper. Mostly she devoted herself to raising her boys.

That all changed in 1985, when the *Guinness Book of World Records* published her childhood IQ score. How they obtained the record is murky: there are suggestions that a contact at a high IQ society encouraged her to send in her test. Thanks to the publicity, however, vos Savant met her third husband, Robert Jarvik, who had developed a pioneering model of an artificial heart. Jarvik had his own story of being overlooked. He had been rejected by fifteen medical schools after scoring badly on the MCAT tests used to predict academic performance, and was only able to study medicine after transferring in from an architecture course. He wrote to Marilyn after seeing her in a magazine, and she sent him some flattering pictures in return.[1] They quickly became an item.

The couple took up residence in New York and gave joint interviews, emphasising their specialness, and invited reporters to their wedding in 1987. Their wedding rings were made of gold and pyrolytic carbon, a material used in Jarvik's artificial hearts. The science fiction writer Isaac Asimov gave the bride away. Marilyn wore a green dress covered in seed pearls and a peacock feather in her hair. A news report has them telling their guests that they were relieved to meet each other, because they found most people difficult to talk to – the implication being that mere mortals were not on their wavelength. The honeymoon would be spent in Paris, they revealed, where Marilyn would write a screenplay for a futuristic satire and Robert would continue researching his 'grand unification theory' of physics.[2]

The couple were very happy to play up to the role of public intellectuals, embracing what we might now call 'galaxy-brainedness' – that is, a willingness to have opinions on everything. The *New York* profile of the couple's unusual marriage records Robert saying that meeting Marilyn opened his mind. He now thought the theory of relativity is 'probably wrong', the Big Bang theory was 'wrong', the expanding universe was 'wrong', and there was no such thing as black holes. Despite their superior brains, Marilyn never had her screenplay made, and Robert did not revolutionise physics with his theories.

What did happen, though, is that on the back of her Guinness nomination, Marilyn built a career as a professional genius. She published books such as the *Omni IQ Quiz Contest* and *Brain Building: A Guide to More Effective Thinking*. She became an advice columnist for *Parade* magazine, where she was billed as 'the smartest person in the world', setting puzzles and answering readers' queries. Her speciality was logic problems. (In other words, she had the particular type of mental ability most readily identified by IQ tests.) In one column, she provided a solution for an apparently insoluble conundrum. Angry readers wrote in to correct her, but she was right.

Marilyn vos Savant's life perfectly illustrates the idea of genius as a self-fulfilling prophecy. She was normal, overlooked even – a housewife raising her children in total obscurity – until she was labelled a genius. And then she became one.

Her reservations about IQ testing did not stop her from joining Mensa, which is easily the best-known of the high IQ societies. Mensa arose from a chance meeting in 1945 between two men called Roland Berrill and Lancelot Lionel Ware, although in later years Cyril Burt – Mensa's first honorary president – would characteristically take the credit.

Berrill was an eccentric, who was interested in every crankish fad going, from palmistry to phrenology. He had grown up in the shadow of his older brother, the golden boy of the family, who was killed in the First World War. He missed the aristocracy, many of whom had sold up their grand estates in the first half of the twentieth century thanks to financial pressures. He wanted a new kind of aristocracy, composed of the very brightest and best – his original vision for the society was as a high-class brains trust, settling the big issues of the day by polling its super smart members. Mensans were to be drawn from the top 1 per cent of the population in intelligence terms, as measured by an unsupervised test, or 2 per cent on the supervised one.* Berrill, who never married, also decided that Mensa needed a 'Queen', so at least one early gathering featured a young woman sitting uncomfortably on a throne among the (majority male) fellowship. His personal wealth sustained the early years of the society – at one point he had special Mensa tiles made, which he wanted members to install unobtrusively in their fireplaces in order to recognise each other. (Later, members were instructed to wear yellow map pins in their lapel as a 'sign of genius'.) Eventually, even Berrill's deep pockets were not enough to offset his eccentricities, and he was forced out in January 1952.

Berrill's crank tendencies were not the only problem faced by the fledgling society. Victor Serebriakoff's highly entertaining – and highly partisan, because he was a senior officer of Mensa – history records that one early plan was for all volunteer roles to be randomly assigned to members. Inevitably, though, that led to unmotivated people failing to fulfil their allotted tasks. 'High intelligence is a poor defence against collective stupidity,' wrote Serebriakoff. Later on, Mensa's magazine was plagued by complaints from members whose articles were edited down, because they were far too long. They saw that process as censorship.

Mensa was a product of its time. When it was launched, few people went to university, and for some members, this was their

---

* This would be an IQ of 130–140 upwards, depending on the particular test used.

first chance to talk about books, or art, or philosophy – their first chance to meet other nerds, really. The other important current of the 1940s and 1950s was an increased interest in equality. In the post-war years, British class-based deference was breaking down and that translated to wider revulsion with anyone who seemed to think they were better than other people. Mensa was countercultural, and unafraid to be elitist. Serebriakoff's book is full of little jabs at the 'egalitarian age' in which Mensa was launched. The society was 'a partial counter-thrust to the over-egalitarian trend which was beginning, as all such trends do, to overshoot itself'. At the same time, it was obvious that many early Mensans were not conventionally successful. That meant the society attracted snobbery from those who saw it, in Serebriakoff's words, as the home of 'brain-proud Quarrelsome Underachievers Limited'. In writing the society's history, he added, 'I look forward with complacent zest to the condescension of established academe.'

If we can thank the high IQ societies for anything, it is for proving that a 'genius-level IQ' does not perfectly correlate with achievement. These societies were set up to demonstrate that their members were superior people with superior brains. But the polls run by Mensa were quickly revealed to be useless – simply having a high IQ does not make you an expert on foreign policy, or economics, or any of a thousand other political questions. In many cases, a self-image as a 'clever person' simply makes you more likely to hold your incorrect opinions extremely forcefully.

Mensa is the best-known of the high IQ societies, but there are plenty of others – although some of them were very short-lived indeed. After coming out as a genius, Marilyn vos Savant joined an even more exclusive society called Mega, which is limited to those within the top 0.0001 per cent of IQ scores.

From the start, Mega was riven by infighting. In the 1990s, it merged with another society and announced that members would have to retake the entry test. This prompted something close to a civil war, and by 2003, the various factions were so splintered that the dispute ended up in court. The loser in that case, Mega co-founder Christopher Langan, was forbidden from using the name.[3] (Langan has a Facebook group where he outlines his 'Cognitive Theoretical Model of the Universe', as well as his belief that George W. Bush staged 9/11 to stop people learning about his cognitive-theoretical model of the universe. In another post, he wrote that humanity was failing because 'rich libtards' were 'pandering like two-dollar whores to the degenerate tastes, preferences, and delusions of the genetic underclass, the future of humanity be damned.'[4]) Another one-time member of Mega was Keith Raniere, whose local paper claimed that his at-home test proved his brain was 'one in 10 million'.[5] In 2020, he was sentenced to 120 years in prison over the abuse he perpetrated as the leader of the NXIVM cult.

Today, because of their infighting and their members' lack of worldly success, high IQ groups have become kind of a joke. An exhaustive online history of the high IQ movement, compiled by a blogger called Darryl Miyaguchi in the 1990s, recounts the story of all their various schisms. For example, the Cincinnatus Society, which admitted only those at the 99.9 percentile of IQ, usurped a previous group with these criteria, called the Triple Nine Society or TNS. The Cincinnatus leader Grady Ward 'declared himself Dictator, which some found preferable to the chaos in TNS,' Miyaguchi writes.[6] The Triple Nine Society was itself a breakaway faction from *another* group, the International Society for Philosophical Inquiry.

Even as someone who has reported on the hard left of politics, I find the frequency of schisms among self-styled genius collectives impressive. Anyone wondering why high IQ does not necessarily lead to works of genius would be well-advised to spend a few hours reading the history of high IQ societies. Two notes from Miyaguchi's list tell the story better than I can:

> **10/16/97**: Paul Maxim [an aspirant member of Mega] has roughly estimated my IQ at about the 150 level, and wonders if I have the proper credentials (which appear to be well below the 'Mega level') to write this history as it applies to the Mega Society and to pass judgment on important issues confronting it. My response is that what is required to place these events in perspective is not an IQ of 176, but rather an understanding of human nature . . .

> **11/6/97**: Paul Maxim now believes that my intelligence is adequate to the task at hand. My comments about not needing IQ 'credentials' to understand the issues still stand.

In the 1980s, when various high IQ societies were surveyed for their thoughts on a collective name for their members, very few suggested 'geniuses', according to another stalwart of the high IQ community, Grady Towers. 'When asked what [their ability] should be called, they produced a number of suggestions, sometimes esoteric, sometimes witty, and often remarkably vulgar,' wrote Towers in *Gift of Fire*, the journal of another group called the Prometheus Society, in 1987.[7] 'But one term was suggested independently again and again. Many thought that the most appropriate term for people like themselves was Outsider.'

Towers believed those with unusually high intelligence fell into three groups: the well-adjusted middle class, who were able to use their talents; those living marginal lives, working in manual or low-paid jobs and reading textbooks by night; and finally the dropouts, whose families had no idea how to support their brilliant children, and might even have treated them as a 'performing animal, or even an experiment'. The first group did not get involved with high IQ societies, Towers thought, because their intellectual and social lives were already full. 'It's the exceptionally gifted adult who feels stifled that stands most in need of a high IQ society,' he wrote. 'The tragedy is that none of the super high IQ societies created thus far have been able to meet those needs, and the reason for this is simple. None of these groups is willing to acknowledge or come to terms with the fact that much of their membership belong to the psychological walking wounded. This alone is enough to explain the constant schisms that develop, the frequent vendettas, and the mediocre level of their publications. But those are not immutable facts; they can be changed. And the first step in doing so is to see ourselves as we are.'

Grady Towers was murdered on 20 March 2000 while investigating a break-in at the park where he worked as a security guard. He was fifty-five.

In 1990, the *Guinness Book of World Records* retired the highest-IQ category, conceding that none of the tests were able to produce a definitive ranking.* Mainstream psychologists have fallen out of love with measuring IQ, because of the many caveats needed when approaching its findings. One highly productive technique in genetic research – genome-wide association studies or GWAS – stresses not only that many genes are involved even in apparently simple biological mechanisms, but also that genes interact with each other and with the environment. We now know that eye colour is influenced by multiple genes, when

---

* The original IQ tests were also linked to age, and so an impressive score early in life could lead to artificially high results.

textbooks used to present it as one, so imagine how complicated the picture is for intelligence.

This new mood of caution means that Marilyn vos Savant's record will remain untouched. If, that is, it was a record at all – the St Louis school board had the date of her test as March 1957, not September 1956, which would affect the calculation of her 'mental age' versus her calendar age. The education authorities claimed that she hit the ceiling with the test, giving her a 'perfect' score of 167. Vos Savant told *New York* magazine she had answered additional questions from the adult portion of the test to take her score above 200.

Why does that matter? Because Marilyn couldn't and wouldn't have become a 'genius' without the label being pinned on her first. Here's how it works: attention is paid, and then more attention follows, because if people are looking, then there must be something worth looking at, surely? Marilyn vos Savant made a career of being the smartest person alive because she had a number to prove it. That should make us wonder if the same process happens in reverse. Does a child who struggles at school with dyslexia (or even just a mental block on a particular subject) get the message that they aren't 'academic', and lose interest and enthusiasm?

The difference between Marilyn vos Savant the stay-at-home mother, writing essays for the local newspaper under a pseudonym, and Marilyn vos Savant the 'brainiest woman in the world' was an arbitrary, unscientific anointing. That wasn't how IQ tests were supposed to work. As Lewis Terman discovered, childhood tests cannot identify a genius. But perhaps they can manufacture one.

The fundamental grossness of the twentieth-century fetishisation of IQ was brought home to me on a car trip a few months into writing this book. A friend of mine, Adam, and I were off to talk about eugenics at a literary festival. He offered to drive me there. We got to talking about the history of IQ tests – about Galton's belief in hereditary genius, about the corruption of Binet's attempt to help underachieving children, about Henry Goddard's race-baiting, about Cyril Burt and Hans Eysenck's cavalier attitude to data – when Adam revealed that his parents had made him take IQ tests throughout his childhood.

'And?' I said.

'And what?'

'What was your IQ?'

The instant the words came out of my mouth I regretted them. It felt . . . obscene, somehow. Like asking for his inside leg measurement, or worse. As if everything he was – a successful academic, a broadcaster, a father, a husband, a friend – could be reduced to a single number. And that if my own number was higher, then I was *better* than him, somehow.

In that instant, I understood the appeal of IQ: its glorious simplicity, and the promise it offers that the complexity of the human spirit can be quantified in a single numerical value. Several months later, I decided to take a supervised Mensa test in London and see for myself whether it measured anything beyond being good at IQ tests. When I arrived at the adult education college Birkbeck in London, I was one of two dozen adults, plus a couple of children. One was reading a book called *Why the West Rules (For Now)*, which didn't assuage my worries about the political overtones of this debate. The email instructing us where to go had carried a warning, in bold type: 'Please be advised that you will not be allowed to take the test if you do not bring your own black pen with you.' This struck me as both slightly cheap, and revealing: Mensa does not expect its applicants to have common sense or organisational ability. In the queue, the boy next to me started to talk to his mother about doing 'some maths in my head to warm me up'. As someone who now uses her iPhone calculator to multiply seven by eight, that stressed me out.

I took two tests that day, both designed by Raymond Cattell, a former pupil of Cyril Burt. The first was a 1963 test designed to be 'culture fair', meaning that there were no language- or logic-based questions, only shape rotation. What became immediately apparent is that the test selects heavily for *speed*. The strict time limits mean there is simply not enough time to luxuriate over questions, turning them over in your head. Now, you could argue that quickly grasping concepts is exactly what intelligence is. But you'd also have to admit that some of history's greatest breakthroughs came from years of careful observation and rumination. That first test convinced me that whatever an IQ test is measuring, it can't be genius. It doesn't measure showing up day after day. It doesn't measure the ego needed to insist that you're right and everyone else is wrong. And it doesn't measure the ability to market yourself as the spirit of the age.

The second test was more recent, from 1993, and leaned heavily into verbal reasoning. What I noticed here, first, was how arguable some of these questions were. We were asked to look at words and then choose the one with the opposite meaning from a list of four. I was pretty confident, as someone who writes thousands of words every week, that this would be easy. But the questions made me furrow my forehead. Is 'idle' a synonym for 'inactive', or a synonym of 'lazy'? Both, surely – it can be used as a pure descriptor, as in 'an idle engine', or to convey a value judgement, as in 'the idle rich'. My desire to argue with the test setter only increased when we hit the analogies section, where the example given was: 'Trousers are to boy as skirt is to . . . ?' The supervisor read this out with some embarrassment, assuring us that the language was 'traditional'. Things got worse. The logic puzzles in the final section included one about an explorer who might have been eaten by either lions or 'savages'. (And this was from 1993, a year when John Grisham was at the top of the best-seller lists and Cypress Hill's *Insane in the Brain* was released, not some long-forgotten colonial past.) Another question asked me to work out what my surname would be based on clues about family relationships, and clearly rested on the assumption that women all took their husband's names, and so would their children. Full of feminist zeal, I prissily ticked the box labelled, 'It is not possible to know what my surname is', and resigned myself to losing the marks.

What did I learn from my time with the genius hunters? Most of all, that attempts to define *genius* objectively have failed. You can't measure genius by measuring someone's biography with a ruler, or by asking them questions about fried eggs when they are ten years old. You aren't being scientific when comparing someone's achievements with winning the boat race or being given a state funeral. You have to be keenly aware of the confounding factors, whether that's the tendency of wealthy middle-aged men to suffer from gout, or the possibilities for fraud created by letting one journal editor gatekeep an entire discipline.

The genius hunters were a motley bunch, ranging from genuine truth-seekers bemused by the data in front of them, all the way to ageing men frightened that the world was leaving them behind. This is a story of big egos, grand claims and large dollops of self-justification. Many of the genius hunters were really making the case for *themselves*. It is no accident that so many IQ researchers have ended up endorsing scientific racism or sexism. If humans can be reduced to a number, and some numbers are higher than others, it is not a long walk to deciding that some humans are better than others, too. That 'better' is as badly defined as the word *genius* – it doesn't mean kinder, or more loved, or even more successful. Like the idea of genius, the concept of IQ can become an excuse. A way of claiming potential when the world sees only failure.

In 2018, the loser of the Mega civil war, Christopher Langan, wrote an obituary for Koko the gorilla, a zoo animal which could sign 1,000 words and therefore had an IQ between 75 and 95. 'Koko's elevated level of thought would have been all but incomprehensible to half the population of Somalia (average IQ 68),' wrote Langan on Facebook.[8] 'Obviously, this raises a question. Why is Western civilisation not admitting gorillas? They too are from Africa, and probably have a group mean IQ at least equal to that of Somalia.' There it was, a century and a half after Galton ranked the races by intelligence – another smart man using IQ to dehumanise and dismiss.* Langan ended the post with the words: 'Some of you might wonder whether this is a joke. The truth is that I'm not quite sure.'

Langan was featured in Malcolm Gladwell's book *Outliers*, which attributed his lack of academic success to his chaotic, violent upbringing and the reluctance of educational authorities to extend him the same sort of grace and understanding a middle-class child might receive. But Langan has found another answer for why he did not fulfil the glorious destiny written in his genes. He blames affirmative action, the 'New World Order', and a society controlled by 'globalists' and 'banksters'. Inevitably, he has a Substack.

IQ testing has narrow, scientific uses, but it is a false god. It

---

* Average IQs are indeed lower in developing countries, but since the average IQ in America has risen by 3 points per decade in the twentieth century – the Flynn Effect – extreme caution should be exercised when suggesting that national IQ statistics reflect anything other than educational opportunities, political stability, childhood nutrition and other environmental factors.

makes people believe they are special, even as they fudge their research, or fall out with everyone around them. Marilyn vos Savant is a living symbol of the problem with IQ worship. Once she was hailed as a genius, vos Savant *was* one. Nothing about *her* changed, but her life did. Stephen Hawking had little time for this kind of thinking. In a Q&A with the *New York Times* in 2004, he was asked what his IQ was. 'I have no idea,' he replied. 'People who boast about their IQ are losers.'

PART TWO

The Myths of Genius

So You Want to Be a Genius?

'The principal mark of genius is not perfection, but originality, the opening of new frontiers; once this is done, the conquered territory becomes common property.'

Arthur Koestler, *The Act of Creation*

Just for a minute, let's return to our old friend Hans Eysenck, and his list of qualities that make a genius. 'Clearly, he should be male, of middle or upper-middle parentage, and preferably come from a Jewish background. He should receive intellectual stimulation at home, but ought to lose one parent before the age of 10. He should be born in February, and die at 30 or 90, but on no account at 60! He should so arrange it that at the time of his maximum creative powers (between 35 and 45, or even younger for mathematicians and poets) there should be a minimum of solar activity.'

Once you flip this round, even the odder parts of it make sense. (Admittedly, not the sunspots.)* These are not necessarily qualities that *make* someone a genius, but qualities that

---

* This list is a mix of the obvious, the quirky and the bonkers. One of the few widely accepted population-level findings in IQ studies is that Ashkenazi Jews have higher than average intelligence (but also higher rates of some genetic diseases). Several researchers argued that losing a parent is correlated with high achievement: in *Fracture*, Matthew Parris writes that he began to notice the pattern when presenting his BBC series *Great Lives*.

will be picked out from his biography if they exist, to justify his anointing in retrospect. Eysenck was identifying some of the most appealing myths of genius: the struggle narrative of losing a parent, or the bittersweet archetype of the early promise extinguished too soon.

Before we go on, I want to talk a little bit more about the other distortions that affect whether someone is hailed as a genius. The criteria for this decision can be extremely wonky and unfair. Take what I call the 'Potus problem', after the acronym for President of the United States. Today, this is a word that appears in news stories every day. But on 22 September 1999, it was obscure enough to be a plot point in the first episode of *The West Wing*. One by one, the characters – who all work at the White House – receive a pager message: 'Potus in a bicycle accident. Come to the office.' One of these high-powered staffers is told by the person he is with: 'Tell your friend Potus that he's got a funny name.'

The West Wing went on to be a huge commercial hit, with 17 million US viewers every week[1] – and in the process, the word 'Potus' became a normal part of American political discussion. In 2015, when Barack Obama decided it was time to get a Twitter account, guess what handle he chose? @POTUS. *The West Wing*, to misquote *Mean Girls*, made 'Potus' happen.

Great discoveries often have this effect, too. They create the conditions for their own under-appreciation. When we watch a Shakespeare play today, we do so as an audience whose entire experience of theatre has been shaped by *all drama since the seventeenth century*. We do not find ambiguity confusing, or feel surprise when characters are psychologically complex individuals rather than personifications of biblical virtues. Hollywood now has to work very hard to make twist endings shock us – of course the protagonist can have been dead all along; that's something that happens in movies. But once it wasn't.

In *Men of Mathematics*, a history of the subject published in 1937, Eric Bell notices the Potus problem without giving it a name. In compiling a book of great lives, Bell realises he does not have the ability to judge the truly great mathematicians from the ancient world. 'Nearly everything useful that was done in mathematics before the seventeenth century has suffered one of two fates,' he writes. 'Either it has been so greatly simplified that it is now part of every regular school course, or it was long since absorbed as a detail in work of greater generality.'[2]

Imagine the intellectual effort that went into the creation of numbers – one, two, three – and the introduction of a symbol for zero. The first use of a zero-like symbol arose in Babylon (modern day Iraq) around the third century BCE; a similar concept developed independently in Mayan calendars in South America. (Zero was 'in the air', or what theorists of creativity now call *the adjacent possible*.) In the early Middle Ages, zero followed the path of the Silk Roads across Asia. We owe the idea not just to the mathematicians who described it but also the weary merchant loading up his goods for a long journey to the next settlement. Zero travelled like a trade wind across the world. These developments took centuries, and yet they are now so much part of our common mathematical language that unthinking them is impossible. Today, a primary school child can understand something it took ancient mathematicians great labour to articulate: *if I have two oranges and give you two oranges, then I have zero oranges*. 'It must have taken many ages to discover that a brace of pheasants and a couple of days were both instances of the number two,' the philosopher Bertrand Russell once wrote. If you ever want to fry your brain, take a moment to imagine not understanding the concept of zero – or that there is a transferable way to count the passage of time and a number of objects.

The American philosopher Thomas Kuhn called discoveries as

important as these 'paradigm shifts' – so momentous that everything that follows depends on that insight.[3] We now associate genius with creativity and originality, but many commonplace ideas were once startlingly original – perhaps alarmingly so. The modern world is heavily shaped by classification, which helps abstract thinking. We know that some animals have spines and others don't, or that some breathe water and others breathe air. We know that some chemicals are organic – containing carbon – and others aren't. We know that visible light is a spectrum – and that it is part of a larger spectrum we cannot see. But even the cleverest person in 1025 knew none of this.

We can never properly appreciate the geniuses of the past if we can't understand the world before they changed it. This part of the book begins with the Potus problem to show how unfair the distribution of the label *genius* can be. It's not a straightforward reward for high achievement or innovation, or even influence. It is not a consequence of a high IQ. You can't pass it on through top-quality sperm, as William Shockley believed, or spot its emergence early, as Lewis Terman hoped. Some people change the world and are forgotten. The ones who linger in our minds do so because they weave a story around themselves – a mythology.

Before we go on, I want to tell you about one of the most arresting research papers I've ever read – and the even more arresting fact that it was written in 1922. This paper presents a huge challenge to the idea of the lone genius, which is one of the most enduring myths we have. 'It is an interesting phenomenon that many inventions have been made two or more times by different inventors, each working without knowledge of the other's research,' wrote the sociologists William F. Ogburn and Dorothy Thomas more than a century ago. Then, in casual, detached prose, they listed some of the many instances of the 'multiple problem', where two or more people arrived at the same invention at the same time.[4]

These multiples include the telephone (Alexander Graham Bell and Elisha Gray); evolution by natural selection (Charles Darwin and Alfred Russel Wallace); calculus (Isaac Newton and Gottfried Leibniz); and the aeroplane (Samuel Langley and the Wright brothers). In case those weren't convincing enough, the researchers added logarithms, photography, the existence of Neptune, sunspots, the law of the conservation of energy, thermometers, telescopes, typewriters and the steamboat. The index contained 148 cases in all. Looking at the sheer number of examples they had gathered, Ogburn and Thomas wondered if 'inventions are inevitable'. Essentially, they argue, at a certain point the steamboat had to come into existence: we knew about boats, we knew about steam power, and now we just needed someone – or many someones – to combine the two. Support for this idea is provided by Soviet mathematicians stuck behind the Iron Curtain in the twentieth century, who made many of the same discoveries as their counterparts in the West, without knowing it. That's why some maths problems have double names, such as the Chaitin-Kolmogorov complexities or the Cook-Levin theorem.

Look back at that list, though, and you'll see that, in most cases, we only remember one of the two names. The winners claimed the credit more vigorously, or won the race to file a patent, or sought publicity and created a mythology around themselves. If you want to be hailed as a genius, take a tip from Isaac Newton, who trashed the reputation of his German rival Gottfried Leibniz by accusing him of plagiarism, when both men claimed to have discovered calculus. Don't do what Alfred Russel Wallace did, after he and Charles Darwin independently discovered the theory of evolution by natural selection: call your subsequent book *Darwinism*.

The idea of multiple discoveries is a challenge to how we think about geniuses as unique and special. 'The evidence and analysis show the tremendous importance of the cultural factor for invention,' Thomas and Ogburn wrote. Since then, others have taken their idea further: if inventions are inevitable, we can work out where they come from – which preconditions have to be fulfilled for them to happen. The zone in which great discoveries take place is now known as the *adjacent possible*.* The printing press needed moveable type, paper and ink – and the already extant wine press. Once those all existed, someone would put them all together.

In the same way, the video streaming platform YouTube could not exist until enough people had video cameras with which to make content, and high-speed internet connections with which to consume it. But once those conditions were in place, YouTube moved into the adjacent possible, waiting to be brought into existence. Some ideas really are ahead of their time. The Victorian inventor Charles Babbage could dream up the 'difference engine' – the first mechanical computer – but never managed to build one. The idea of the lightbulb existed long before the technology required to produce a successful model; as we will find out later, Thomas Edison is remembered for being an inventor, when he should be remembered as a manufacturer.

Both the idea of multiples and the adjacent possible suggest that there is an element of luck to great discoveries. It's all about timing. In *Outliers*, Malcolm Gladwell suggested that early

---

* The label was popularised by Steven Johnson in his 2010 book *Where Good Ideas Come From*.

computer pioneers such as Bill Gates had the great good luck to be born at a time when computing was becoming more accessible. Something similar is true of paradigm shifts: if you start work in a discipline soon after one, bad luck. You might have a fertile career, but you probably won't make a world-changing breakthrough. Time is against you.

What if you were the one who made the paradigm shift happen? Albert Einstein and Pablo Picasso reoccur throughout this book because they have become the towering figures of genius; one in the sciences, the other in the arts. Picasso broke the formal conventions of representational art with his abstract pieces of the 1900s, such as *Les Demoiselles d'Avignon* – those piglike pink figures with distorted faces. Around the same time, Einstein overturned centuries of Newtonian physics, with its idea of a 'clockwork universe'.

The two men are examples of 'conceptual innovators' – proponents of a big idea that changed the world.* These are the type of figures most likely to be hailed as geniuses. Yet both Einstein and Picasso, talented though they were, challenge the idea of a genius as a superior sort of person whose judgement will always be vindicated. 'Pure abstraction was a Rubicon that Picasso never crossed, and Einstein never agreed with the high abstractions of quantum theory,' wrote Arthur I. Miller (the history professor, not the playwright).[5] 'Each man ultimately lost contact with the implications of his own revolution.'

Picasso and Einstein, as talented as they were, prospered at a particular time and place. In fact, each created the conditions for

---

* The phrase comes from the economist David Galenson, and its opposite is an 'experimental innovator', someone who perfects their craft or hones their research incrementally, by trial and error.

their own surpassing; because of the breakthroughs they made, others went where they could not follow.

What else distorts our estimation of geniuses? What about the fact that, once you have received some acclaim in a particular field, the material and social conditions of your life change, making it easier to succeed further? Marilyn vos Savant is an obvious example of this phenomenon: she was called a genius, and so . . . she started to play one in public.

In 1968, the sociologist Robert Merton wrote a paper with a simple but provocative question: do the best people in a field get the most recognition?[6] He argued strongly that they do not. Look, Merton said, at the Académie Française, set up in 1635 to recognise excellence in French culture. From the start, it had only forty members at a time, known as *les immortels*, who were elected for life. But as early as the Victorian era, critics spoke of the 'forty-first seat', which could have been filled with dozens of illustrious thinkers who somehow never made it into the academy. The list of philosophers and writers who missed out on membership includes René Descartes, Pascal, Molière, Pierre Bayle, Jean-Jacques Rousseau, Henri de Saint-Simon, Denis Diderot, Stendhal, Gustave Flaubert, Émile Zola and Marcel Proust.

Merton was relatively relaxed about these omissions. He reckoned that posterity would sort it all out: 'History serves as an appellate court, ready to reverse the judgments of the lower courts, which are limited by the myopia of contemporaneity.' But the existence of the forty-first seat did make him wonder why some reputations grow and others stall. He decided that reputations tend to snowball, distorting our ideas of genius. He called this the Matthew Effect, after a verse in the Gospels: 'For unto every one that hath shall be given, and he shall have abundance:

but from him that hath not, shall be taken away even that which he hath.'

Under the Matthew Effect, scientists who achieve a particular level of recognition never drop below it: 'Once a Nobel laureate, always a Nobel laureate.' Merton also suggested that scientists develop a taste for recognition, and work harder once they achieve their first success. But there was one other thing that happened, he thought, and it's key to how the mythology of genius develops: 'Recognition can be converted into an instrumental asset as enlarged facilities are made available to the honored scientist for further work.' In other words, if you win a Nobel Prize, you might get a better lab as a result. You might get the money for more research assistants. You might find it easier to secure grants. You will be invited to give lectures abroad. You will be interviewed by the press. Everyone will look out for your next paper – and yours will be the first name on it, regardless of who did most of the work. If a discovery occurs in your lab, it will be attributed to you. Success is a self-fulfilling prophecy.

Many Nobel laureates are aware of this bias, according to research by another sociologist, Harriet Zuckerman.[7] She found that the moral ones sometimes asked to be the second author on a paper rather than the first, in an attempt not to hog the limelight. That is extremely laudable – and perhaps those laureates retire happily, beloved by their students and respected by their colleagues. But what about their peers who get one honour and promptly become a credit-hogging diva? Well, the entire world is set up to enable them to do so. Genius is a form of celebrity; it draws attention and creates profits. Why isn't James Clerk Maxwell – the physicist cited by Shockley, who made exceptional breakthroughs in light and electromagnetism – as well known as Einstein or Newton? Think of his fame like a snowfall that wasn't quite big enough to start an avalanche.

The Matthew Effect plays into the Great Man theory of history, which you might remember from the introduction. We find it intuitively easy to understand human-sized stories, where *someone* does *something*, whereas vague wafts of social change driven by multiple factors might get academics excited ... but tend to leave everyone else bored to tears.

As it happens, Merton was relaxed about great men – he thought big figures like the psychiatrist Sigmund Freud and the physicist Enrico Fermi played a 'focalising' role in their disciplines. Their ideas excited and stimulated their contemporaries, and their disciples created institutions to carry on their work. But he could see the downsides, too. A handful of big beasts in a discipline can suck up all the resources, long after they have done their best work. That applies in the humanities, too: bad writers and artists keep getting commissions and awards even when their fame has outlasted their inspiration. A genius can first help their field, and then hinder it. Sometimes, science really does advance one funeral at a time.*

If you become famous enough during your lifetime – if your genius mythology is strong enough – then future generations will tend to ignore your many failed ideas and focus on your successes. Even better, your setbacks and personal eccentricities will be written into your personal story to provide a moral lesson. *Believe in yourself. Being odd can be a superpower.* That sort of thing.

So the next piece of advice is: *be weird*. Now, it's impossible

---

* This is often credited to Max Planck, but what he actually wrote, in his autobiography, was this: 'A new scientific truth does not triumph by convincing its opponents and making them see the light, but rather because its opponents eventually die and a new generation grows up that is familiar with it.'

to know if geniuses are more likely to be weird or whether we are just more likely to use that word for weird people than for their equally talented but dull rivals. Take Benjamin Franklin, who was, by any measure, an extraordinary scientist – the inventor of bifocal glasses, improved fireplaces and the flexible urinary catheter, and a student of demographics, oceanography and electricity. But he also believed in 'transmigration', or reincarnation. In a letter to his wife Deborah in September 1773, Franklin noticed that her god-daughter's new baby was very kind to him, adding that the child 'is withal so very like its Grandmother, that I am half inclin'd to think there has been a Transmigration, and that she remember'd an old Friend'. That's the kind of thing that makes biographers cry in ecstasy; the opposite of the Austen Problem.

Or perhaps a certain childlike wonder is an incubator of genius. 'Only geniuses preserve their infantile voracity for "becauses" – and the naive hope that there *are* real answers to every question,' suggested the author Arthur Koestler.[8] Other theorists go further, asking whether creativity is a mild form of psychoticism. You see things other people can't, but luckily they turn out to be *an invisible force could be used to create light* rather than *a talking dog which is telling me to kill my neighbour*. Either way, if you have ninety-nine insane ideas and the other one is gravity, congratulations. History will remember gravity. But that does suggest that there are many people out there who simply had the misfortune to have a hundred insane ideas and no good ones. Again, that distorts our idea of achievement.

Next question: what sort of work should you do to be hailed a genius? Should you be a *fox* or a *hedgehog*, to use the terms explored by the philosopher Isaiah Berlin?

In 1953, Berlin began an essay with a quotation from the Greek poet Archilochus: 'The fox knows many things, but the hedgehog knows one big thing.'[9] He wondered whether the meaning of that aphorism was relatively banal – even the cunning fox can be defeated by the hedgehog's simple spines – or whether it illuminated something profound about human nature. Perhaps, thought Berlin, there were two types of people: those who pursued a single idea, or related all their work to a central organising principle, and those whose brains were more scattershot and their work more fragmented. The Italian poet Dante was a hedgehog, he suggested, while Shakespeare was a fox – able to move through genres, equally adept at sonnets, comedies and dramas. 'Plato, Lucretius, Pascal, Hegel, Dostoevsky, Nietzsche, Ibsen, Proust are, in varying degrees, hedgehogs; Herodotus, Aristotle, Montaigne, Erasmus, Molière, Goethe, Pushkin, Balzac, Joyce are foxes.'

This taxonomy feels like a precursor to those lists of top albums and novels that now generate so much discussion online, because the two categories are extremely arguable. In my view, James Joyce had one big idea – *what if novels, but harder to read* – but you could equally argue that *Ulysses* and *Finnegans Wake* are strange and groundbreaking in completely different ways. Even Berlin admits that he can't quite work out where to place Tolstoy: 'The hypothesis I wish to offer is that Tolstoy was by nature a fox, but believed in being a hedgehog.'

To my mind, modern culture is more likely to acclaim hedgehogs – people who devote their lives to a single idea – than foxes. (Unless the sheer range of a person's talents can be woven into the story, as with Leonardo da Vinci.) We prefer someone who fits neatly into a category, who plugged away at one topic for their entire career. Dilettantes seem somehow frivolous. Recently, however, there have been efforts to salvage the reputation of the foxes. The super-forecaster Philip Tetlock urges anyone who wants to make better predictions to sample widely, instead of relying on narrow subject expertise. The hedgehogs fall into a classic genius trap: assuming that deep knowledge in one area makes them a person of superior judgement in general. They are overconfident about their abilities, and more likely to be wrong as a result.

OK, so you have found your one big idea. Now should you make *termite art* or *white elephant art*? In 1962, the painter and critic Manny Farber attacked what currently passed for 'Great Art', accusing those who aspired to create it of squandering their talent by producing self-conscious masterpieces: 'a yawning production of over-ripe technique, shrieking with precocity, fame, ambition'.[10] This was white elephant art, like the fabled gift designed to be expensive and useless. Instead, he championed 'termite tapeworm-moss-fungus-art . . . that goes always forwards eating its boundaries, and likely as not leaves nothing in its path other than the signs of eager, industrious, unkempt activity'.

Farber's particular target was movies, where he was bored by art that announced itself as a masterpiece, treating 'every inch of the screen and film as a potential area for prizewinning creativity'. That tendency persists today, with directors and actors stressing the great effort involved in their work – *I lost five stone to play this role*; *I basically learned to be a fighter pilot in six weeks*; *I got so into my character that I went mad*; and so on – where our enjoyment of what's on-screen is supposed to be boosted by the knowledge of how difficult it was to accomplish. The awards campaigns for Alejandro G. Iñárritu's films often position them as white elephant art – we heard a lot about the challenges of filming only in natural light for *The Revenant*, while *Birdman* was constructed to look as though it was filmed in one take. This is self-conscious precocity and ambition.

Farber has little time for this approach, unfavourably contrasting Orson Welles' *Citizen Kane* ('exciting but hammy') with Akira Kurosawa's *Ikuru*, which concentrates 'on nailing down one moment without glamorizing it, but forgetting this accomplishment as soon as it has passed'.

In the literary world, *Ulysses* is perhaps the most obvious example of a work that is not afraid to announce itself as a masterpiece. You praise it to show not just that you enjoyed it, but also that you are the sort of person to enjoy it. If you want to be called a genius, white elephant art is the best route to the label.

If all else fails, work as hard as you can, and then hope for sheer dumb luck to save you. 'It is often by a trivial, even an accidental decision, that we direct our activities into a certain channel, and thus determine which of the potential expressions of our individuality become manifest,' wrote René Dubos in his 1950 biography of Louis Pasteur. 'Every decision is like a murder, and our march forward is over the stillborn bodies of all our possible selves that will never be.'[11]

This is a beautiful and eerie sentiment, and Arthur Koestler thought it was true of Alexander Fleming's discovery of penicillin. The story we usually hear about penicillin is that a flake of mould drifted through the window of Fleming's lab while he was out and landed on a neglected bacterial culture. When Fleming arrived back in his lab, the bacteria had retreated from around the mould. Hey presto – a method of curing diseases that claimed millions of lives.

That is true, but it's only part of the story. When Fleming saw the culture, he did not immediately appreciate its significance. He spent several months calling the substance 'mould juice' before settling on *penicillin*. It took his lab assistant, Merlin Pryce, reminding him of an earlier experiment to realise the potential uses of the mould. Previously, Fleming had a cold and accidentally let his nose drip into a microbial culture – which had also retreated from the nasal mucus, because it contained an enzyme which attacked bacteria. Pryce and Fleming connected the two. You can call that fortune favouring the prepared mind, or you can call it double luck, that one of the greatest microbial scientists of all time was also a total slattern. (Do not try Fleming's slapdash approach to biosafety if you are researching Ebola.)

Fleming's career reveals even more fragile threads of happenstance. He picked medicine only because his brother was a doctor. He attended medical school at St Mary's in London – where he spent the rest of his career – only because he had played water polo against their team as a teenager. He chose bacterial research because his supervisor wanted to keep him in the St Mary's rifle club, where he was an excellent shot. Fleming was both a brilliant man and the end of a long chain of strange events.

The chapters that follow outline some of the other things that influence whether a person gets called a genius or not – and show how those myths can become poisonous. We love to contemplate lone rebels, indulge tortured artists and downplay the contributions of those around the genius to paint a more satisfying portrait of superhuman achievement. But the more satisfying we make these myths, the less they are *true*. These myths are like sunlight – any individual story yearns to grow towards them. They have to be resisted, challenged, their contents deliberately returned to complexity from an appealing state of simplicity. Otherwise, we end up living in a world of myths that does not reflect reality – a world where every iconoclast is right, a world where power is abused, and where everyone is told that they are getting what they deserve.

The Rebel

'I have met several psychologists who thought they had been selected by providence to be the Newton of psychology, but turned out rather to be the Newton of alchemy!'

Hans Eysenck, *Genius*

During the coronavirus pandemic, many otherwise smart people became what's known as 'ivermectin truthers'. Ivermectin is a deworming agent, which has been brilliantly useful in treating river blindness among humans in the developing world. It is also given to livestock in richer countries. You can therefore get it pretty easily from a vet. It is a 'wonder drug' – for deworming. What it *doesn't* do is alleviate Covid-19.

Despite this awkward fact – eventually confirmed by multiple studies – internet-friendly public intellectuals began to advocate for ivermectin as a treatment. In a 2021 article for *Areo* magazine, the biologist Heather Heying wondered if ivermectin might not even be a 'better alternative' to the new mRNA vaccines produced by Pfizer and Moderna, which have saved hundreds of thousands of lives. She spent a moment considering that she might be wrong: 'For every [Louis] Pasteur, there must be thousands of people who have had an idea that didn't pan out.'[1] Then she concluded that she was probably right.

What had happened? Heying (and her husband and podcast co-host Bret Weinstein) had fallen prey to one of the most seductive myths of genius out there: the myth of the lone rebel, the iconoclast, the heroic dissenter against the orthodoxy. 'You've got a bunch of heretics who are saying things about ivermectin, about the hazards of vaccines, about all of these topics,' Weinstein told the podcaster Joe Rogan in June 2021. 'Who do you believe? You're going to believe the heretics? Well, the heretics actually are an interesting group and the thing that unites them seems to be their independence of the structures that are controlling others, right?'

We absolutely love these stories, because they give us an underdog protagonist squaring up to the establishment. Exaggerating the opposition to a discovery also has the effect of magnifying the bravery and insight of the heretic. In storytelling terms, it raises the stakes. And that is why, for every Newton of mathematics there is a Newton of alchemy – someone who becomes convinced that because everyone is against them, they must be right. The myth of the rebellious genius is a seductive one, but its effects can be poisonous.

As it happens, I was initially sympathetic to some of the arguments made by the 'Covid contrarians', including those asking for the potential of ivermectin to be taken seriously. In the early days of the pandemic, the World Health Organisation advised against mask-wearing. Then its stance changed – *masks were great!* That led to 'mask mandates', with airline passengers, restaurant diners and schoolchildren obliged to mask up, sometimes even outside. More recently, though, studies have emerged which showed that mask-wearing in real life (where many people wore them incorrectly, used cloth masks instead of medical-grade varieties and so on) is less useful than it first seemed. Particularly in that first, frightening year, worried people clung to the World Health Organisation guidance – these were the experts, after all – and verbally attacked dissenters for being cavalier about public health. But the science kept evolving, from *no masks* to *yes masks* to *maybe masks in certain settings*, and reasonable scepticism aided that process.

It wasn't ridiculous to wonder if the advice on ivermectin might change, too; some of the most useful Covid treatments were repurposed generic drugs, such as the bog-standard steroid dexamethasone. But then science did what it should do, and carefully studied the evidence. By the middle of 2021, the pharmaceutical company Merck – which stood to make millions if its brand of ivermectin proved to be a useful treatment – published a statement saying there was 'no meaningful evidence for clinical activity or clinical efficacy in patients with COVID-19 disease'. In September, *Nature* reported that ivermectin had 'an evidence base that has substantially evaporated under close scrutiny'.[2]

And yet some intellectuals, such as Heying and Weinstein, couldn't let go. They were original members of a loose group of dissident liberals, mixed in with some straightforward conservatives, who were christened the 'Intellectual Dark Web' by the *New York Times* in 2018. This group prided itself on disrespecting taboos in academia and journalism, speculating on the origins of sexual and racial disparities (were they biological?), pushing back on the liberal pieties about gender, and decrying the phenomenon known as 'wokeness'. Weinstein had been forced out of his job at Evergreen State university because he objected to a day when all white people were asked to stay away from campus. Sam Harris, a New Atheist, was critical of Islamism to a degree that saw him accused of Islamophobia. Douglas Murray worried about the decline of Western civilisation thanks to Muslim immigration from the Middle East, in a book called *The Strange Death of Europe*. The entire brand of the Intellectual Dark Web was built on opposition to the mainstream. They were anti-orthodox: 'heterodox'.

Perhaps you can already spot the problem. *Sometimes, the mainstream is right.* There's a popular saying in the social sciences: 'When you hear hoofbeats, think horses, not zebras.' In other words, assume the most obvious explanation – while keeping your mind open to other possibilities. The members of the Intellectual Dark Web who went all-in on ivermectin didn't do that – and when presented with evidence that challenged their beliefs, they doubled down. They had been seduced by the idea of the genius as rebel.

The idea that most great discoveries were rejected at first is an appealing one: the record executive who passed on the Beatles (more on him later), for example, or the hundred scientists who signed an open letter denouncing the theory of general relativity in 1931. ('Why a hundred?' replied Albert Einstein. 'If they were right, one would have been enough.') There's a whole Ella Fitzgerald and Louis Armstrong song based on this faulty premise: 'They all laughed at Christopher Columbus when he said the world was round / They all laughed when Edison recorded sound.' *Except they didn't.* As we'll find out later, the phonogram was a resounding success, making pots of cash and turning Edison into an immediate celebrity. And Columbus didn't need to prove the world wasn't flat; everyone knew that already, although he personally thought it was pear-shaped. In fact, that's why he thought he could open up a new route to India by sailing west from Spain. (Don't make me fact-check the rest of the song; it's a beautiful piece of music, and doesn't deserve to be footnoted.)

This story template – this mythology – is nonetheless deeply appealing. My own favourite example of a heretic proved right is Ignaz Semmelweis, a Hungarian doctor who noticed that mothers who gave birth on wards run by midwives had rates of childbed fever three times lower than the women attended by doctors.

(The doctors came to the ward straight from dissecting cadavers, bringing bacteria on their hands.) Unfortunately for Semmelweis, he could not fully explain the mechanism behind this difference in mortality rates – because the germ theory of disease was not yet accepted. He just knew what he was seeing.

To his contemporaries, Semmelweis' suggestion that 'corpse particles' were being carried on doctors' hands sounded like superstition, exactly the sort of backwards thinking they were trying to escape. He was ignored. The women kept dying. Eventually, he fell into a downward spiral of drinking, ranting and writing open letters. In 1865, he was confined to an asylum. There, in a final brutal irony, he appears to have died of blood poisoning after being beaten by guards. Today, however, his ideas are utterly uncontroversial: the National Health Service has a 'bare below the elbows' (BBE) policy because of the possibility of germ transfer.[3]

The fate of poor Ignaz is so well-known among historians of science that they coined the phrase 'Semmelweis reflex'. That phrase describes the knee-jerk reaction of medical and scientific authorities to challenges to their authority and established practices. But the Semmelweis reflex sometimes has its place: in 2022, I watched Mark Rylance – probably the greatest actor of his generation – play the poor overlooked Hungarian doctor, in a production where the ghosts of women killed by childbirth fever danced around him. I noticed one small problem with this artistic celebration of a medical heretic: Rylance is sceptical of chemotherapy for cancer, and initially took a 'distilled garlic solution' instead of the Covid vaccine. 'The body knows how to heal itself,' he told the *Sunday Times* a year later.[4] (Well, it didn't from childbirth fever, did it?) The seductive myth of the rebel genius had led him into falling for pseudoscience.

The same idea of generational resistance – the sense that the avant-garde has to smash the previous consensus – also exists in art. (Thankfully, no one dies because of it.) Notoriously, the Impressionists were considered to be low-quality daubers by the French artistic establishment of the time. They were forced to hold their own exhibition outside the official one at the Académie des Beaux-Arts, at a photographer's studio on the Boulevard des Capucines. Rarely has a single room held so many exquisite paintings: ten by Edgar Degas, nine by Claude Monet, seven by Auguste Renoir, five by Camille Pissarro, three by Paul Cézanne and nine by Berthe Morisot. Here were ballerinas by Degas and striking female figures from Renoir, alongside one of Morisot's tender paintings of maternal love. Monet's offerings included a spectacular sunrise over water, as well as his study of poppies at Argenteuil, which you can now see in the Musée d'Orsay in Paris. Against a muted countryside palette of greens and browns, the flower-heads are represented by the most delicate red dabs.

To a modern observer, these paintings (and the accompanying bronzes and sketches) demonstrate incredible vision paired with impressive skill. But the reviews were *appalling*. People reacted like I do when confronted with *another* video installation of someone beheading a chicken or screaming on a street corner. Ugh. One critic said the group had 'declared war on beauty'. Another called them 'lunatics'. The exhibition became a sort of anti-tourist attraction; the Parisian bourgeoisie brought their friends just to scream in horror at the paintings.

An infamously nasty review by the critic Louis Leroy took on the voice of an older, traditional artist, dismissing Monet's minimalist portrayal of figures in a crowd as 'innumerable black tongue lickings' and Camille Pissarro's depiction of ploughed earth as 'palette-scrapings placed uniformly on a dirty canvas'. It ended by damning Monet's seascape by declaring: 'Wallpaper in its early stages is much more finished than that.'[5] The title of that painting was *Impression, Sunrise*, giving the review its headline – and the artistic movement its name.

Very few of the paintings sold, and those that did went for pitiful sums: in the hundreds or low thousands of francs. For comparison, that year the classicist Ernest Meissonier sold a military painting called *1805, Cuirassiers Before the Charge* for 300,000 francs. A collector bought Monet's *Impression, Sunrise* for 800 francs, and resold it four years later at a loss. It is now held by the Musée Marmottan Monet in Paris, where it is insured for millions of euros. (A sidenote: some of its current aura of specialness was created in 1985, when it was stolen from the museum by a masked gunman. Similarly, the two-year quest to recover the *Mona Lisa* after it was stolen in 1911 made Leonardo's masterpiece into the most famous painting in the world.)

The rejection story of the Impressionists is now famous – part of their mythology. It provides the archetypal example of rebellious artists ahead of their time. Think of it as the Marty McFly gambit: when the hero of *Back to the Future* travels back to his parents' youth, he stuns the crowd by shredding his way through 'Johnny B. Goode'. At the end, the ballroom is silent. McFly shrugs: 'I guess you guys aren't ready for that yet. But your kids are gonna love it.'

Marty McFly expresses a popular idea, essential to the mythology of genius: rebellion is more exciting than conventional wisdom, and that the avant-garde are often vindicated by history. You can draw a line from there to the ivermectin truthers.

Here's the story of Galileo you might have heard at school, or in popular culture. Galileo was an astronomer – a watcher of the skies. He lived in Italy, under the jurisdiction of the Catholic Church, which had outlawed the idea that the earth revolved around the sun. God had made the universe with the earth at its centre, the Church said, as befitting his finest creation. But Galileo looked up at the stars, and the other planets, and he realised that this couldn't be true. He was compelled to publish his results, which demonstrated the heliocentric universe. The Church banned his book, put him on trial for heresy and ordered him to recant. In response, Galileo gasped out: '*Eppur si muove*' – 'And yet it moves'.

You can tell this phrase has cachet among a certain type of Western liberal intellectual, because 'Eppur Si Muove' is the title of a *West Wing* episode (season five, where the president's daughter Ellie gets attacked by Republicans for working on sexual health). But it's almost certainly apocryphal. The science historian Antonio Favaro traced its first appearance to a book called *The Italian Library*, published in 1757, more than a century after the trial. Here is the story as told by its author Giuseppe Baretti:

> This is the celebrated Galileo, who was in the inquisition for six years, and put to the torture, for saying, that the earth moved. The moment he was set at liberty, he looked up to the sky and down to the ground, and, stamping with his foot, in contemplative mood, said, Eppur si muove; that is, still it moves, meaning the earth.[6]

So much of drama and literature sides with the true-eyed individual against the crowd: Hamlet, Winston Smith in *1984*, John Proctor in *The Crucible*. This myth of the lone rebel is incredibly appealing – which is exactly why we should be suspicious of it. There is an emotional charge in contemplating one man, alone against the state, refusing to capitulate when asked to renounce his beliefs. This is the story of the underdog, and it has become essential to our idea of genius. *He knew he was right – and he was!*

As always, there are grains of truth here: research suggests that high achievers often have what's known as *strong intrinsic motivation*. That is, they are driven by an engine inside themselves – curiosity, compulsion, sheer orneriness – even when the world is uninterested or dismissive. (The opposite is extrinsic motivation, where the thought of money, power or other external rewards drives a person onwards.) Galileo did follow his observations even though they took him to an uncomfortable conclusion. But the great astronomer died in his own bed, not on a pyre or at a gallows. He sought the Pope's permission – through the exquisitely named Father Monster – to publish his *Dialogue* in 1632. He was a risk-taker but he did not have a death wish.[7]

Reducing Galileo's story to heresy and vindication also obscures the reality of his achievements. He is presented as a thinker rather than a maker – a frame which reflects our own prejudices. But there is another model of scientific progress, apart from the Great Man theory of history, suggested by the historian Peter Galison. That is the idea that progress is driven not just by ideas, but by new technology. Galileo could see Jupiter's moons, and what he called Saturn's 'ears' – its rings – not just because he dared to imagine a heliocentric universe, but because he was a superb lens-maker. He rejected the lenses made by spectacle merchants, which only gave him three times magnification, in favour of a bespoke setup which gave him eight, then fifteen, then twenty times magnification. He called this last telescope 'the discoverer'. (When his fellow astronomer Johannes Kepler wanted to confirm one of his own hunches, he had to borrow Galileo's telescope to do so.) This new technology allowed him to observe the fluctuating brightness of Venus, which proved that the Copernican model – the planets orbiting the sun – was correct. When he heard that Jesuit priests were developing their own high-powered telescope, Galileo scrambled to put his discoveries on record, so that he could claim the credit. He documented the phases of Venus in a letter to Kepler, using an anagram to disguise his discovery.*

Why do we hear so little about this version of the story? Life is a mess, like a vat of noodle soup dumped on the floor, and biographers, journalists and academics pick out the most appealing strands. The myth of Galileo the iconoclast genius has overtaken the reality of Galileo the careful empiricist – and Galileo the canny self-publicist, and Galileo the subtle politician.

Freeman Dyson, one of the most influential physicists of the twentieth century, identified the power of iconoclasm in an essay called 'The Scientist as Rebel', adapted from a talk given when he was nearing seventy.[8] Dyson had lately watched the film *Dead Poets Society*, which depicts a brilliant teacher who bends the rules to inspire his students.

During his own youth at Winchester, an expensive private school in England, Dyson said, 'we took advantage of the wartime blackout to climb over the rooftops and up the chapel tower'. His chemistry teacher, Eric James, forgot about his own subject and instead tutored the boys in avant-garde literature: W. H. Auden, Christopher Isherwood, Dylan Thomas, Cecil Day Lewis – 'the poets who were then speaking for the younger generation in the first desperate years of World War II'. (You can see how seductive this idea is – a rebellious teacher throwing away his lesson planner to inspire his boys with charismatic iconoclasm – by

---

* The anagram was 'Haec immatura a me iam frustra leguntur o.y.' (These are at present too early to be read by me.) It unscrambled to 'Cynthiae figures emulator mater amorum': the mother of love, i.e. Venus, imitates the shape of Cynthia, the moon. Unfortunately, Kepler – who thought that since Venus was so bright it must generate its own light – didn't understand Galileo's code. Or maybe he just wasn't very good at anagrams.

reflecting that it is also the premise of Alan Bennett's *The History Boys*, first performed in 2004.)

In *The Scientist as Rebel*, Dyson asserts that 'science is an alliance of free spirits in all cultures rebelling against the local tyranny that each culture imposes on its children'. He traces an intellectual lineage of heretics, starting with the Arab poet and mathematician Omar Khayyam, for whom 'science was a rebellion against the intellectual constraints of Islam'.

In a later essay, 'The Modern Heretic', Dyson's prime example of the rebel genius is Thomas Gold, who 'proved that pitch discrimination [the ability to tell high notes from low notes] is mainly done in the ear and not the brain', thanks to experiments performed in 1948. The mainstream took thirty years to accept Gold's theory, Dyson observes, until the evidence became overwhelming. Then, almost as an aside, he notes that Gold also proposed that the moon was covered in squishy dust. Oh, and that oil and natural gas are not biological in origin. (By the time Dyson was writing, the moon missions had proven Gold's dust theory wrong, and his ideas about fossil fuels have since been debunked, too.) 'About once every five years, [Gold] invades a new field of research and proposes an outrageous new theory that arouses intense opposition from the professional experts in the field,' writes Dyson. 'He then works very hard to prove the experts wrong.' For Dyson, this is genius – a talented amateur plunging into unknown territory, offering no respect to its gatekeepers and stuffy traditions, and forging onwards with no fear of failure.

This is an emotionally appealing framework for science but it has drawbacks. For every Semmelweis there is an unknown scientist whose great hunch was wrong. People laughed at it . . . because it was laughable. Ever heard of phlogiston? The eighteenth century was obsessed with this 'firelike element' – until it turned out not to exist. How about 'mesmerism', invented by

Franz Anton Mesmer, who put his patients in a trance to access their animal magnetism? Or phrenology, the measurement of head lumps which so captivated the young Lewis Terman? Or even 'polywater', a form of water discovered in the 1960s with a lower freezing point than H_2O. (The amazing properties of polywater mysteriously disappeared when labs introduced better glassware, which stopped contaminating their samples.) Great minds are open minds, by necessity – it's why some researchers link mild psychoticism to creativity – but if you open your mind too much, your brains will fall out.

During the pandemic, I started to call this tendency 'Galileo syndrome'. His story is one of the earliest examples of the myth that if everyone is telling you that you're wrong, it will be all the sweeter when you are proved right. Others have called it the 'Galileo gambit'. In 2021, the anthropologist Chris Kavanagh and the psychologist Matthew Browne wrote an article about Bret Weinstein and his wife Heather Heying for *The Skeptic* magazine, with the headline: 'You're Probably Not Galileo'. Surveying the evidence against ivermectin, they concluded: 'For every Einstein, there are legions of deluded dilettantes, whose revolutionary ideas amount to nothing more than hot air . . . the lone voice in the wilderness, the unrecognised genius – these are seductive personas, and ones enthusiastically inhabited by contrarian "public intellectuals".' This is the dark side of the mythology of genius: it makes a fetish of contrarianism, and flatters the 'free thinker' or 'heterodox intellectual' into moving from scepticism to conspiracism.

Bret Weinstein, who started off by objecting to an overzealous campus diversity effort, has since drifted off into the heterodox podcast space, where the wilder your opinions are, the better. In the podcast he hosts with Heying, he speculated that there was more to Hamas' attack on Israel on 7 October 2023 than met the eye. Perhaps, he said on *Dark Horse* that month, 'something had gotten into the Israeli system that is ready to sacrifice civilians', which would not surprise him since the country's government had 'betrayed' its population by vaccinating them against Covid. Weinstein has also called for a version of the Nuremberg trials, which prosecuted Nazi war criminals, to be held for advocates of the Covid vaccine for children.

Freeman Dyson, like Cyril Burt and Hans Eysenck, ended up poisoned by his own mythology. At the end of his career – one marked by genuine breakthroughs, and clearly the product of a towering intellect – he became best-known for questioning the scientific consensus on climate change. By the 2000s, he was suggesting that higher carbon in the atmosphere might even be beneficial, because it would help trees to grow. 'There is suspicion that, at age 65, a great scientist of the 20th century is no longer just far out, he is far gone – out of his beautiful mind,' wrote Nicholas Dawidoff in the *New York Times* in 2009. Dyson called environmentalism a 'worldwide secular religion'. He attacked Al Gore as its 'chief propagandist' and insisted after watching *An Inconvenient Truth* that 'the polar bears will be fine'.[9] (Polar bears are currently listed as vulnerable to extinction because of the disappearance of sea-ice at the North Pole.) Dyson's rebellion wasn't just some intellectual flight of fancy; it had real consequences. His views aligned with the interests of fossil fuel producers during a crucial period when climate change was often still dismissed as a mere theory or an overblown irrelevance. The rebel is not as powerless as he sometimes pretends.

And neither is our next archetype: the tortured artist.

Monsters and Tortured Artists

'When you're a star, they let you do it.'

Donald Trump

For people who watch plays at the Edinburgh Fringe and think, *this is just too well-edited and coherent*, there's something called 'devised theatre'. The format is beloved by students, because it seems more anarchic, playful and immediate than a piece performed from a published play-text – which can feel like a meal cooked from someone else's recipe.

If you were around in England at the start of the 2010s, there was one maker of devised theatre whose name you needed to know: Chris Goode. A tall, shy man, he cultivated the air of an outsider, a deep thinker, a tortured artist. 'Physically he was a big guy, but its effect was offset by that conspicuous gentleness bordering on courtliness,' Brian Logan, his successor as artistic director at Camden People's Theatre, told me. 'I knew from his social media feed that he had episodes of depression, futility and so on, and – even though he was cheerful on the occasions I met him – he did, even in person, wear his sensitivity on his sleeve.' He was seen by some of his contemporaries as a dark, Byronic figure. One frequent collaborator told me that 'talking to Chris was like being let into a secret society of clever, interesting artist people. He knew how to light a fire under people's egos.'

You almost certainly haven't heard of Chris Goode, for reasons which will soon become apparent. Yet he was once the darling of London's artistic avant-garde. In the *Guardian*, Lyn Gardner described him as a 'theatre maker of infinite talent and infinite compassion'. *Time Out* called him 'a star of intelligent, left field theatre'. He was a rebel – even by the standards of subsidised theatre, his work was too punkish, personal and sexually explicit to be commercially successful. Since his death in 2021, though, most traces of Chris Goode have been erased from the internet, and his plays are unlikely to be staged again. Because as well as a gifted playwright, he was a paedophile.

You might be wondering why a minor talent – and one with such a dark secret – belongs in a book that has otherwise dealt with such giant figures. He belongs in this gallery because you don't have to be a world-bestriding genius to benefit from the genius myth. You just have to convince a group of people that you are a special person, who deserves special rules. Goode's story demonstrates how an aura of tortured talent can draw a crowd of admirers – and then stifle their doubts about what they are seeing in front of them. One of the great questions of genius studies is this: *why do people put up with the bad behaviour?* His story offers an answer. 'He would target young, impressionable and vulnerable men who wanted a break in the sector or who were in awe of his work and "genius",' Goode's producer Xavier de Sousa wrote later.[1]

'I was so happy to be working with a "genuine writer"', one of his collaborators told me. 'He would come into rehearsals and he hadn't slept all night, but he had written fifty pages, it was so impressive. We were like moths looking at a flame.'

Chris Goode was born in 1973, and made his name during the explosion of social media and blogs in the late 2000s. 'He was there and active in the heroic age of Twitter and theatre blogging,' the academic and critic Aleks Sierz told me. Goode wrote a blog called 'Thompson's Bank of Communicable Desire', filled with alternately joking, obscure, straightforward, teasing prose – a verbal dance of the seven veils. He once described his style as 'insufferably prolix, strenuously performative, slightly arch sometimes, a bit camp here and there'. His biggest admirers clustered around an independent theatre website, Exeunt, run by students and young critics. 'It's a bit of a bold statement, but I think Chris Goode's *Hippo World Guest Book* might just be the best piece of theatre to be made about the internet to date,' wrote Catherine Love, an Exeunt regular, on her own site in 2014. 'There's a very low-fi aesthetic to the piece – so low-fi, in fact, that it would be easy not to think of it as an aesthetic at all, just to accept it as a man reading from a stand.' The man reading from the stand was Goode himself. The play explored the internet's ability to reduce us all to shrieking polarisation by quoting an online slap fight on a website about hippos.

In 2009, Goode wrote and starred in a play called *The Adventures of Wound Man and Shirley*, about the relationship between a superhero covered in lacerations (Wound Man) and a fourteen-year-old boy called Shirley. 'Goode was able to access a world of magical realism which softened the blow of a story that the *Daily Mail* would have had a field day with,' Exeunt's Honour Bayes wrote. Goode told her that the surrealism of the premise 'helps people to get to a place where at the end of the show they are really rooting for essentially a relationship between a 14-year-old boy and a 40-something-year-old man who just wears pants all day'.

The theme of forbidden relationships occurs across his work. Even his most celebrated play, *Men in the Cities*, finds the subject of sex between adult men and children irresistible. An adult called Graeme watches a boy called Rufus take a selfie outside his house: 'He starts to pull up his T-shirt. Graeme shuts the blind in a hurry.' Rufus bunks off school and is sexually awakened by photos of leather daddies at an art gallery; he later watches porn on his phone at school. Eventually, Rufus drops a note through Graeme's door, an obscene drawing: 'It's like a physical assault. Which is to say, not unwelcome.' In other scenes, a bereaved father asks his dead son's boyfriend if it's OK to look at a website called Gay Twink Angels: 'I don't want to get my door kicked in at six in the morning. Or any time of the morning.'

There is no doubt that *Men in the Cities* is a powerful play, precisely because it flirts with taboos like child sexuality, sadism and rape. (Goode's work reminds me of the paintings of Francis Bacon, another artist who felt an erotic charge from male violence.) High on its success, he decided it was time to establish his own ensemble – a group of actors he could work with across multiple projects. In 2014, he created Ponyboy Curtis. This is where the story spirals into a very dark place indeed.

'Some basics,' read one recruitment notice, posted online in early 2016. 'We are generally looking for performers who are:

- probably in their early 20s, though they might be anything from 18 up to late 20s / early 30s
- male / male-identifying
- able to be part of a working and artistic culture that includes physically demanding activity (though we are keen for this to include people with different abilities, needs and body types).'

The 'Ponyboys' of Goode's all-male ensemble would be largely unpaid, and would be identified in programmes only by their first names. In rehearsals, they were expected to get naked and touch each other. 'Nudity is a fundamental part of the company's working language,' the advert stated. 'At its best the room is suffused with a feeling of erotic possibility and openness... Without going into detail, the room has, right from the start, sometimes had real sexual contact in it.' One member of the collective later told *The Face* magazine that at his audition, at the age of eighteen, he was asked to masturbate into a mirror.[2] Many rehearsals involved performers going into 'the Field', a taped-off portion of the rehearsal room, and being asked to carry out an escalating series of erotic acts.

Goode managed this delicate situation, according to collaborators, through 'check-ins'. Performers and fellow artists – assistant directors, production managers, set designers – were asked how they were feeling in the morning, and again after lunch. The idea was that anyone who was uncomfortable could speak out. In return, performers were asked 'that you consistently work as close to your line as you can, in a critical way, so that you are interested to analyse and maybe, seek to explore and maybe shift it'. The advert ended with a warning that the room was 'sex-positive' and those who were ethically opposed to pornography would find it 'inhospitable'. Those who found the idea of Ponyboy Curtis disquieting were advised to read an attached review from Exeunt, which called Goode's work 'a theatre of bodies and noise and feeling, not a theatre of words... I don't yet have words – let alone sentences – to describe or respond to it.'

With the promise of this kind of transcendence, Goode had no trouble recruiting his Ponyboys. The company began to prepare for a show called *Vs* at The Yard theatre, where the Ponyboys tore off their clothes to Stravinsky's *Rite of Spring*. The show received four stars from *The Stage*, with the critic noting that it challenged 'the sensibilities of an audience, who necessarily become a voyeuristic presence'. The nudity and sexual contact of *Vs* provoked wildly different reactions in the audience. 'It didn't feel especially lurid or provocative in performance,' one fringe theatre regular told me. 'I know it's a bit of a cop-out or cliché to say it, but . . . it felt more awkward or boring or theatrically unfruitful than it did lurid.' However, a previous collaborator of Goode's told me that she was unable to talk to him after the performance because she was so affected by what she had seen. 'It was shocking how explicit it was: blow jobs, hand-jobs, whatever,' she said. 'But couched in this beautifully paced outer casing of a show that had these moments of – *whoa* – transgressiveness.' Did it feel as though you were watching one man's bespoke porn? 'Yes. His bespoke porn with its own playlist.'

The argument smuggled inside calling Goode a genius was that you, the viewer, were cool. You were sufficiently sophisticated to understand that plays about fourteen-year-old boys having relationships with adult men, or plays where a group of twinks touched each other on command, were conveying a more sophisticated message than . . . well, that their author liked that sort of thing. Some reviewers were conscious of this bargain. The blogger Meg Vaughan wrote an imagined dialogue between two speakers after seeing a Ponyboy Curtis performance:[3]

> B: I just feel so uncertain about everything.
> A: Because of the Tories?
> B: Yeah, definitely . . . But it's because of Ponyboy Curtis too I think.
> A: I heard that show was basically just dick.
> B: Well . . .
> A: I heard it was just a load of pretty young boys waggling their cocks about with all these fucking performance crowd hipsters jizzing all over it because it's a Chris Goode project and they're all too scared of pissing off their guru to tell it like it is.

B: Your whole face looks like the nail varnish emoji right now.

The dialogue continues with B insisting that although the nudity was 'gratuitous', it was also powerful.

A: OMG was it live porn????
B: Calm down Mary Whitehouse. Not live porn, but there were naked boys doing TOUCHING. Which is okay. Which is totally okay. Because we are mature, arts-literate women of the world who are open to the creative experiments of others.

The name of Mary Whitehouse is resonant here, because in the 1980s she tried to have a play banned for featuring a gay rape. She has become an emblem of social conservatism, and of philistinism; Whitehouse eventually revealed that she had not even seen the play before condemning it. Meg Vaughan's dialogue ends with B hoping that she can shrug off her Whitehouse tendencies and become the audience that the Ponyboys deserve: 'I've always thought that I'm so brave, so liberal, so accepting, and so ready to embrace all the wonderful batshit ideas that artists bring to life, but actually I was a bit frightened.'

The gendered overtones of the situation are worth mentioning here. The arts industry is not only full of demanding, brilliant men, but women who like to be around those sorts of men. Goode and his male performers were intensely sexual, kinky and transgressive – while his most ardent cheerleaders were middle-class women with a taste for the dark side. His queerness was a shield against left-wing criticism. 'There are *many* moments when I was told that my objections were actually a sign of an inner hatred of myself and my self-directed homophobia,' one female collaborator wrote later.[4] Had Goode been a fortysomething man overseeing a roomful of naked women, more eyebrows would have been raised. As it was, people were reluctant to ask out loud if they were watching an act of genius or sexualised coercion.

Chris Goode's work was presented as a challenge to bourgeois norms. He was an outsider, a rebel – a true artist. Calling him a genius was a way of excusing him from the demands of 'polite' society.

George Orwell called this impulse the 'benefit of clergy', after a medieval practice where priests and nuns were spared the death penalty because they claimed that civil courts could not judge them. Reviewing the work of Salvador Dalí, Orwell described his art as an insistent confession, full of symbolic objects such as high heels, images of death and putrefaction, and even flirtations with coprophilia. Because he was writing in the 1940s, Orwell felt able to offer a moral conclusion: Dalí was 'a symptom of the world's illness. The important thing is not to denounce him as a cad who ought to be horse-whipped, or to defend him as a genius who ought not to be questioned, but to find out *why* he exhibits that particular set of aberrations.' To Orwell, being an artist – being a special person – was no excuse for abusive behaviour. 'If Shakespeare returned to the earth tomorrow, and if it were found that his favourite recreation was raping little girls in railway carriages, we should not tell him to go ahead with it on the ground that he might write another *King Lear*.'

In theory, most of us would agree with this sentiment. But in practice, it's different. The film producer Harvey Weinstein's predatory behaviour was well-known enough to be the subject of jokes on a mainstream sitcom, *30 Rock*, years before his trial and conviction. Money-grabbing mercenaries turned a blind eye, because his films made money. But so did sensitive left-wing types who wanted to be good people. For them, the appeal of

Weinstein was that he could raise the funds for beautiful, intelligent independent films.

This debate over the personal ethics of geniuses began long before the MeToo movement of the late 2010s, but that feminist reckoning gave it extra ferocity. In a viral essay in 2017, the critic Claire Dederer asked: 'What do we do with the art of monstrous men?'[5] The question was unavoidable, she said, because of the sheer number of abusers, racists and even murderers among the ranks of the mega-talented – and because their art often implicitly made the case for their particular perversion. 'They did or said something awful, and made something great,' she wrote. 'They are monster geniuses, and I don't know what to do about them.' (As a parallel question, Dederer wonders if she is not monstrous *enough* to achieve something wonderful. 'A book is made out of small selfishnesses,' she writes. 'If I were more selfish, would my work be better? Should I aspire to greater selfishness?')

These conversations have left us in a cultural bind. We implicitly accept that geniuses are *not like us* – that's the point of the label – but does that mean they should get the 'benefit of clergy'? If you claim that you will never condone or ignore abuse, violence and discrimination, then either half the canon is closed to you . . . or you must make yourself a hypocrite. These choices are deeply personal and rarely coherent. I would happily dance to 'Billie Jean' at a wedding, but I walked out of *MJ*, the recent Michael Jackson musical, at the interval. Having to sit through a number about how unfair the media were to him ruined my ability to enjoy the performance. (The musical is cannily set on the *Dangerous* tour in 1992, just before the first child abuse allegations became public in August 1993.) Poor Michael, hounded by the press as weird, simply because he wanted to build a theme park at his home and invite children there for sleepovers. The spell of his music broke, and suddenly the whole enterprise seemed obscene; an attempt to scrub clean the life of this troubled, talented man so that he could continue to make money from beyond the grave.

With living artists, these questions are even more uncomfortable. I know lots of people who think the current vogue for 'cancellation' has gone too far. Sometimes I agree with them. But it's also important to remember that, within living memory, even the most appalling crimes were overlooked if the perpetrator was talented enough. One of Dederer's examples is Roman Polanski. In 1977, the 43-year-old director took a 13-year-old girl to Jack Nicholson's house, gave her champagne (and, she says, stronger drugs) and then had vaginal and anal sex with her. When he faced legal action, he fled America rather than face jail time. (He had pleaded guilty to a lesser charge of statutory rape in exchange for the other charges of rape, sodomy and supplying the girl with drugs being dropped, but became worried that the plea bargain would not be upheld.) Since then, Polanski has not returned to the States, and has even avoided visiting countries which might extradite him.

A year after leaving America, Polanski released *Tess*, his version of the Thomas Hardy novel. 'This is a wonderful film; the kind of exploration of doomed young sexuality that . . . makes us agree that the lovers should never grow old,' wrote Roger Ebert, which is not the happiest phrasing in the circumstances.[6] The film was nominated for six Oscars – including Best Director. It won three of the categories, as well as three Césars, two Golden Globes and a Bafta. In the next three decades, a parade of stars lined up to explain that what Polanski had done wasn't really that bad – not 'rape rape', as Whoopi Goldberg phrased it. When Polanski won the Best Director award at the 2003 Oscars, Hollywood heavyweights including Martin Scorsese, Meryl Streep and Harvey Weinstein gave him a standing ovation. He wasn't there, of course.

Polanski has worked steadily in the decades following his self-imposed exile, occasionally suing someone he feels has defamed him – including another woman who accused him of rape. According to his memoir, he considers himself a victim of American prudishness. As for his defenders in the acting world, the journalist Hadley Freeman has written, 'questions about why they were working with a convicted child rapist were seen as tacky, proof of a rigid mind more focused on gossip than art'.[7] You also have to wonder – did his status as an outlaw add a certain titillating lustre to his work? The actor Debra Winger described Polanski's arrest in Switzerland, over the 1977 case, as 'philistine collusion' and said that 'the whole art world suffers'.

What finally changed these laissez-faire attitudes was the MeToo movement, which made defending predators commercial suicide. The fall of Harvey Weinstein made a lot of people in Hollywood state loudly that they were and had always been opposed to sexual predation. In that spirit, the Academy finally voted to remove Polanski from its membership in 2019. His ostracism was a slow process with many resisters, both passive and active.

And during that time, he made many films – some of which, as one of my friends put it, were 'celebrations of sexual sadism'. For me, this is the line. I try to separate the art and the artist. But that's impossible when – as with Polanski, and as with Chris Goode – the art is propaganda for the crime.

For decades, if Hollywood were pressed about Orwell's question about *King Lear* being worth the rape of a few little girls, the answer would have been a shamefaced 'yes'.

What destroyed Chris Goode was love. In 2015, he met a young American actor called Griffyn Gilligan. Fine-boned, slim and with delicate features, Gilligan was the first transgender man to join the Ponyboy Curtis collective. The fans liked that; they had worried that Goode's vision was too 'cisnormative'.

I knew before Goode's death that he had been the subject of an open letter in early 2018, complaining about the working practices in the Ponyboy rehearsal room. That document has now disappeared from the internet, but those who saw it remember its central allegation: that one member of the collective had harassed another member, and that Goode had done nothing to intervene. When it was published, Goode was in the middle of working on a theatrical adaptation of Derek Jarman's *Jubilee* for Manchester's Royal Exchange Theatre – his biggest stage commission for many years.

The allegations weighed on Goode. He was distracted and absent during the *Jubilee* rehearsals, people who were present told me. The actors and other creatives salvaged what they could; the resulting show was a mess. Sometimes, half the audience walked out at the interval; many in the remaining half prided themselves on not doing so. 'In the Saturday matinee performance I was in, many of my fellow audience members weren't that keen on being showered with sparks at all,' wrote Meg Vaughan.[8] 'They left in significant numbers in the interval, and left Amyl Nitrate – the WONDERFUL Travis Alabanza – to say good riddance on all our behalfs. Here was another relief – the exit of a stony-faced minority giving the rest of us permission to have a good time.'

The open letter came in the middle of the MeToo movement, which also brought down Out of Joint's Max Stafford-Clark and the Old Vic's Kevin Spacey. Privately, some in the theatre world thought that the new mood was going beyond redress for years of sexism and over the line into fastidiousness. (A proposed harassment policy spearheaded by the Royal Court warned against 'staring' and 'meaningful glances'.) Was Chris Goode's work abusive, people whispered, or merely out of step with a newly puritan ethos? These questions were deeply awkward for his most fervent fans, described to me by one theatre-maker as 'the wokest of the woke'. People began to drift away from him. His health declined.

The end of the year brought one of the most significant abandonments. Maddy Costa was an irregular theatre critic who had given up reviewing to have children in 2007. Four years later, she returned to blogging with a site called Deliq. And two weeks after that, Chris Goode asked her if she would become his 'critic-in-residence'. He was the storyteller, she was his 'bridge'. Her role was 'telling the story of the company back to itself'. Her work would be funded by the Arts Council (and subsidised by her husband's much-better-paid job). Initially, Costa loved Goode's work for 'its queerness, its delicacy, its anti-capitalist politics, its romance, its empathy with outsiders, the rejected of society, those in pain, its desire to open space for those outsiders within theatre'. This is part of what proximity to genius – or what people call genius – offers to the rest of us. A fingertip touch with the extraordinary; a few moments of fleeting awe to leaven a humdrum existence. But, Costa wrote later, 'somewhere along the line of the company I stopped saying *I love his work* and started saying *I love him*. Which is part of what's made writing this so difficult.' The final straw was that Ponyboy Curtis show, *Vs*, at the Yard. It was too much for her – she could not be his vicar on earth any more, laundering his transgressions into artistic provocations.

The next year, the investigation into Chris Goode and Company delivered its verdict. It identified 'safeguarding issues' in the rehearsal room. (The full report was never made public.) The finding ended Ponyboy Curtis and put the rest of Goode's work 'on hold'. There was a promise to institute a new code of conduct before he could work again. But that wasn't enough: former collaborators contacted the company to express their disappointment, and the person who sent the initial open letter turned it into a formal complaint. Goode tried to keep working on other projects. He had a plan for an autobiographical play, and another work about men who deliberately infected themselves with HIV. But, he told friends, he could no longer make the work he wanted to make.

After Goode's death, I discovered who had brought Goode's offending out into the open. The discovery was a shock: it was his husband, Griffyn Gilligan. One night, when Gilligan was using Goode's computer, he found a stash of child abuse images. At 1 a.m. on 5 May 2021, officers arrested Chris Goode. On 1 June, while out on bail, he killed himself.

This is where I enter the story. As I said, I had been only vaguely aware of Goode's work during his life, but his death shook me. At the time Goode's death was announced, there was a mood running through London theatre – a sudden sense that the 'benefit of clergy' had been removed, and that abusive practices were no longer acceptable in the name of creativity.

I expected a reckoning. Instead there was a burial. When I began to investigate this story – reasoning that Goode was an example of someone who had consciously played up to the image of the tortured genius – one acquaintance warned me to 'save everything'. Goode's collaborators and friends were busy wiping him from the internet, he said. The Chris Goode and Company website disappeared, his Twitter account was deleted, and then Gilligan's confessional blog was set to password-protected. Another mutual acquaintance told me that the disappearance of Goode's Twitter account meant that their private message exchanges 'vaporised', which had upset him. Gilligan wrote a pair of blog posts, called 'There Will Be No Archive' and 'There Will Be No Memorial', which argued that Goode's work could never be performed again. But there *was* a memorial, in 2022, which Gilligan said was 'not to celebrate him or ritualise/bolster his legacy. Simply to acknowledge that for many people, his presence and work did affect their lives'.

Maddy Costa and others have tried to reckon with their participation in Goode's work – her archived posts on their collaboration carry a note at the top, recording his crimes. 'I acknowledge that I was complicit in some of the harms he caused, for instance by erasing the work of other women who worked with him, fuelling a cult of genius around him, and consistently asking people who criticised his work (particularly the sexually explicit work) to see it in softer ways,' she wrote. In 2022, she and others published 'personal accounts and a call to action'. One of the other three writers, a former Ponyboy called Paul Paschal, warned that any post-mortem criticism of Goode's working practices could fuel his political opponents. 'The story', wrote Paschal, 'is ripe to be appropriated by right-wing commentators seeking to attack queer experimental art.'[9] What could not be questioned, even now, was whether Goode had used his political stances and personal identity as fuel for his self-mythology as an outsider genius. As a shield against questions. As 'benefit of clergy'.

As I was about to set aside the story of Chris Goode's life and death, someone passed me a remarkable document. A few days before he died, Goode had written to his friends, sending them a nineteen-page confession. 'Shall we agree straight away, from the very beginning, that reading this is not compulsory?', it began.

The letter was brutal in its honesty; I have never read a paedophile explain their psychology and offending patterns so clearly. Goode contradicted anyone who might be tempted to plead that there was no link between his work and his personal life. He himself thought that his art and his sexual orientation towards children were indivisible: what made him a paedophile also made him a playwright. What made him a genius also made him an outcast. After a sexual encounter with another boy at the age of nine, Goode wondered: 'How could I feel like that all the time? – One way was to write about it, of course.' Eventually, he wrote, he found a therapist. 'In the first session we had following my arrest, my therapist made the link perfectly, between the intense and exciting sex games I'd played with my friends at the age of seven or eight, and the work I'd done with Ponyboy, which was perhaps the only thing I ever found to match those early experiences for intensity and excitement,' wrote Goode. 'He couldn't have put it more succinctly. "It's all about getting other boys to do things, isn't it?"'

In the summer of 2022, Goode's collaborator and friend, the playwright Simon Stephens, agreed to speak to me about the link between art and artist. We had lunch, and he seemed to want to confess, too. 'There's a lot I need to tell you,' he said, at one point, when the conversation wandered off-topic. Stephens had once been a guest performer in the Ponyboy Curtis show, which he found 'exhilarating', and he had subsequently written a monologue for a sixteen-year-old actor to deliver on the climate emergency. Chris Goode directed the teenager's performance; Stephens visited the rehearsal room without noticing anything untoward. After Goode suspended his company's work, the other playwright agreed to collaborate with him.

This was during the pandemic, and rehearsal space was 'at a premium', so Goode hired an Airbnb in Stratford, east London. 'Chris had just had half his foot removed,' Stephens told me. 'Whatever it was, it was the same illness that killed his mother in her fifties.' He turned up wearing a ski boot, and the pair went to work. Goode wanted to make a work about hope – or rather the absence of it. 'I want to make the audience sit with their hopelessness,' he told Stephens.

Then Stephens got a text message – from Gilligan. It asked him to call immediately, when Goode wasn't around. So he called back that night, and Griffyn told him what he had found on the hard drives. What should a person do in that situation? Perhaps, for some people, it would have been easy – Goode himself wrote about how many friends 'ghosted' him when the allegations came out. Stephens felt differently; he had worked in prisons himself, as a writing teacher, and felt strongly that although he could no longer work with Goode, he couldn't cut him off completely.

That led to what Stephens really wanted to tell me – the coda to the story. While Goode was on bail, they met in Victoria Park, east London. Stephens turned up with a croissant, and was immediately attacked by the park's hungry geese, a comic moment in a tragic episode. Over two hours, Chris told him everything. He remembered one exchange:

> **SIMON:** I will visit you in prison.
> **CHRIS:** That's not going to happen.

And then, Simon told me, 'I did something that as a fortysomething man from the north, I had never done before. I reached over and held his hand.' Without having to say it, they both knew what was coming next.

Stephens rejects Goode's belief that his terrible secret fuelled his creative drive. That what made him a monster also made him a writer; that all his art was a confession, a desire to hide and also to be seen. The idea that, as one friend told me: 'All his plays were suicide notes.' *That's bullshit*, Stephens said, which should not be tolerated. Such thinking feeds a dangerous cult of the individual, and messes up artists themselves, if they begin to believe it. 'It reminds me of notions of alcoholism and their connection with art,' he wrote to me. 'Some people make great art and are alcoholics. But they don't make great art *because* they are alcoholics. Nor are they alcoholics *because* they make great art. That's a specious romantic myth that leads to the sentimentalisation of addiction.'

Chris Goode, he said, was 'both a criminal and a good friend. He engaged in child sex abuse and was a kind mentor to many. He perpetuated horrifying abuse and made good art. I don't think one atones for the other . . . And I don't think one caused the other. I think they exist side by side. In contradiction not causality.' He wondered if those who lionised Goode needed him to be a hero, while others, later, needed him to be a villain. 'The cult of the individual is a lie because there is no such thing as individuals. We are, instead, *dividuals*. There is no such thing as an authentic self.'

Did Chris Goode tell himself that his offending was the price he paid for his talent – is that how he reconciled it to himself? Did the 'cult of genius', as Maddy Costa called it, prevent those around him from seeing clearly and speaking out? I was touched by what Simon Stephens had said to Goode, that last time they spoke – and I wished that Goode had fewer fans, and more friends.

Great Wives

'Feminism has made us rethink musedom as a career choice.'
Francine Prose, *The Lives of the Muses*

'I was wondering today why there were no women writers, artists or composers of genius,' wrote Sofia Tolstaya in 1898, when she was in her fifties. 'It's because all the passion ... of an energetic woman is consumed by her family, love, her husband – and especially her children ... When she has finished bearing and educating her children, her artistic needs awaken, but by then it's too late.'[1]

By the time she wrote these words, Tolstaya had been pregnant sixteen times. Three years earlier, her final child, Vanechka, had died at the age of seven, plunging her into terrible misery. By then, her husband Lev (or Leo) Tolstoy was not the same man who had written *War and Peace* and *Anna Karenina*. He was now a prophet, preaching the renunciation of property – although he continued to live on the family's aristocratic estate – and sexual abstinence. The arrival of little Vanechka had shown that principle to be hollow.

Sofia had known Tolstoy all her life. Her mother was one of his childhood friends, and the writer loved her family, the Behrs. His own mother had died before he was two years old and he lived a disconnected, peripatetic childhood, passed between relatives. He had tried university, but could never knuckle down, and that experiment ended when he caught a venereal disease that hospitalised him. Before he proposed to Sofia at the age of thirty-four – she was eighteen – he had served in the army, visited dozens of brothels and fathered a child with one of the peasants on his estate.

To students of Russian literature, the Tolstoy marriage is notorious. Lev was a born aristocrat, an unquestioned patriarch and a depressive, capable both of extraordinary empathy – he organised a famine relief effort in the 1890s – and brutal callousness. Sofia was a self-conscious martyr, deeply conservative and more highly strung with every passing year. Lev turned to anarchism and wanted to live like a peasant; Sofia wanted to make sure their children were fed and housed. He was excommunicated by the Orthodox Church; she was deeply religious.

Tolstoy's pen gave him power in the relationship. When Sofia struggled to breastfeed their first child, he wrote a five-act play called *The Infected Family* arguing that women who used wet nurses were unnatural. As an old man, he wrote a book, *The Kreutzer Sonata*, whose discussion of abstinence embarrassed her greatly. But she still went to the Tsar to protest the novella being banned. The Tolstoys were bound together by his words – at first, by his struggle to write his two great novels, and later by his struggle to avoid the censors.

The sacrifices that Sofia Tolstaya made were obvious to her. 'A genius must be fed, washed and dressed, must have his works copied innumerable times, must be loved and spared all cause for jealousy, so he can be calm,' she wrote in her diary. 'A man of genius is always so much better in his works than in his life!' Yet when Tolstoy peeled away from her – first getting his daughters to copy out his works, and then falling for a charismatic young disciple called Vladimir Chertkov – his wife was devastated. She wanted to possess him, no matter how much pain it caused her.

'She was his reader,' writes A. N. Wilson in his biography of Lev. 'She survived all the ups and downs of married life until this fact came to be challenged, and rival readers tried to move in and take her place.'[2]

Sofia Tolstaya's first wifely role was as a muse. Tolstoy saw in the easy camaraderie and care of her family everything he had missed in his own upbringing. He also saw *material*. In the short few weeks of their courtship, the couple swapped diaries and other writing. At sixteen, Sofia had written a novella called *Natasha*, which she gave to Tolstoy to read (before burning it along with her other supposedly youthful fripperies). She regretted that destruction later, because it removed the proof for her claim that Tolstoy borrowed her heroine's name and experiences for Natasha Rostova in *War and Peace*.

While Lev was captivated by what he saw as Sofia's naive outpourings on love, she was rather less captivated by his diary. The first entry recorded him being treated for gonorrhoea caught from a prostituted woman. Sofia wrote later that she cried when reading the book because it 'shattered' her vision of the great man. But Lev wanted to be *known* – he wanted his wife to be a second heart, a second brain and a second pair of hands. Much of their later unhappiness surely springs from the mess of contradictions he expected from a woman. He wanted an uncorrupted being with no sexual feelings. He wanted a substitute mother. He wanted someone who could express feelings that he could not, and to maintain a purity he felt he had lost. He wanted a secretary, but he also wanted that secretary to love him.

In the early years of their marriage, Sofia became pregnant far more often than she would have chosen. (Lev was opposed to all contraception.) While she was still a teenager, stuck at home nursing their children, he took her younger unmarried sister Tanya to balls and shooting expeditions. 'Tolstoy "mixed" Sophia with her sister to create his Natasha [Rostova],' writes Alexandra Popoff in her biography of Tolstaya.[3] 'Tanya was the model for the heroine's youth, and Sophia, who never had a chance to be carefree, was used for her motherhood.' Tolstoy encouraged his wife to write a diary, as well as regular letters to him while he was away. He wanted to drink in her interior world. In return, he trusted her with his own secrets, including his attraction to her sister. When he was away from their remote estate of Yasnaya Polyana, he wrote to her telling her that his writing had suffered. Everything felt drab and the words didn't flow. He needed to be at home, where everything was arranged to spur his creativity.

The heartbeat of their marriage was writing. She spent seven years copying out *War and Peace*, with Lev bringing her new pages every evening as he revised scenes obsessively. (She preferred the family sections to the military campaigns.) Sometimes he read out chapters to her, or the work of other authors he thought she should appreciate. This is what A. N. Wilson means by the idea of Tolstaya as her husband's *reader*; they were knotted together by the project of his work, which they both acknowledged to be greater than themselves. She believed in him. He borrowed from her. She gave up everything for him – her interest in art and music, her closeness with her family, her time, her body – and he fed on it, swelled himself with her sacrifice. He wrote for her.

During the great years – the time when he wrote *Anna Karenina* and *War and Peace* – Sofia Tolstaya believed the sacrifice was worth it. They were in love. He was an artist. She was put on earth to serve him. To outsiders, the imbalance in this relationship might seem profound, and the details can seem gothic; Tolstaya's copying duties were not to be interrupted by her frequent pregnancies, and she kept working while in bed, recovering from childbirth. But for a while, this was a vocation she felt privileged to have, and she accepted it. Tolstoy had a vision of how life should be – he wanted to be a rural lord, surrounded by happy, simple peasants and an idyllic family, free from the taint of modernity or sophistication. And because he had money and status, he could make that happen. What sustained Lev Tolstoy was a giant organic machine built to sustain him – his beehive.

Few artists can have been more indulged in their whims than Lev Tolstoy was once *Anna Karenina* and *War and Peace* had turned him into Russia's 'second tsar'. His second great work had not come easily; after *War and Peace* was published, Tolstoy became depressed. He spent months studying Greek, travelling to the steppes to drink wild horse milk for his health, and opening a neighbourhood school. Sofia was always pregnant or nursing a baby. In March 1873, however, he found a collection of Pushkin stories that Sofia had left out for their son to read; the plain style enthralled him and that evening he composed the opening paragraphs of *Anna Karenina*. But halfway into writing, he lost interest and started back on his school project again. Sofia desperately wanted him to go back to the novel. She wrote to her sister that writing was Lev's 'vocation' and she was miserable when he was not following his heart: 'What's lacking in my life now is Lyovochka's work, which I always enjoyed and admired. You see, Tanya, I am a true writer's wife, so close to my heart do I keep our creative work.' (Note that 'our'.)

What unlocked *Anna Karenina* was grief: in 1875, the couple's son Nikolai died from meningitis. Lev started writing again, borrowing Sofia's anguish for his novel, in which a mother speaks of the 'eternal fear' of raising children. Once again, he wrote and she copied. She worked so hard – while, of course, pregnant again – that she collapsed. Her right arm was agony, and the doctor ordered her to rest. In the autumn, she caught whooping cough and gave birth to a premature baby daughter, who died. Then she contracted peritonitis and came close to death herself. Tolstoy's reaction to all this is worth noting. 'All this time – two weeks – I've been looking after a sick wife who gave birth to a stillborn child and has been at death's door,' he wrote to a friend. 'But it's a strange thing – I've never thought with such vigour about the problems which interest me as at this time.'[4]

Once Sofia recovered, she was back to copying all night. Despite this terrible gestation – or perhaps because of it – the novel was instantly recognised as a major work. Some early reviewers carped about the length – 'tedious, verbose to somnolency', intoned the *New York Tribune* – but just as many were captivated by the lavish detail of Tolstoy's countryside, the insights of his omniscient narrator and the subtle characterisation of Anna and the people around her. Readers also understood that it was a novel about the clash between old and new Russia, which captured Tolstoy's own ambivalence. 'I'm not sure Tolstoy ever worked out how he actually felt about love and desire, or how he should feel about it,' wrote the novelist James Meek in 2012.[5] 'He was torn between compassion and moral rigour, between lust and self-denial, between loving his wife and being bored by her. His uncertainty is reflected in the dual portrayal of his wife in *Anna Karenina* – as the virtuous, somewhat frumpy Dolly, worn out by childbearing, like the woman his wife was when he was writing the book, and as the feisty, pretty teenager Kitty, like the woman his wife was when he married her.'

In celebration of the book's success, Lev bought Sofia a ruby and diamond ring as a gift. But their strange compact, the communion of minds that had bound them together through Tolstoy's two greatest works, was beginning to dissolve. After years of struggling with his faith, Tolstoy had visited a monastery and come back full of religious enthusiasm. As ever, his wife reordered their lives to accommodate his new passion: strict fasts and Gospel readings were introduced at Yasnaya Polyana. (Tolstoy gave up smoking and hunting, and even became vegetarian for a while.) He started work on a novel about the Decembrists, a group of Russian rebels earlier in the century, but abandoned it after three chapters. Then he abandoned his newfound piety, too, and became anti-religious instead. He had given up literature altogether, he declared. He *was* a writer, but no longer. From now on, he would write improving books. Tolstaya found his new work 'insufferably boring', she wrote to her sister in 1880. The golden thread of their life – his work and her enjoyment of it – was fraying.

The next few decades of Tolstoy's life are notorious. He developed a hatred of Moscow and became ever more fanatical about the joys of the countryside. As his philosophical interests deepened, he became Russia's foremost critic of the Orthodox Church, and of the sluggish bureaucracy of the country's government. His fame protected him from the censorship or even imprisonment that a lesser writer would have experienced as a result. He was acclaimed as a sage, a prophet, a holy man – and his personal behaviour changed to match. He became even more attached to his peasant costume. He rejected medicine. He visited prisons. He gave away their money. His wife could not follow him down this path; she couldn't even understand it. 'It was as if he was intentionally looking for places where he could see human suffering and abuse,' she wrote in her memoir. 'His disapproval and condemnation turned also against me, our family, and everyone who was rich and not unhappy.'[6] Once, Tolstoy had used the figure of Sofia – the pure virgin – as fuel for his female characters. Now he could resent her for keeping him fed and housed, relying on the material support she provided while simultaneously despising her for being less committed to his philosophy than him.

The alienation between them was played out through words. 'I wonder why I no longer blindly believe in him as a writer,' Tolstaya confided in her diary in 1886, eight years after the publication of *Anna Karenina*. They both wrote journals and left them around the house for the other to read. Lev threatened to walk out on Sofia when she was in labour with their twelfth child, Sasha. She refused to have sex with Lev, which made him even angrier, even though he confided in his diary that living with her was vile. Their alienation created a void, which was filled by admirers, who called themselves Tolstoyans, and hung around the estate complaining about Sofia. (She, in turn, became ever more highly strung and unreasonable.)

The foremost of these Tolstoyans was a young ex-Guards officer named Vladimir Chertkov, whom Tolstoy met when he was fifty-five. The pair exchanged more than 2,000 letters, and he was allowed to read Tolstoy's diary. Their relationship went beyond friendship into a mixture of spirituality, coercive control and eroticism. Chertkov effectively supplanted Sofia Tolstaya as Tolstoy's greatest *reader*. And unlike Tolstaya, he did not discourage the author's religious enthusiasms and rejection of the material world – not least because it wasn't *his* children who had to live off the copyright of *Anna Karenina*. Chertkov hired secretaries to copy out Tolstoy's diary and letters, and even told him what to write.[7] By the end, Chertkov had created a secret will giving him control of the author's legacy.

If you want to know why the great Tolstoy of *War and Peace* became the unreadable author of dreary religious tracts, there is a simple answer. He swapped Sofia Tolstaya for Vladimir Chertkov. He swapped domestic life for saintly preaching. He swapped a relationship built around support for one founded on control. Anyone who disbelieves the importance of a great wife to a genius, who thinks that a solitary figure is all that matters, is invited to read *Anna Karenina*. And then read anything that Tolstoy wrote after the age of fifty-five.

The wife holds a unique position in the mythology of genius. I say 'wife' because most people we recognise as geniuses are men, and most of them have been in heterosexual marriages. But you can see a similar dynamic in the relationship between, say, the American author Gertrude Stein and her partner Alice B. Toklas. Stein didn't just plunder Toklas' real life for her work, as Tolstoy did – she stole her partner's *voice*, writing a book called *The Autobiography of Alice B. Toklas*. And then used it to have 'Alice' say that Gertrude was a genius.

This is partly about practical considerations – who feeds and waters the innovator, the author, the painter, the heroic protagonist engaged in an epic struggle with his muse? In the absence of a wife, institutions can cover these needs. The early female writers, such as Hildegard of Bingen, lived in nunneries. Isaac Newton, a deeply strange man, prospered within the Cambridge college system, a cross between prison, a gentleman's club and a monastic cell. The Japanese artist Yayoi Kusama checked herself into a mental hospital in Tokyo in 1977 and has lived there ever since. (Her studio is across the street.) A wife offers more, however. No other figure in a great man's life can hold quite such influence, or can be so intimately intertwined with every aspect of his existence. In a *Baffler* essay called 'The Wife Glitch', the American writer Jennifer Schaffer lays out these unique properties of a spouse:[8]

> Someone to think ahead about our needs; someone to make our homes and our lives orderly; someone to tend to our

emotions when they're raw and sore. Someone to track and manage the infinite details of living; someone to be responsible for our moods; someone to balance the books. We all want someone who knows us so intimately they can predict what we'll want; someone who picks up our loose ends without complaint; someone who fills in our weaknesses with her strength . . . Someone who means it.

Tolstaya is the demonstration of this principle. She was a talented artist – as she discovered in middle age when she took up photography – and her diaries reveal her to have been a compelling writer, too. She gave notes on her husband's work, and more than that, she was endlessly interested in it. Tolstoy could have married a simpler, less intellectual woman, but then he could not have leaned on that woman so heavily. What made the Tolstoy marriage work – while it did work – was that Tolstaya was in love with her husband's writing, and her care and attention nourished him. It would be simplistic to say that he 'stole' from her novella *Natasha* to create *War and Peace*, but it would also be simplistic to say the novel was his achievement alone. He needed his wife, their children, her copying, their country estate. He was a genius, and a parasite. Did those around him think their sacrifice was worth it? And do we, as Tolstoy's readers today? When you admire an artwork or a scientific innovation, what duty do you owe to those harmed in its production?*

A wife is also a mirror, reflecting the genius back at himself (or herself) but magnified in size. Gertrude Stein's claim to genius was bolstered by having a wife who could talk to the other wives. She has Toklas say: 'Before I decided to write this

---

* Several recent books attempt to wrestle with this question, including Claire Dederer's *Monsters*, and Erich Hatala Matthes' *Drawing the Line*.

book, my twenty-five years with Gertrude Stein, I had often said that I would write, *The wives of geniuses I have sat with*. I have sat with so many. I have sat with wives who were not wives, of geniuses who were real geniuses. I have sat with real wives of geniuses who were not real geniuses. I have sat with wives of geniuses, of near geniuses, of would-be geniuses; in short, I have sat very often and very long with many wives and wives of many geniuses.' When the couple are with Pablo Picasso, Gertrude talks to the artist. Alice talks to his partner, Fernande, who also paints: 'She was not in the least amusing. We talked hats.'[9]

The unique role of the wife in the history of genius became clear to me in 2021, when I made a radio series called *Great Wives*. It was intended as a companion to the BBC's long-running series *Great Lives*, which has featured everyone from Neville Chamberlain to Donna Summer. In the 450th episode of the programme, its producer noted a recurrent problem: that female guests often picked a man as their Great Life, but male guests rarely picked a woman. (Well done to unexpectedly woke Bernard Manning, who picked Mother Teresa.) That was a sobering reminder even now that the two categories seem to be 'history' and 'women's history', but I had taken something else from the programme. Very often, the great man benefited from an unseen support system. Usually a wife, but sometimes a mother, a sister or a housekeeper. In 2015, Katrine Marçal's book title asked *Who Cooked Adam Smith's Dinner?* The answer was his mother, Margaret Douglas, and after her death, his cousin Janet. Marçal saw the humour of Adam Smith's situation: a man who had the free time to write about capitalism because of the unpaid labour that kept him fed and watered.

How many more women through history would be hailed as geniuses if they had been able to take a wife? Because a wife can do *everything*. Véra Nabokov certainly did; she famously sat at the side of the stage when her husband Vladimir was giving lectures, for moral support. She also acted as his agent, translator and secretary. She cooked and cleaned for him, drove him around the country and even taught his classes at the university when he couldn't make them. She went butterfly collecting with him, and they played Scrabble together. He dreamed of playing the piano, while she turned the pages; a neat metaphor for the symbiosis of great man and great wife. The skill is his, but it can't be demonstrated without her. Véra was the first reader of all Vladimir's novels. When Vladimir became infamous after the publication of *Lolita* – a novel about a man who lusts over a twelve-year-old girl – Véra carried a pistol in her handbag, ready to take on any would-be assassins. In return, she received Vladimir's gratitude, and his extraordinary love letters: 'I love you very much,' read one. 'Love you in a bad way (don't be angry, my happiness). Love you in a good way. Love your teeth . . . I love you, my sun, my life, I love your eyes – closed – all the little tails of your thoughts, your stretchy vowels, your whole soul from head to heels.' This was their bargain.

Not every great wife experiences her life as drudgery, as Sofia Tolstaya did. But it is notable how rarely women receive such unstinting, sacrificial support for their careers, and we have to factor that into any discussion of the male dominance of the category of 'genius'. If a genius is selfish, their partner must be selfless. And the joy of a wife is that when she does everything, she can make it seem effortless. She can do it with a smile, and a shake of the head: *really, it was nothing*. She can become, as Martha Gellhorn said she refused to be, 'a footnote in someone else's life'.

Tolstoy wasn't the only author to rely on his wife for secretarial support. Dostoevsky married his stenographer, Anna, and she became his editor, too. So did T. S. Eliot, who met his second wife Valerie when she was employed in the Faber typing pool. In 2017, a professor of English called Bruce Holsinger did a search of academic texts and posted the results on Twitter under the hashtag #thanksfortyping.[10] He looked for the words 'my wife typed' and found an unexpected store of treasure. 'The plain fact is that I wrote the book 22 times, always trying to clarify and simplify it, and my wife typed and re-typed the whole manuscript five times (on a decrepit old typewriter),' wrote one author. Another offered this gem: 'My wife typed my manuscript drafts as soon as I gave them to her, even though she was caring for our first child, born in June 1946, and was also teaching part-time in the chemistry department.' The South African economist Don Ross thanked his wife and fellow academic like this: 'Finally, my greatest debt is to my wife, Professor Nelleke Bak, for (inter alia): proofreading and formatting the entire manuscript; handling editorial correspondence while I wandered around the globe for long periods; putting up with my wandering around the globe for long periods; managing the entire infrastructure of our lives with very little help, but many calls for this and that improvement to it, while I sat in the study thinking about utility maximisation.' He certainly maximised the utility of having a wife.

When we talk about geniuses, we often knock away these invisible support structures. In 2021, a *New Yorker* cartoon went viral: it showed two women looking at paintings in a museum. One was saying to the other: 'It's all significantly less impressive once you realise these guys had free child care.'

From the eighteenth century onwards, when female education became more widespread, it's notable how many artists and scientists had talented wives: William Blake made prints with his wife Catherine; Harriet Taylor's handwriting is all over John

Stuart Mill's notes. As a young man, Albert Einstein married Mileva Marić, a fellow student at the Zurich polytechnic where he was a mediocre academic performer. Marić had fought hard to be allowed to study physics, and initially Einstein liked having someone to fulfil the role of both domestic servant – he jokingly sent her a drawing of his foot, so she could make him socks – and intellectual sparring partner. In the 1900s, they discussed physics and maths together while he was working on the theory of general relativity. And even when their intellectual relationship broke down, after the birth of their illegitimate child Lieserl Marić was still expected to supply his material needs. Einstein wrote out a contract for her:

A. You will make sure:

- that my clothes and laundry are kept in good order;
- that I will receive my three meals regularly in my room;

B. You will renounce all personal relations with me insofar as they are not completely necessary for social reasons.

C. You will stop talking to me if I request it.

Like Tolstoy and his Tolstoyans, Einstein ended up with a cult around him – the 'Einstein priests'. They jealously guarded his legacy, and wanted Marić gone from the story. She was easy to write out: in 1914, Einstein left her for his first cousin Elsa, who had no intellectual ambitions of her own. When he moved to the United States, Marić stayed in Europe with their two sons. He gave her the money from his Nobel Prize, but otherwise kept his distance. After Einstein died in 1955, the executors of his will even refused to let his older son, Hans Albert, publish a book about the family's fractious relationship.

Sometimes, great wives choose to stay in the shadows. Nick Harkaway, son of David Cornwell – better known as the spy writer John le Carré – records that his mother Jane even stepped out of family photographs because she hated attention so much. After his parents died in 2020, within three months of each other, Harkaway wrote: 'For as long as I can remember, my parents have been defined by the work they did together, and by a working relationship so interwoven with their personal one that the two were actually inseparable . . . he produced, they edited; he burned, she fanned. It was their conspiracy, the thing that no one else could ever offer him, in which they both connived.' (At the same time, le Carré was an incorrigible adulterer; his faithfulness to Jane was limited to the page.)

A wife can fulfil many roles, then, or just one. She can be a muse, inspiring poetry or plays. She can be an uncredited collaborator, typing up book drafts or tidying up errant prose. She can be a domestic servant. She can be a secretary. She can be an advocate. She can be a confidante. She can be a breadwinner during the lean years. She can do it all, and smile throughout.

The story of the Tolstoys' marriage ends on a bitterly cold day in November 1910. The Russian Revolution was only a few years away, and already the country was febrile. The Tsar was widely hated, the Orthodox Church had lost much of its authority, and eighty-two-year-old Lev Tolstoy had become the voice of the country's alienation. But today, he was dying.

The scene is Astapovo, a rural railway station more than 200 miles south-east of Moscow. A few days earlier, Lev Tolstoy had snuck out of the house he shared with Sofia, having decided he could no longer bear to live with her. 'I am doing what old men of my age usually do: leaving worldly life to spend the last days of my life in solitude and quiet,' read his departure note.

As his health began to decline, Tolstoy's will – and therefore his money and the rights to his books – became a flashpoint between Sofia and the Tolstoyans. Both sides of the argument thought Tolstoy was a genius. The question was what made him one: the novels, or the philosophy.

And so, in November 1910, when Tolstoy boarded the train that took him away from Yasnaya Polyana, the Tolstoyans thought they had finally won. The writer was quickly recognised by the passengers, and he began to preach. His late-life elopement from the family home was soon reported in newspapers, and by the time he reached Astapovo, one of the first ever news cameras, from Pathé, had arrived on the scene. It was a circus, a spectacle. Lev Tolstoy had always had a flair for self-dramatisation, even as he claimed to reject fame and fortune.

As for his wife, when she first heard the news, she threw herself into the pond at Yasnaya Polyana. Having been fished out again, she hired her own train – a special service – to take her to Astapovo. And there she waited, outside the room in the station house where her husband was dying, pleading with her husband's fans to let her inside. She was only allowed in to say goodbye after he had already lost consciousness.

Two things strike me about Sofia Tolstaya's story: first, that she spent her life in the service of a man whom everyone around him considered to be a genius. This made her profoundly unhappy. The second is that she was jealous of anyone who threatened to take her torment away. He was *her* husband, *her* problem. She was the guardian of his flame.

In the Tolstoy story, you can also see another angle: to the Tolstoyans, Sofia was the enemy. She was dragging her husband back towards domesticity and bourgeois normality, instead of letting him be the anarchic saint they worshipped. This conflict between the wife and the fans is a staple of genius myths: just look at Yoko Ono. Who *really* understands the great man? Who *does* he belong to? The wife is often hated because she distracts the genius, or makes demands on him: how dare she ask for help at home when his time is so precious? Particular hatred is reserved for those women who complain: you get to be so near to greatness, and are still so ungrateful? The implication is that the fans would cheerfully put up with cheating, or temper tantrums, or neglect, or any of the other galaxy of misdemeanours that might bedevil a marriage. Some of the more extreme might even consider it an honour to be beaten, abused or even killed by the great man.

Tolstoy's secret final testament made Vladimir Chertkov his literary executor. This was the prize that Chertkov was determined to snatch from Sofia Tolstaya, because of the power it gave him. Her memoir went unpublished, and her papers were not made available to researchers for eight decades after her death in 1919. In the absence of her voice, she was thoroughly Yoko-ed: Tolstoy was not a hypocrite, unable to follow his stated principles. Instead, his wife held him back.

Sofia Tolstaya was acutely aware of the sacrifices she had made so that the world could have *Anna Karenina* and *War and Peace.* (As well as Tolstoy's overwrought religious tracts and bizarre takedown of Shakespeare.) 'I have served a genius for almost forty years,' she wrote in the memoir that was suppressed by the Tolstoyans. 'Hundreds of times I have felt my intellectual energy stir within me, and all sorts of desires . . . and time and again I have crushed and smothered all these longings. Everyone asks: *But why should a worthless woman like you need an intellectual or artistic life?* To this question I can only reply: *I don't know, but eternally suppressing it to serve a genius is a great misfortune.*'

Keepers of the Flame

'My last request: Everything I leave behind me ... in the way of diaries, manuscripts, letters (my own and others'), sketches and so on, to be burned unread.'

Franz Kafka to his friend Max Brod

In November 1950, *Life* magazine brought together fifteen avant-garde artists for a photoshoot. It was one of those stunts that magazines have always used to create a zeitgeist, or christen a movement – while bolstering their own importance as tastemakers. The group was largely drawn from the 'Irascible Eighteen', who had lately protested the Metropolitan Museum in New York for mounting a show of contemporary American painting that, they felt, paid insufficient attention to abstract works. Four decades after Picasso shocked the art world with *Les Demoiselles d'Avignon*, many leading dealers and artists felt that museums were slow to recognise how art had continued to change. Once, Impressionism had shocked onlookers, with what they saw as its smudgy daubs. Now, the frontier was abstract expressionism, where there were often no recognisable figures at all, and artists experimented with pure colours, or clean lines, and even found objects.

Life magazine gathered fifteen of the Irascible Eighteen, including Mark Rothko, Willem de Kooning and Jackson Pollock – who had started making his drip paintings three years earlier, but struggled to sell them. For a portrait of alleged artistic revolutionaries, it is curiously drab: almost everyone is wearing a suit and tie. The only visual relief comes from the sole woman in the photograph, Hedda Sterne, who looms over the men in a jet-black coat and hat. (She had arrived late, and stood on a table.) Nonetheless, when the portrait was published in January 1951, it succeeded in exactly the way that *Life* magazine had hoped. Abstract expressionism now existed, and these fifteen artists were its core proponents. The sense of excitement created by the anointing of this new wave translated to greater fame, bigger sales and more exhibition opportunities. It created a legacy: the photograph, art historian Irving Sandler wrote more than half a century later, 'has become *the* image whereby we invision [sic] the artists who achieved the triumph of American painting'.

Inevitably, though, many of the artists involved chafed against this loss of individuality. Within a few years, several of them had fallen out, and others had broken away from their shared gallerist. One of them, Ad Reinhardt, was so rude about his fellow artists that he got sued for libel. Hedda Sterne always regretted the photo, noting both that the group portrait had annoyed the male artists – who felt their seriousness was compromised by the inclusion of a woman – and that it had overshadowed her career. 'I am known more for that darn photo than for eighty years of work,' she told the writer Sarah Boxer a few years before her hundredth birthday. 'It is a lie . . . I was not an Abstract Expressionist. Nor was I an Irascible.' She thought that the men around her had succumbed to a cult of personality – they had leaned into the genius myth, in other words. Sterne saw her art, Boxer writes, 'as a diary, her eye as a camera finding the extraordinary in the ordinary'.[1]

Contrast that with Jackson Pollock, a self-destructive drunk who lived out almost every cliché of the tortured artist. (Like

Chris Goode, he was self-consciously dark and depressive.) The other Irascibles agreed to the photoshoot because they had seen the interest generated by Pollock's earlier *Life* feature in 1949. The double-page spread showed a thirty-seven-year-old Pollock, arms folded, legs crossed, a cigarette dangling from his lips, wearing head-to-toe denim, staring accusingly at the reader. Behind him was his biggest painting yet, *Number 9*, an eighteen-foot swirl of black, yellow, red and blue. The headline read: 'Jackson Pollock: Is he the greatest living painter in the United States?' The accompanying article took the same adulatory tone. But hints of something more complicated peeked through: 'Exhibiting in New York last year, he sold 12 out of 18 paintings,' we are told. Then comes the tale of how Pollock's 'grocer bought one' and now tells travelling salesmen it depicts an aerial view of Siberia. In reality, the grocer didn't so much buy the painting as accept it in lieu of payment for Pollock's debts at his store. This is the mythology of genius in action, and it explains why more than a dozen artists – who are somewhat harder to herd than cats – agreed to the subsequent *Life* shoot.

The group portrait is also notable for another reason: because of whom it excludes. In 1950, there was another trained artist who had embraced the new style, who had exhibited paintings, and who had helped organise earlier protests in favour of abstract art. And who, despite these recommendations, did not make the cut for the Irascible Eighteen. That artist was Lee Krasner, otherwise known as Jackson Pollock's wife.

Lee – born Lena – was the fifth child of a devout Jewish couple, Joseph and Anna, who left Odessa (in what is now Ukraine) for America in the first decade of the 1900s. The family dutifully attended synagogue, spoke Yiddish at home and hoped to rise to middle-class comfort thanks to Joseph's fish stall in Brooklyn.

Only one of Lee's siblings was a boy, Irving, and the family gradually began to revolve around him. She rebelled at fourteen by applying for a high school that would allow her to study art, and then going on to further study in Manhattan. Her work was precocious, daring and formally accomplished. 'Yet early on it became clear that the steely self-confidence Krasner conveyed in her work, and in the pursuit of her career, seemed to crumble when it came to her relations with men,' the biographer Andrea Gabor writes.[2]

Krasner spent a decade living with the Russian artist Igor Pantuhoff, but the relationship fell apart as their creative interests diverged. (He was happy to be a society painter, and she wanted to keep up with the avant-garde.) After their break-up, Krasner threw herself into the new movement: she took classes with Hans Hofmann, who championed many abstract expressionists, and joined the American Abstract Artists group. She met Mondrian at an exhibition where she was showing her work, and he praised her 'very strong inner rhythm'.

Lee Krasner's success came despite the macho mood of the New York scene, which was firmly delineated into what Gertrude Stein would have identified as the geniuses and the wives. When she met Pollock, she was better-known than he was. But when they became a couple, professional opportunities kept eluding her. Krasner always believed that Peggy Guggenheim deliberately excluded her from the influential 'Art of This Century' show because the art collector was jealous of her relationship with Pollock.

And Jackson Pollock was a needy man. His drinking was so out of control that he was a frequent visitor to emergency departments and rehab clinics. He relied on Krasner to keep his appointment schedule and cook his meals. In the first months of their relationship, his volatile, rule-breaking creativity – which later broke through in the drip paintings – drove her to a 'blackout period' where she could not produce anything worthwhile. Nonetheless, the couple married in October 1945. (Peggy Guggenheim was supposed to be a witness but failed to show up.)

Now, you might argue that Pollock was simply a more talented artist than his wife. His drip paintings have a strange power to them – a fusion of colour and form that seems right, somehow, even though they stubbornly refuse to resolve into anything as obvious as a subject. But many of the people around the couple saw it another way: while Lee Krasner could have been an artist without Jackson Pollock, without Lee Krasner, Jackson Pollock would have been nothing more than a non-functioning alcoholic. 'Without Lee, he probably wouldn't have been able to create his work,' said Krasner's nephew Ronnie Stein. 'He would have died falling down drunk in Greenwich Village.'[3]

For her husband's sake, Krasner decided that the couple should move out of New York City to Long Island. There, writes Gabor, 'Krasner found a creative haven for Pollock and a shallow grave for her own artistic ambitions.' The eighteen-foot drip painting that accompanied the *Life* feature on Pollock would not have been possible without the space afforded to them in Long Island, where property was cheaper and they could afford to have a barn across the lawn from their main house. In the barn, Pollock could stretch out huge canvases and pour paint on them from above. By contrast, Krasner worked on a tabletop in a bedroom to create her Little Image series, which took in hieroglyphs, drips and tightly packed squares. These abstract paintings have an incredible energy, with every inch of the surface packed with colour or texture, emphasising the two-dimensional plane of the canvas. But their small size is a reflection of the conditions in which they were made. The couple's friends often assumed that Krasner had given up art – and she didn't always correct them. In fact, she was painting in the mornings, before her husband woke up. In 1947, she turned two wagon wheels into mosaic tables, one of which was exhibited, earning positive reviews. When the couple went to dinner with a female gallerist as a result, though, Pollock drank three bottles of wine, became violent and insulted their host.

Then came his great success: the *Life* profile, the 1951 photoshoot, a chance to show his work at the Venice Biennale. He was famous now, but still prone to multi-day binges and terrible arguments. He had several affairs, and flirted with their mutual friends. Dealers were reluctant to take him on. Krasner helped him to find representation, but she also started to become more independent: in 1954, in her mid forties, she finally learned to drive. She began to exhibit her work again. In 1955, Pollock met a twenty-five-year-old fan and began a very public affair with her. Krasner left him, and left America – she was in Europe when she received a call saying that her husband had died in a car accident. He was drunk and out of control, and skidded into a tree.

Lee Krasner was no longer a great wife. In the years that followed, she took over the barn studio at their house, and began to produce her own vast canvases. Her painting *The Seasons*, from 1957, is seventeen feet wide. Her Umber paintings, made between 1959 and 1962, are sweeping, confident, perhaps even imposing – made of controlled swirls of browns and cream. She rejected her previous bright colour palette, she later said, because she painted these works by artificial light while suffering from insomnia. Was she inspired by Pollock in these grand canvases? Or liberated from him? Mourning him? Exorcising him? Perhaps all four. 'It's too bad that women's liberation didn't occur 30 years earlier in my life,' she told *Artforum* a decade later. 'I couldn't run out and do a one-woman job on the sexist aspects of the art world, continue my painting, and stay in the role I was in as Mrs. Pollock.'

It was a role she could never fully escape.

This is probably a good point to go back to the toothpicks allegedly made from wood grown in Shakespeare's garden – the ones that featured in the jubilee celebrations in Stratford-upon-Avon that cemented him as England's national poet. Posthumous reputation management is an integral part of the marketing of a genius – selling off relics, tidying up the record and preventing the brand from being devalued. A genius' partner is perfectly placed to market their departed spouse – a great wife can become a great widow. (Historically, a smaller number of men have fulfilled this role, such as Andreas Kronthaler, who now runs the Vivienne Westwood brand founded by his late wife.) An artist's widow can help produce a catalogue raisonné – the authorised list of all authentic works. A businessman's widow can pay to endow university chairs and name buildings after the dear departed. A literary widow can keep her late husband's works in print, make the life of unauthorised biographers extremely hard indeed – covering up unwholesome incidents or erasing the contributions of others – or she can help, by selling his papers to a library. Sonia Brownell spent fourteen weeks as Mrs Orwell, and thirty years as his widow, managing his literary estate (and helping to violate the no-biography clause in his will). Without her, the Orwell industry – which includes a foundation, a series of prizes and a statue outside the BBC – would not exist in its current resplendent form.

The literary critic Ian Hamilton has identified a dozen other guardians who were crucial to the creation of genius myths.[4] John Donne's son possibly stole the poet's papers from his executor, who had done nothing with them, in order to publish them, while his friends helped burnish his reputation by pushing a repentance narrative of a young rambunctious poet turned into a sober cleric. Andrew Marvell's *Miscellaneous Poems* were published in 1681 by a woman called Mary who claimed to be his widow, but was quickly accused of being his landlady. Alexander Pope's celebrity was bolstered by his long-running feud with the publisher Edmund Curll, who published his unauthorised letters and poems. (In return, Pope mildly poisoned Curll.) Samuel Johnson's luck in meeting his biographer, James Boswell, is well-known; without Boswell, the great polymath would be far less remembered. Patriotic admirers of Robert Burns sanitised his life, airbrushing out his womanising and drinking, and playing up the image of a raw peasant genius, allowing him to become Scotland's national poet. Thanks to his early biographers, 'a new Robert Burns was born: cleaned up, detoxed and pitiably the victim of a lifelong sickness contracted during his famously disadvantaged childhood,' writes Hamilton. 'At long last the Burns Club could adore their hero without reservation.' (In 1930, the Glaswegian author Catherine Carswell published a revisionist biography that laid bare the poet's sex life. She became a pariah in Scotland and was sent a bullet in the post.)

More recently, literary estates have been able to manage the dead genius' reputation through copyright: if you're an actress who wants to be in *Waiting for Godot*, tough. The Samuel Beckett estate forbids women to play his male roles. Research access to documents can be limited by jealous heirs, and executors can decide what material to put into the public domain. Authorised biographers are drafted to keep the story straight, to tidy away any jilted lovers or unfortunate legal wrangles. Sometimes, however, this backfires. In 2015, Adam Sisman brought out an authorised life of John le Carré while his subject was still alive. Discovering a trove of material he was not allowed to include, he squirrelled it away – and eight years later, with the author safely dead, he published a second version, which revealed le Carré's incessant womanising.

In light of all this, here is another prescription for anyone who wants to bolster their genius myth: find either a wife, or a younger peer, and impress upon them the importance of preserving all your work and maintaining the approved version of your life. That version does not need to be blameless; in fact, as discussed in earlier chapters, being an absolute shit is sometimes helpful to the construction of genius. Alcoholism, family abandonment, unfaithfulness, abuse, weirdness, failure to take responsibility – all of these can be rewritten as evidence of your greatness.

The phrase 'Art Widow', as applied to Lee Krasner, comes from the influential critic Harold Rosenberg. Pollock had left his wife everything, including all his paintings, and the manner of his death had cemented his reputation as the untameable spirit of American art; the Romantic genius who could not be contained by markets, or bourgeois propriety, or rigid dogmas about naturalism. His American citizenship was key to his posthumous fame: 'It was the first time that an American artist had been hailed as worthy of talking about in the same breath as the European Modernists,' writes his biographer Evelyn Toynton.[5] Tennessee Williams wrote a play about him. His friends – even his analyst – spoke about him in the press. A biopic, *Pollock*, was released in 2000. The house in East Hampton has become a museum, where you can pay to see the splatters of his paint on the floor.

After Pollock's death, Krasner held on to most of the paintings, selling only one or two a year, preferably to museums rather than private collections. In doing so, she raised their value – and the reputation of the entire abstract expressionist movement. Harold Rosenberg once said that Krasner had 'almost single-handedly forced up prices for contemporary American abstract art'. In 1973, Pollock's *Blue Poles* became the most expensive contemporary painting when it was sold for $2 million. Three decades later, another Pollock, *No. 5, 1948*, took the record again, at a reported $140 million.

Toynton compares Pollock to Vincent van Gogh, who was also 'romanticised as a wild-man painter, a tormented genius, who applied paint with a passionate directness and immediacy expressive of intense feeling – [and] also as a man destroyed by the very sensitivity that enabled him to create great art; the "clam without a shell," for whom the world was too cruel and abrasive a place for him ever to be at home in it.'[6] And sure enough, there are two people who were vitally important to the creation and survival of van Gogh's works. The first is his brother Theo, who provided encouragement and financial support to his depressive, penniless brother. The other is Vincent's sister-in-law Johanna – another Art Widow.

If one modest boarding-house in Bussum, a small town south of Amsterdam, had caught on fire any time in the 1890s, then Vincent van Gogh would be forgotten today. That house belonged to a young woman called Johanna, who found herself widowed before the age of thirty, with a baby son. In April 1889, at the age of twenty-six, when Johanna Bonger had married the art dealer Theo van Gogh, she already knew how close he was to his brilliant, unstable brother Vincent. Five months earlier, on the day before Theo proposed to Johanna, Vincent had taken a razor to his ear after an altercation with Paul Gauguin, wrapped it in paper, and presented it to a maid at a nearby brothel. He ended up at an asylum, where he had two cells: one for sleeping and one for painting. Soon after her marriage, Jo wrote to Vincent, letting him know that she was pregnant and that they would name the baby after him. He wrote to a friend that he would paint almond blossom to celebrate.

What followed then was all in a rush: within the space of eighteen months, Jo had Theo's baby, and then lost both Vincent (to suicide) and Theo (to grief, and possibly syphilis). She was left alone with her son and a vast collection of artworks: her husband had bought his brother's paintings in return for giving Vincent 15 per cent of his salary. When Johanna opened a boarding-house to support herself, she hung every wall with van Goghs, in a collection that would now be worth hundreds of millions. The almond blossom went in her and baby Vincent's bedroom. 'As well as the child,' she wrote in her diary, '[Theo] has left me another task – Vincent's work – getting it seen and appreciated as much as possible.' In 1891, the insurance policy mentioned 200 paintings and a portfolio of drawings, but even that seems to have been an underestimate.[7] The house also held the brothers' letters, photographs and sketchbooks – all the raw materials to build a cult of van Gogh that blended biography with artistry. And one cooking accident or careless tenant could have meant the entire collection was lost for ever.

Jo van Gogh-Bonger was one of the most successful and important Art Widows in history – albeit at one remove. As she looked through the collection of Theo's letters and Vincent's paintings, she realised that the brothers' love story could help sell the paintings. She also decided that Vincent could become the spirit of the age: he had wanted to get away from drawing-room niceties and art for the elite. That chimed with the fin-de-siècle mood of Northern Europe.

She showed both the letters and the paintings to an influential art critic called Jan Veth, who initially dismissed them as 'nearly vulgar'. But he was eventually won over by the idea of van Gogh as a painter of peasants and raw nature – an outsider who was too sensitive for Paris salons and, eventually, this cruel world. The fashionable art world followed Veth's lead, and began to see the work and the life as a package. 'When they looked at the paintings, they saw not just the art but Vincent, toiling and suffering, cutting off his ear, clawing at the act of creation,' writes journalist Russell Shorto.[8] 'They fused art and artist. They saw what Jo van Gogh-Bonger wanted them to see.' In 1905, she organised an exhibition of 484 works at the Stedelijk Museum in Amsterdam, the largest ever exhibition of van Goghs. *Starry Night*, one of the painter's later works, made many critics uncomfortable – they felt that the whorls of the sky reflected van Gogh's disintegrating mental condition. But Jo van Gogh-Bonger realised something: uncomfortable is good. She bought the painting back from its owner, reasoning that it had the potential to become an icon of an unstable genius. (*Starry Night* is now one of the prized exhibits in the Museum of Modern Art in New York.)

Emilie Gordenker, the director of the van Gogh museum in Amsterdam, was given a biography of Jo van Gogh-Bonger by her staff when she arrived for the job. She told Shorto that van Gogh-Bonger helped create the 'notion of the starving artist in the garret' even though many artists through history lived comfortable lives. 'It doesn't work for the early modern period, when someone like Rembrandt was a master working with apprentices and had many wealthy clients,' she said. 'In a sense Jo helped shape the image that is still with us.'

Why did her role in creating Brand Vincent go unmentioned for so long? Because her family did not make her diary available to researchers until 2009, possibly to downplay her later relationship with another painter. Today, the van Gogh family still controls Vincent's legacy: three of Jo's descendants sit on the board of the van Gogh museum, whose core collection is drawn from the works that once hung in her boarding-house, or were tucked away in its attic. That has turned van Gogh into a *national* artist – he belongs to Holland in the same way that Shakespeare belongs to England. Bolstering his brand now becomes the work of the state.

But if a legacy can be made, then it can be unmade. Jackson Pollock's reputation was challenged first by pop art, where rigid, geometric lines were 'an almost voluntary reaction to the frustration of being unable to ape the legendary spontaneity of Pollock in the studio'.[9] More recently, art critics have expressed discomfort with the glorification of his macho lifestyle. They saw him instead as 'an old fashioned-brute: Stanley Kowalski with a paintbrush'.

The high-status opinion within the art world is now championing Krasner, the underdog, rather than her husband. The mythology of the unsung female genius has now taken hold. Nine years after Pollock's death, Lee Krasner had a solo show at the Whitechapel Gallery, and ten years later there was another at the Whitney Museum of American Art. She died in 1984, just months before a major retrospective at MoMA in New York. In 2019, the Barbican showed a hundred of her works, calling her 'a formidable artist, whose importance has too often been eclipsed by her marriage to Jackson Pollock'.

Krasner might have been excluded from the Irascible Eighteen and that iconic *Life* shot, but she is now recognised by the art world as a major figure in abstract expressionism. She is a critical darling – the beneficiary of a new myth; an updated version of the stories about contemporary critics recoiling from the Impressionists. Krasner was not appreciated in her own time – not because her art was too challenging, but because her sex was. Just as it flatters us to think that we have better taste than the nineteenth-century Parisians who didn't get the beauty of Monet's sunrise, we can also congratulate ourselves for rehabilitating an overlooked female artist.

The giant-killing impulse is now a major force in contemporary art – but it has limits. The art market operates on a different value system to critics and curators. In 2015, one of Jackson Pollock's works sold for $200 million. Four years later, Krasner's 1960 work *The Eye Is the First Circle* became one of the most expensive paintings ever sold by a female artist. It went for $11 million.

A Cover Version

'Talent is insignificant. I know a lot of talented ruins.'

James Baldwin

There's a man – not quite in the first flush of youth, but not yet middle-aged either. He has musical talent but he's getting nowhere. He pours his heart into his music but no one cares. He's frustrated and beginning to feel bitter. What separates him from all those other men, who have taken their anguish and heartbreak and spun them into gold discs? Why did they succeed where he is failing?

And then something miraculous happens. A flash. A slippage in reality. Suddenly that youngish man is the only person alive who can remember the Beatles. So what does he do? He can't help himself – he knows how brilliant 'Hey Jude' is, how the world pulsed to 'I Wanna Hold Your Hand', how a million tears fell to 'Eleanor Rigby'. He picks up his guitar, stands in front of the microphone, and plays the Beatles.

That is a description of the film *Yesterday*, written by Richard Curtis. Released in 2019, it was a solid success, taking $154 million at the box office on a budget of less than $50 million. The film's protagonist Jack initially plays 'Let It Be' to his unimpressed family – they think it's called 'Leave It Be' – but eventually, the sheer power of the Beatles cannot be denied. The world hears the Fab Four for the first time, and falls in love all over again. Jack becomes famous.

The paragraphs above also describe another film – *Cover Version*, by a little-known screenwriter called Jack Barth. In *Cover Version*, the lead character Dan never makes it. He is the lead singer of a band called Clay Enema whose biggest hit, 'Walk Tall', was a cover version. After the rupture happens, and everyone forgets, Dan starts playing Beatles songs to his bandmates but they are only mildly impressed. When the band performs 'Day Tripper' at a noughties nostalgia night, the crowd *fails* to go wild. The promoter tells off Dan for not playing 'Walk Tall'.

The resemblance between the two films is not a coincidence: Jack Barth's original idea was bought by Working Title and reworked by Curtis and director Danny Boyle.

The biggest difference between *Yesterday* and *Cover Version* is that they provide opposite answers to the same questions. How much does talent matter? Is genius unstoppable? Perhaps the lives and careers of Jack Barth and Richard Curtis led them to opposite conclusions. *Yesterday* is a film about authenticity, about staying true to yourself despite the superficial rewards of fame. It's a film about how to deal with success. The idea for *Cover Version*, however, came from Barth's belief that 'if *Star Wars* hadn't been made and I just came up with the idea for *Star Wars*, I bet I wouldn't be able to sell it.'[1] *Cover Version* is a story about how talent isn't enough. It's a story about failure.

In person, Jack Barth hums slightly, a vibration of nervous energy that he says stems from his intense social awkwardness. I have met many people more socially inept than he is, but it doesn't matter – this is how he sees himself. 'I mean, most writers are pretty introverted in real life, but I'm really, really socially inept,' he told me over lunch in Soho one summer day. "Until ten or twenty years ago, I couldn't even speak to people, I'd always put my head down . . . the whole ego of it made me really sick. And I know that's crazy. Because you can't get by in this world if you don't try and sell yourself. But then the people I hate the most are the ones that are always selling themselves. So if I paid the price for that – for like, being cool. I've always been really true to myself.'

Barth's life hasn't been a failure by most of our standards – he has a wife and a daughter, and has worked consistently in his adopted country of Britain – but to him, it feels like a series of near misses. In the 1990s, he was asked to pitch an episode of *The Simpsons*. He did, and it was accepted, resulting in 'A Fish Called Selma'. But *The Simpsons* producers never called again.

By the time Barth began *Cover Version*, he was already the author of twenty-five unproduced scripts. And he *loved* the Beatles. He could remember seeing *Help!* at the cinema at the height of Beatlemania. 'All the girls in the audience were screaming every time there was a close up of one of the Beatles,' he told me. 'And there's a lot of shots where they winked at the camera, because they know this is going to have an effect.'

Putting together that kind of fandom and his own experiences as a creative artist caused a chain reaction in his brain. If the Beatles didn't exist, could you invent them? Would the songs be just as enjoyable without the Fab Four? Or would we listen to 'In My Life' and think: what does a twentysomething know about loss and nostalgia?

Jack Barth poured all his love and frustration into the story of Dan, the thirty-two-year-old lead singer of Clay Enema, which once had a hit with someone else's song. Dan's bandmates have grown up and are ready to accept that music is a hobby rather than a career. The bassist is Dan's girlfriend Ella, who also has a job as a teacher. Cesar, the other guitarist, works in finance. But Dan won't abandon his dream, and his feelings of failure poison his relationships with Ella and Cesar. (He is also snobbish. He sees a girl in a Ramones T-shirt and sniffs that she probably doesn't even like their music.) Everything around Dan reminds him that success is out of reach. His former roadie Justin becomes a star with a 'lame, anodyne pop' song. Someone else records another version of the cover that gave Clay Enema its biggest hit – and does it better. (Strangely, at no point does anyone suggest that Clay Enema is a terrible name for a band and Dan could improve his chances of success by changing it.)

For my taste, Dan is too much of a sulky man-child to be an entirely sympathetic character; lump him in with the Judd Apatow-era loser bros of the 2000s, angry with the world for not giving them their due. (At least, unlike the women in their lives, they got to be protagonists.) But *Cover Version* nonetheless taps into a feeling that many of us have, that success isn't fair or fairly apportioned, and that part of the pain of ageing is accepting your limitations and quietly shelving your dreams. Hitting your thirties means a narrowing of options, no matter how great those remaining options are. You are no longer a person who 'could be'. You are a person who is, inescapably, whatever you are.

So there Dan is, ruing his fate, when some wibbly-wobbly timey-wimey stuff happens – a strange limousine drives past, a snatch of music haunts the air, the colours go psychedelic – and the universe shifts. Next time he's at band practice he begins to play 'Yesterday' – and Cesar and Ella don't recognise it. They don't recognise any of the Beatles back catalogue. It has all gone. Only Dan remembers.

He is immediately excited. Those songs are proven winners, the soundtrack to a thousand girls screaming, the first dance at a thousand weddings, the first choice for the car stereo on a long journey with the family. Except – that's not how it works out. The Beatles songs don't get much attention – although Alex from Franz Ferdinand tells him one of them would sound good on a car advert. He comes to a realisation.

> **DAN:** I just realised. You know who I've become? Townes Van Zandt.
> **JOEY ESSEX:** That's a funny name.
> **DAN:** (ignoring) Great songwriter, gets name-checked all the time . . . Never had a hit record, never made a dime. (BEAT) I don't want to be Townes Van Zandt.

Dan is bemused, and then angry, at how things have turned out. Townes Van Zandt has been cited as an influence by Bob Dylan, Willie Nelson, Sonic Youth and Norah Jones, but he died of a heart attack in 1997, aged fifty-two, without having had a breakthrough hit. (In 1983, Nelson and Merle Haggard took Van Zandt's song 'Pancho and Lefty' to number one on the Billboard country music chart.)

Why, Dan asks himself, does the universe hate him? Why doesn't it want him to be happy? He alienates the band – we discover he had no idea Cesar's partner left him a year before, so he was clearly a self-involved jerk even before he became the sole bearer of the Lennon-McCartney gospel. He breaks up with Ella. In a moment of exquisite derangement, he hires two young Scousers to replace his departed bandmates: maybe the moptops and the accents are the missing pieces of the puzzle! Still nothing. Eventually, he comes to the realisation that it's all pointless. He will never make it. In this world, Ringo (as Richard Starkey) was a one-hit wonder. But what about John Lennon? Dan remembers that John once gave an interview saying that if he wasn't famous, he would be a fisherman – and as a good union man, he would surely be traceable by his union. And so he tracks down Fisherman John, who tells him to be true to himself. Life isn't a cover version. You have to make up the notes yourself.

Dan does what any British person would do after receiving a philosophical revelation of this magnitude, and goes to the pub. He sees a procession of famous faces – Helen Mirren, Bobby Charlton, Judi Dench – or rather versions of them for whom fame never happened. 'What stopped all the people in this pub from doing countless other things with their lives?' he wonders. Why didn't Charlton ever pick up a football? Why did Dench miss her audition? Who forgot to inspire this version of David Attenborough with a love of the natural world?

And finally: 'Why am I not a rock star?'

Cover Version ends with Dan renouncing the Beatles songs – well, up to a point. He sells some of them to his former roadie so he can buy John Lennon the vintage car that the old fisherman always wanted. But Dan stays living with his dad, who has taken up painting again after previously abandoning the hobby, and who provides him with the artwork for his album of original songs. He only has a few fans, but they are 'serious musos'. Best of all, when he finishes his gig, Ella is waiting outside for him, ready to joke that his new song is good: 'Not even a bit shit. Reminded me of . . . Townes Van Zandt.'

The plot of *Yesterday* has similarities to *Cover Version* – more on that later, because it's a source of some distress to Jack Barth – but the differences are just as important.

Yesterday's lead character Jack Malik is twenty-seven, for a start, rather than thirty-two – old for a potential popstar, but closer to wannabe than has-been. He is only beginning to get bitter about doing pub gigs and festival bookings in front of a dozen unimpressed children in the breakout tent. His manager

Ellie is played by Lily James, so you know from the start she's going to be the love interest, although Jack Malik seems blissfully unaware of this. He moans to her constantly and has no interest in *her* life, but this is what women in mainstream Hollywood films have always, inexplicably, put up with from men. Ellie is no exception.

Then the event happens. Jack is knocked off his bike at exactly the same moment the world seems to reboot – the lights dim and then restart. He wakes up in hospital with no front teeth, and Ellie is there to hold his hand. When he has recovered enough to go to the pub, his female friends have bought him a recovery gift – a replacement guitar! – while one male friend is too stoned to engage and the other male friend apologises for his lack of involvement, because he had a 'big work week'. Jack strums away, and – just like in *Cover Version* – his friends go: hang on, that's good. Why haven't you played us that one before? And so he discovers that this is a universe without the Beatles; a Google search brings up only insects, and Pope John Paul II. And so Jack begins to perform their songs in public. At first, he gets nowhere, because Curtis also has fun with the idea of listening to Beatles songs stripped of reverence. Can something be a masterpiece if it is received with indifference? A kids' birthday party is unmoved by 'I Wanna Hold Your Hand'.

At this point the two films diverge, however. In *Yesterday*, Ed Sheeran – yes, Ed Sheeran – hears Jack playing 'In My Life' on a local news programme, and asks him to open his show in Moscow. This section is pure wish-fulfilment. Jack turns up and plays 'Back in the U.S.S.R.', prompting an offhand comment that this is a weird way to refer to Russia thirty years after the fall of the Soviet Union, and then Ed challenges him to a songwriting battle. They must each retire to a room for a few minutes and return with a song. Ed returns with a pleasant, forgettable track. Jack comes back with 'The Long and Winding Road'.

Let's pause here for a moment to note another trope about genius which has been casually smuggled past us, aside from the noble, misunderstood male. Like most modern songwriters, Ed Sheeran does not work alone. (My friend Rob never ceases to find it funny that Beyoncé's 'Who Run the World (Girls)' credits two male co-writers and heavily samples a song written by four men. I always tell him this is incredibly feminist, actually: *who run the world?* Girls – who delegate the legwork to men.) In 2022, Sheeran won a plagiarism case over his song 'Shape of You', which had been accused of ripping off a Turkish track called 'Oh Why'. He was ruled not to have unduly copied the earlier song; however, the trial was a reminder that 'Shape of You' was co-written by Snow Patrol's Johnny McDaid and producer Steve McCutcheon. Responding to the judgement, Sheeran said: 'Coincidence is bound to happen if 60,000 songs are being released every day on Spotify. That's 22 million songs a year and there's only 12 notes that are available.' He is right, but those statistics only highlight the incredible pyramid of the music industry. So many songs, so many songwriters – and so few stars at Sheeran's level.

Yesterday is well-aware of this fetishisation of the auteur, because Richard Curtis has Jack Malik's management design an eye-catching campaign for his first album of Beatles tracks. It will be billed as the work of 'One Man Only'. This makes Jack feel guilty, because he knows damn well that he didn't write these songs, alone or otherwise. Add in the fact that Lily James' Ellie has confessed her love for him, but also that she doesn't want to be a rockstar's girlfriend, and poor Jack starts to hate his celebrity lifestyle. Ahead of a rooftop concert – in Gorleston-on-Sea rather than the top of the Apple building – he meets the few other people who remember the Beatles. They don't want to out him as a thief, though. They are just happy that he's given the Beatles back to the world.

Racked with guilt, worried about his love life and wondering what the point of fame is if you're unhappy, what does Jack Malik do? He goes to meet John Lennon, who, in this universe, is a fisherman.

Hmm. When *Yesterday* was released, Richard Curtis gave a series of interviews talking about how the film had come about. He had seen Jack Barth's pitch, he said, but never read his script. 'I had the one-sentence, then said I don't want any more information because I sometimes found when I worked with original material that it doesn't come from the heart', Curtis told the website Den of Geek. 'So I tried to write a whole film that meant something to me, rather than having too much extra information.' He told *SlashFilm*: 'Someone rang me and said, you know, would you be interested – and I think maybe even directing – the film with this one line plot: a musician who's the only person to remember The Beatles. And so, what happened after that is I said well no, don't tell me anymore. Let me just write my own film.'

If it's true that Curtis didn't read Jack Barth's script, two fisherman John Lennons are quite the coincidence. As is the ending: both films finish on a throwaway joke that no one remembers Harry Potter, either. (Curtis credits that gag to the US comedian Sarah Silverman. When Uproxx put these similarities to Richard Curtis' team, the website did not receive a response.)[2] These ironies are what initially attracted me to Jack Barth's story – this was a film about taking the credit for someone else's work, and . . . well, that seems to have happened to him. But *Yesterday* is also a film that makes the case that the content is what matters – *talent will out*. And yet we all know there's a readymade audience for a 'Richard Curtis' film, while no one is queuing up to see a movie with Jack Barth's name on it. So it turns out that it really does matter whose name you attach to the product.

Yesterday ends with Jack Malik performing a concert at Wembley, declaring his love for Ellie and confessing that the Beatles songs aren't his own work. Instead of making money from the album, he uploads it to the internet for free. He marries Ellie and becomes a teacher. The moral of the story is that snogging Lily James beats a stadium tour and 10 million downloads on Spotify.

When *Yesterday* came out, Jack Barth initially stayed quiet about his involvement – or, as he would have it, he simply wasn't asked to contribute. He did score some tickets for the premiere, but he only got a joint 'Story by' credit on the film. He didn't become rich from the film's success, because he was promised only a share of *net* profits. (Despite making far more at the box office than its budget, *Yesterday* technically ran a loss, thanks to typical Hollywood accounting.) The experience of being sidelined has left him increasingly bitter. It is very rare for screenwriters to talk about the brutal experience of 'collaboration' in the film industry, where writers regularly get bounced off projects with very little notice. The money is good, and no one wants to be blacklisted. Whisper it, but some films credited to a particular director were taken over during production by others. Writer credits can be the result of tough negotiations between agents. Until 2000, there was even a generally accepted pseudonym – Alan Smithee – for directors to use when they thought the film was such dreck that they didn't want to be associated with it.

In this environment, Barth's outspoken defence of his original script, and his criticism of the Hollywood content machine, is unusual. It springs from the same impulse that made him write *Cover Version* in the first place. Richard Curtis, he told me, 'thinks he's honouring the Beatles by saying these songs would be a hit even today. And it's not [true], it was also their personalities and their performance and the way they looked, their time and place. It was all of those things.' By focusing on Jack Malik as a reincarnated Beatle, the film also deprecates the importance of George Martin, the producer whose musical innovations were so crucial to the band's development, and Brian Epstein, whose careful management launched these precocious, spirited Scouse lads. In *Yesterday*, Jack Malik's manager, played by Kate McKinnon, is a shark. She doesn't care about the music except as a way to make money. 'Brian Epstein was really committed to these guys,' says Barth. 'He always had integrity, which is pretty rare. And to say that someone like the Kate McKinnon character could have made this guy a big star just as easily, even though she's horrible, and doesn't care about his music at all. It's an insult.'

Talking to Uproxx, Barth had attributed the difference between the two scripts, and the attitudes they embody, to the accident of biography. For him, writing had always been a struggle – not the act of creation itself, but finding ways to make his work commercial. Richard Curtis, by contrast, has succeeded from the start. He learned to write comedy and direct plays at the private school Harrow, and met Rowan Atkinson at university, where they were both in the Experimental Theatre Club. Curtis co-starred in Atkinson's breakout Edinburgh Fringe show, and they co-wrote a BBC radio series together. From there, he moved to *Not the Nine O'Clock News* and then *Blackadder*, both of which were produced by the exceptionally talented John Lloyd. (The theme tune for the latter was written by Howard Goodall, who had also attended Oxford.) *Blackadder*'s first series was a notable disaster – with no audience, the actors couldn't time their lines, and the first iteration of Edmund Blackadder was a weedy prick rather than a devilish schemer. Nonetheless, the BBC renewed it. For the second season, Ben Elton replaced Rowan Atkinson as a co-writer, and other stars of the fashionable Oxbridge comedy set – Hugh Laurie, Stephen Fry – became regulars. In 1994, Curtis conquered the film world with *Four Weddings and a Funeral*, which made a star of floppy-haired Hugh Grant and became the top-grossing British film of the time. *Four Weddings* was produced by Working Title, where Curtis has stayed ever since – another creative collaboration which has lasted throughout his career.

I say all this not to dismiss Richard Curtis' talent (my husband watches *Love Actually* every Christmas, as do I if I don't run away fast enough). The point is that even a talent as big as that of Richard Curtis – or of the Beatles – is not enough. You need the right collaborators, the right environment in which to flourish and a dollop of plain old good luck.

'I've been thinking about this a lot,' Jack Barth told the website Uproxx when it asked him about the difference between *Cover Version* and *Yesterday*. 'And I think that the reason that Richard turned [Jack Malik] into the most successful songwriter of all time is because that's how Richard's life is going. He met Rowan Atkinson at Oxford, he came out of Oxford and immediately rode Rowan Atkinson to huge success in his early twenties, he's never been knocked out, as far as I know. Why *wouldn't* this guy become the most successful songwriter in the world?'

In my mind, *Yesterday* was more commercially successful than *Cover Version* would have been – even if you stripped off the writers' names. And that's because it peddles a more attractive version of the genius myth: that great talent cannot be repressed. That's the story we want to hear . . . not the suggestion that in some other time or other universe John, Paul, George and Ringo could have come up with the songs they did, and the world would simply not have cared. But there has always been more to the story of the Beatles than sheer talent – so let's dig a little deeper into their mythology.

Alchemy

'Masterpieces are not single and solitary births; they are the outcome of many years of thinking in common.'

Virginia Woolf, *A Room of One's Own*

Lunchtime in Aldeburgh, and Craig Brown has just committed heresy. 'With pop, I think it's very interesting how virtually everyone, including Paul and John, they kind of lose it,' he tells me. Unwittingly, the journalist and parodist has just echoed a rhetorical question Jack Barth asked me: 'Why is it that none of the great old bands have had a hit album in the last twenty years, even though they're probably better than they used to be? Technically better, anyway.'

Barth's answer was that Springsteen, the Stones and all the rest 'don't look right' – that the arts are a fickle business, where raw sex appeal is more important than sophisticated critics might like to admit. Brown's answer is different, although perhaps complementary: that the best musicians, like artists and other creative sorts, have a *moment*. Like a sustained note, it can be beautiful, but it can't be held for ever.

We are sitting in Brown's living room, overlooking the sea, close to the study where he wrote his biography of the Beatles, *One Two Three Four*. Of all the books I read in lockdown, it's the one I remember best. The structure is exquisite: Brown developed a technique he pioneered writing about Princess Margaret, another mythologised figure, by telling the story in 'glimpses'. In the case of the Beatles, these glimpses run from their schooldays to the death of their manager Brian Epstein on 27 August 1967. It is a well-chosen time frame: Epstein's accidental drug overdose was a watershed for the Beatles. Peter Jackson's immersive documentary, *Get Back*, shows them seventeen months later still wondering how to go on without the guiding sensibility of 'Mr Epstein'.

Brown's book captured the importance of the contrast between the four men: 'There was a Beatle to suit every taste,' he wrote. 'As a fan, you expressed yourself by picking one over the others.'[1] (The record industry repeated the trick with the Spice Girls in the 1990s.) And he particularly noticed the partnership between John and Paul, which has sustained innumerable articles and books on creativity. 'Sometimes their contributions to the same song were so keenly differentiated that they seemed to be playing up to their caricatures,' Brown observed. 'Paul comes up with "we can work it out," and John immediately undercuts it: "Life is very short." Paul sings "It's getting better" and John butts in with "Can't get much worse"'. This tendency is taken to the extreme in 'A Day in the Life', where a story about an aristocrat's car crash is yoked to a jaunty rendition of a man's morning routine.

The reason I wanted to talk to Brown, however, was because of something else that the book does more perfectly than I've ever seen a genius biography do before. It shows the many ways the Beatles nearly *didn't* happen.

Liverpool, in wartime. Paul McCartney's parents, Mary and Jim, met when both were old by the standards of the time: thirty and thirty-eight. Mary was living with Jim's sister Gin, and Craig Brown sketches out two versions of history:

(a) Tonight the Nazi bombers fly overhead. Gin and Mary are visiting Jim's mum in Scargreen Avenue when the sirens sound, so they have to stay over. As the bombs fall, Jim and Mary sit and chat for hours. By the time the all-clear is sounded, they feel they are meant for one another. After a brief engagement, they marry on 15 April 1941; just over a year later, Mary gives birth to their first child, a boy. They christen him James Paul McCartney.

(b) Tonight is quiet. The sirens never sound. As it happens, they will tomorrow night, when Gin and Mary are planning on staying home. So Jim and Mary fail to have their heart-to-heart, and go their separate ways. James Paul McCartney is never born.[2]

There are more flukes and near misses: in real life, John's mother Julia died soon after he met Paul, who had already lost his own mother – a traumatic, bonding experience which brought the two boys closer. A seven-year-old Ritchie Starkey nearly died of peritonitis after his appendix burst. Paul failed his GCE Spanish, so he had to stay down a year at school – allowing him to become friends with a younger boy called George Harrison. The boys just avoided conscription. They found their manager Brian Epstein in the nick of time, as they considered giving up the band. Stuart Sutcliffe, who performed with the group in their early shows in Hamburg, stayed in Germany when the others returned home, because he had found a girlfriend. (He died of a brain haemorrhage in 1962.) Epstein screwed up his courage to fire the band's handsome, charismatic drummer, Pete Best, and replace him with Ringo – and then he had to ignore a petition, and a picket of his offices, demanding that he reinstate Best. Ringo considered emigrating to America, but changed his mind because there were too many forms to fill out. And so on. *Yesterday* and *Cover Version* ask if the Beatles' songs would still be hits without the men behind them; *One Two Three Four* asks us to consider how close the songs came to never happening at all.

The book also investigates the thick layer of mythology smeared over the early days of John and Paul's relationship. Much of it serves to make their friendship – and therefore the existence of the Beatles – seem inevitable. We want there to have been trumpets and angels attending their first meeting. We want it to be meaningful; a hinge in history. But their early bandmate Pete Shotton told an interviewer in 1967 that Paul made little impression on John, who was two years older, when he first introduced himself. *No, that won't do. Try again.* Sixteen years later, Shotton claimed in his memoir that John was 'immediately impressed'. *Better.*

Every biography of a genius must have slippages and smoothings like this, if only we knew where to look. The Beatles are the first band in history to have been so exhaustively documented, allowing us to excavate their lives, appreciate the serendipity of their career and trace the real-time formation of the mythology around them. You could look through any band's career and discover the coincidences, the near misses and the creative friction between individuals which powered their best work. It's just that no one bothers to do this for, say, Kula Shaker or Wizzard.

Which brings us to Craig Brown's heresy: that the Beatles *had it*, oh so gloriously, but somewhere along the way, their individual members lost it. I would assign him to Team *Cover Version*: talent doesn't always out, and there are a million reasons why the Beatles became the Beatles, quite apart from the genius of those involved. 'It is perfectly possible that the Beatles wouldn't [exist],' he tells me. 'If Paul hadn't met John, I suppose he would have been a songwriter. And he might have done some good tunes, but he might not.'

I tell him about the 'adjacent possible'. The Beatles benefited from the arrival of television as a mass medium (they were early pioneers of the music video), and forebears such as Little Richard (with whom both John and Paul were half in love), and the postwar stability of Britain which allowed working-class musicians to make a living. The band was supremely lucky to meet the groundbreaking producer George Martin, who deserves the title of 'Fifth Beatle' more than anyone else. Martin, who was classically trained, had been a comedy producer before he met the group. 'He did the Goons, and Peter Sellers, and that's why the Beatles wanted to be with him originally,' says Brown. 'They were in awe of him because of that.' Martin liked the four musicians because they were cocky Scousers, full of jokes and ready wit; in exchange, the Beatles got someone who could orchestrate a complex arrangement – and who could read music, unlike Paul. 'He was able to translate the thoughts so that if they'd say: Well, I want it to sound like a balloon going up in the air, he'd be able to work it out.'

But here comes *my* heresy. Among Beatles fanatics, there is a blood sport of finding early reviews which missed the band's genius. The band's unsuccessful audition for Decca in January 1962 is infamous enough to have its own Wikipedia page, which notes that the record label instead opted to sign Brian Poole and the Tremeloes. (Decca's rationale was that a local group would need fewer expenses.) Brian Epstein would later claim that an executive called Dick Rowe had declared that 'guitar groups are on the way out' and 'the Beatles have no future in show business'. (Rowe always denied these comments.) But . . . what if those early songs *weren't* very good? The setlist from the Decca audition is mostly cover versions, and the three Lennon-McCartney originals are not songs you will know, unless you are a true fanatic.* What George Martin, who listened to the recording from that day, presumably heard was *potential* – enough potential to convince his employer Parlophone to sign the band.

By chance, the first Beatles album I ever listened to in full was their debut, *Please Please Me*. I heard it as a teenager, and so what strikes me most about it is how *young* they sound – raw, energetic and unfinished. The album was notoriously recorded in a single mammoth session, and John's voice is audibly failing by the last track, 'Twist and Shout'. The songs, a mixture of covers and originals, are straightforward and short: radio stations wanted sub-three-minute tracks. 'There are nice harmonies, their voices are really interesting, and they go well together,' says Brown. 'But I think the songs are very, very simple. And if you think of what Little Richard and people were doing five years before, that was way ahead of the early Beatles. And so I don't go along with this idea that there was sort of a revolution.' However, he does concede that Bruce Springsteen and other future American songwriters *did* experience the Beatles as transformative, right from the start. We will have to chalk that up as a Potus problem we cannot unpick, even sixty years on. 'I don't get it. But you've got to trust them because they were there at the time. And it did change America in some weird way.'

Like me, Brown finds it hard to separate the Beatles from the era in which they worked – the subtitle of *One Two Three Four* is 'The Beatles in Time'. My parents remember having to go to the cinema to watch Queen Elizabeth II's coronation in 1953, but by the 1960s, three-quarters of British people had a television at home. The Beatles' teenage fans were part of a demographic bulge – the Baby Boomers, born after the Second World War.

---

* 'Like Dreamers Do', 'Hello Little Girl' and 'Love of the Loved'.

These Boomers have had an outsize cultural influence throughout their lives, possibly because of the sheer size of their generation. (Brown notes that six-year-olds today know Beatles songs, whereas few of us remember the popular songs of *his* youth, by artists such as George Formby.)

So the Beatles didn't come too soon, but they also didn't turn up too late. The world of music is now fragmented and siloed. The charts still exist, but they are not a cultural force in the way they were in the 1960s. Today, algorithms feed us recommendations, and the great gatekeepers of culture have crumbled. (There is no equivalent today to going on *The Ed Sullivan Show* and waking up the next day as the most famous people in the world.) Several of the geniuses who are most revered today have a sense of an ending about them: Einstein as the last great conceptual innovator in physics, before it shattered into specialised, competing disciplines; Picasso as the king of Cubism, before abstract and modern art made mere paintings look passé; Thomas Edison the inventor burning through patents when low-hanging fruit abounded. Music still produces new superstars, but nostalgia is where the money is: the Rolling Stones are still a touring act after sixty years. That's like the Cavern Club asking the Beatles to support a band of headliners born in the 1880s.

The Beatles existed at a moment when pop music came of age. Craig Brown was ten in 1967, and so can still remember the sense of expectation which attended their every move – an entirely white album cover, for example. Their sheer popularity means they influenced everything that came after them. (A harsh echo of this is provided in *Yesterday*, when Jack Malik does an internet search for Oasis, and finds no trace of the Gallagher brothers.) Somehow, the Beatles became *the* band. The top item on anyone's mental list of pop musicians, as Picasso is for art, Einstein for science, Shakespeare for drama, Edison for invention. The process by which this happens is an alchemical one; a collective act of will. Tastemakers and critics can't do it alone: you can't make people love rubbish in the long term, although you can often persuade them that the emperor is wearing clothes for a while. Disciples can't do it, although they help – as does a younger generation deeply influenced by a particular work, individual or group. Today, the sheer weight of capitalism often plays a part. Some geniuses become brand names; commercial juggernauts whose continued popularity makes their heirs and estate managers very rich indeed. They become a self-perpetuating industry. 'It's a kind of Jungian thing, of a collective unconscious and everyone willing them into greater and greater works,' says Brown. 'And then suddenly that disappears.'

Ah yes. The Beatles obeyed another of the great rules of genius: leave them wanting more. To put it another way: when should a genius die?

In 1874, an American neurologist called George M. Beard studied the biographies of a thousand eminent people, and found that their achievements peaked by the age of forty, before declining over their remaining years. This work sparked others to investigate the phenomenon, leading to a consensus summed up by Hans Eysenck in *Genius*: 'Poets and mathematicians achieve success earliest, scientists later, scholars later still.' The psychological explanation is that younger people are iconoclasts, unencumbered by the weighty burden of tradition and standard practice in their fields. They also have more energy and enthusiasm, which outweigh their comparative lack of technical ability and specialist knowledge. Hans Eysenck, being Hans Eysenck, followed this by arguing that both psychotics and the eminent were more likely to be born in February – which he suggested might be related to seasonal viruses affecting the developing foetus.

A more systematic approach to the problem was taken by the historiographer Dean Simonton, who analysed biographies of the 'eminent'. He traced a curve with a steep upward gradient and a gentle downward roll, with achievement beginning in a creator's twenties, peaking near forty, then dropping off sharply before levelling out: 'Because the decline is not nearly so precipitous as the ascent, creative individuals can be more productive in their 70s than they were in their 20s.'[3] Simonton stressed that his figures were just averages: Darwin published *On the Origin of Species* at fifty, and Copernicus completed *On the Revolutions of the Heavenly Spheres* at seventy. In politics, Benjamin Disraeli believed that 'almost everything that's great has been done by youth', but became prime minister of England at sixty-four.

More recent research has tried to explain this contradictory evidence – the prodigies versus the late bloomers – by suggesting that geniuses fall into two types: conceptual innovators and experimental innovators. The first group have a grand idea, a Big Bang which remakes their field, drawing the attention of outsiders. Then they get bored or exhausted, and move on to something else. The second type, the experimental innovators, are slower and more careful. They persist. They work at the same idea for years, even decades, constantly refining their craft and working towards a goal only they can see. The historian David Galenson uses Picasso and Cézanne as examples of the two types, noting that Picasso's early Cubist works – made after his artistic revolution – are more valuable than those at the end of his career.[4] The auction market has delivered the opposite judgement on Cézanne, however, with higher prices for his later paintings. 'Conceptual innovators historically have been those artists most likely to be described as geniuses, as their early manifestations of brilliance and virtuosity have been taken to indicate that these individuals were born with extraordinary talents,' writes Galenson. '[Conceptual] innovators are often perceived as irreverent and iconoclastic.' The glorification of the conceptual innovator – the genius with the big, paradigm-shifting idea – has distorted our idea of success.

Perhaps we *want* to believe that genius is not, as the quote attributed to Thomas Edison has it, 99 per cent perspiration and 1 per cent inspiration, but instead a special quality that is visited only upon the chosen few.* After all, if Cézanne's genius was to devote decades of his life to a single idea, what's stopping us from doing the same? Far better to believe in talent that declares itself early and loudly. This model of genius makes us feel better, because it explains why *we aren't geniuses*. 'I have asked a lot of my emotions – one hundred and twenty stories,' writes F. Scott Fitzgerald in *The Crack-Up*. 'The price was high, right up with Kipling, because there was one little drop of something – not blood, not a tear, not my seed, but me more intimately than these. Now it has gone and I am just like you now.'[5]

This used to be the standard story told about the Beatles – that they were conceptual innovators; untutored prodigies who transformed the jangly, predictable chords and melodies of the Merseybeat sound into something strange and new. Famously, Malcolm Gladwell's *Outliers* rewrote that narrative, showing the thousands of hours the band spent practicing and performing in Hamburg. (Gladwell's '10,000 hours' thesis was never intended to be the cornerstone of the book's argument, and it is clearly spurious in its precision. But it is certainly true to say that plenty of apparently untutored prodigies merely started their work very

---

* By this point, you may not be surprised to know that this quotation's origin is disputed.

young and very intensively.) Anyone who has watched Peter Jackson's epic documentary *Get Back* will understand how much time the Beatles spent jamming, to no obvious purpose, until a song would begin to emerge as if out of the mist. The most obvious example of this is 'Get Back' itself, which you can watch form on Paul McCartney's fingers in real time. Jackson's documentary is gorgeous to watch, an almost mystical experience, but I should level with you. *I also found it quite boring.* McCartney's tolerance for inhabiting the cloudy, uncertain zone of creativity is as much a part of the band's success as their conceptual innovations, such as experimental recording techniques and the use of non-standard instruments like the sitar. (McCartney's decision to keep writing music after the band's break-up also shows another quality associated with genius: intrinsic motivation. It didn't matter when the critics moaned that the Frog Chorus or 'Mull of Kintyre' weren't a patch on 'Let It Be'. He kept going anyway.)

The thing is, although these models of genius are interesting – and comforting to anyone approaching forty and still hoping to achieve something extraordinary – we don't need them to answer the question I posed a moment ago. When should a genius die? If we treat genius as a story, then the question of lifecycles moves from one of peak creativity to peak *mythology*. A memorable death enhances a reputation, or reflects ironically on the life that preceded it. Both Thomas Jefferson and John Adams died on 4 July, exactly half a century after the signing of the Declaration of Independence. Mozart died composing a requiem, which the play *Amadeus* wove into a parable all of its own. James Dean, the rebel without a cause, died in a car accident on a day when he had earlier been ticketed for speeding. (He crashed his Porsche Spyder into a Ford Tudor driven by a student who was improbably named Donald Turnupseed.) Deaths that attain mythological status aren't always glamorous: Elvis Presley suffered a heart attack in the bathroom of his Graceland mansion, leading to longstanding rumours that he died eating a burger on the toilet.* Instead of his death becoming a symbol of lost promise, it became a fable of the hollowness of fame, and of youthful talent gone to seed.

For a mythology to develop, then, when is the best time for a genius to quit the stage? Go too soon and you haven't had time to do your great work. Stick around too long, and the memory of your later, lesser output might overwhelm your early success. Then again, keep on living to a really ripe old age and you can become a symbol of something greater than yourself – a lost age, a social revolution, an exciting chapter in the history books. 'For the creators who wish to attain the greatest fame, dying at a middling age like 60 is ill-advised,' writes Dean Simonton, with his usual dry wit. 'Their best options are either to die at a tragically young age or else hang in there until they become living monuments to their own past. In the former case, posterity can lament all the promise that was pitifully unrealised. In the latter case, younger contemporaries can make pilgrimages to the great matriarch or patriarch of the national culture. In the first case, we have a Mozart; in the second, a Goethe.'[6]

The Beatles, almost uniquely, fulfilled both halves of this demand. McCartney announced his departure from the band in 1970, effectively ending the group when George Harrison was only twenty-seven – a fact that still has the power to astonish. For the next decade, the Beatles resisted pressure to reform, feeling neither the artistic nor commercial need to do so. The delicate equilibrium of the intense, loving, fraught bond between John and Paul had been ruined. George was relieved to be the

---

* The burger isn't true, but the toilet is – Presley suffered from extreme constipation, presumably as a result of the varied cocktail of drugs he took for insomnia and other ailments. His last words were in reply to his fiancée Ginger Alden, who warned him not to fall asleep on the loo again: 'I won't.'

protagonist of his own life at last, rather than a supporting cast member. Ringo, being Ringo, has never shown any great angst about no longer being in the Beatles. And we got his other great work, Thomas the Tank Engine.

Those decisions meant that although the band's output was prodigious, it was finite. And then on 8 December 1980, a former fan called Mark Chapman shot John Lennon four times in front of his apartment in New York, and there was no possibility the Beatles would ever reform.

Lennon's death turned him into a martyr. The exterior of the Dakota building, where he died, became a shrine. The real Lennon – spiky, sarcastic, difficult – was airbrushed out and 'St John' the bearded prophet of peace took over. The self-indulgent political statements could be forgotten, as could the avant-garde art he made with his wife Yoko Ono. Lennon was now the dead genius who wrote 'Strawberry Fields Forever', not the living celebrity who filmed his buttocks. His death put him firmly in the past – which helped when morals changed, otherwise the abandonment of his son Julian and the violence he handed out to his first wife Cynthia might have tarnished his legacy. After his death, John could no longer trash Paul's contribution to the band – he had called him a 'PR man' after the band split up – or his solo work, which he had once described rudely as 'muzak', the kind of ambient, plodding song that gets played in elevators. 'He could be a manoeuvring swine, which no one ever realised,' McCartney said in an interview with *Woman* magazine five years after the assassination. 'Now since the death he's become "Martin Luther" Lennon. But that wasn't really him either. He wasn't some sort of holy saint. He was really a debunker.'

Constant unfavourable comparisons of Paul with John used to poison discussions of the Beatles. 'His achievement is immense, historic, and will be remembered for centuries if anything will,' wrote the author Ian Leslie in 2020. 'Yet there are people, at least here in Britain, who talk about Paul McCartney the way they might a light entertainment celebrity who once hosted a game show . . . Lennon is soulful, deep, and radical; McCartney is shallow, trivial and bourgeois. That dualism, which took hold in 1970 and was reinforced by Lennon's horribly premature death, still holds sway.'[7] Lennon was more of a self-mythologiser than his songwriting partner; one of my favourite Beatles songs, 'The Ballad of John and Yoko', details how he and his wife were hounded by the press while 'we're only trying to get us some peace'. A classic genius trope: the pure artist under siege from the tainted material world.

Lennon's personal life also more narrowly fit the template of the modern genius. Leslie notes that McCartney's obvious joy in his family was held against him for many years. 'For the back cover of *McCartney I*, his first solo album, McCartney chose a picture taken by Linda of him with [their daughter] Mary peeping out from underneath his brown bomber jacket,' he writes. 'It is easy to under-estimate quite how bizarre this image-making was for a rock star. It was at the height of the counter-culture's contempt for the family man and his petty narrow, blinkered life. Rock stars were meant to be shining examples of a lifestyle liberated from the shackles of bourgeois convention. Revelling in domesticity wasn't cool. It certainly wasn't the kind of thing a *genius* did.'

It is callous to say that the right Beatle survived. But it is true that McCartney has now lived long enough to outlive John's disdain, and his appointment as the Boring Beatle, to become a 'patriarch of the national culture'. His 2022 Glastonbury set brought on relative whippersnappers Bruce Springsteen and Dave Grohl, and he collaborated with Kanye West in 2014. In the four decades since Lennon's death, the 'PR man' has cannily managed the band's image and back catalogue. He has also achieved a kind of peace with the memory of his friend and rival: his Glastonbury set closed with a performance of 'I've Got a Feeling' – a duet with Lennon, whose vocals had been isolated from an original recording. The song was deeply moving. At eighty, with no formal voice training, after a lifetime of tearing into songs, McCartney sometimes sounded thin and reedy, while Lennon's voice was still young. For all that it felt like a reconciliation, it was maudlin, too – Lennon has now been dead longer than he was alive. His childhood friend has spent half a lifetime in his shadow, through years when critics and fans would rank the dark, cruel tones of John above the easy sunshine of Paul, forgetting that the Beatles needed both, as well as the sharpness of George and the steadiness of Ringo.

If genius is a story, we can see how the unique fame of the Beatles was a product of a particular time and place, and of a series of productive collaborations and lucky chances. It also relies on both John and Paul. One to die – and one to stay alive. 'They finished,' Craig Brown told me, just before the end of our interview. 'They had a beginning and middle and end. Whereas the Rolling Stones just carried on.'

The Deficit Model

'If we evolved a race of Isaac Newtons, that would not be progress. For the price Newton had to pay for being a supreme intellect was that he was incapable of friendship, love, fatherhood, and many other desirable things. As a man he was a failure; as a monster he was superb.'

Aldous Huxley

It's 1948, and a young mathematician called John Nash has just arrived at Princeton. He is awkward in company, and stubborn, refusing to take classes. He prefers to read in the library, or study in his bedroom, where he is sometimes interrupted by his roommate, Charles. The talented student is searching, always searching: he wants to find a theory so beautiful and so novel it can compare to Einstein and Newton. Nothing fits. He is failing. And then, one night in a bar with his buddies, the talk turns to women: which of them will ask out the beautiful blonde who has just walked in with her friends? Nash has an epiphany. If they *all* go for the blonde, they will get in each other's way, and all but one of them will strike out. Also, the hot blonde's friends will be annoyed at being overlooked, and will have little time for a rejected man who tries to make one of them his second choice. Instead, all the men should approach a different one of the less good-looking women, ensuring they at least get to dance with *someone*.

This is how Nash's great discovery is presented in the 2001 film *A Beautiful Mind*, directed by Ron Howard and starring Russell Crowe. It's not a perfect description of the 'Nash equilibrium', which occurs in a non-co-operative game when players would normally refuse to change their own strategy even if they knew all the other players' strategies. But the bar scene is worth studying anyway, because it shows us the power of the biopic to create and reinforce myths about genius. John Nash's idea comes to him in a flash, fully formed and coherent, and all he needs to do is write it down. The film depicts his breakthrough as a literal vision.

In the late twentieth century, the biopic outstripped all other media as the great engine of genius mythology. In films like *A Beautiful Mind*, *The Theory of Everything* and *The Imitation Game*, genius myths abound: inspiration as blinding insight; genius as unworldly being; and finally, what I call 'the deficit model of genius'. This is the idea that, in exchange for the precious gift of genius, there is a human price to be paid. Biopics are as powerful today as Vasari's *Lives* were in the Renaissance. Scholars keep trying to bury the Great Man theory of history, and biopics dig it right back up again. Just look at John Nash's roommate, Charles.

Charles is the best character in *A Beautiful Mind*. Played by Paul Bettany, he is a dissolute, pale wraith; a literature student who is both concerned and indulgent. After graduation, Nash meets Charles' niece, Marcee, on a visit to the campus. They are a sweet pair.

By now, though, Nash's life has taken a sinister turn. His incredible skill with numbers makes him a great codebreaker – he can see patterns where no one else can. One night, Nash is summoned to a secret meeting where he quickly cracks a numerical code, working out that it represents co-ordinates in North

THE DEFICIT MODEL

America. He is assigned a handler and shown how to make dead drops in a letterbox. His mission will be to search newspapers and magazines for clues to where Communists are hiding in the United States.

Ron Howard's direction, and Russell Crowe's performance, walk the audience along the line of disbelief throughout this section. Nash is paranoid, and has always been strange. *Is all this spy stuff real?* Eventually, giving a lecture, Nash is surrounded by secret agents and pursued across campus. Kicking and struggling, he is sedated and taken to a psychiatric hospital. *Of course the spy stuff isn't real.* Nash's wife Alicia discovers that he even has an office papered with photographs connected by red string – the surefire visual signifier for 'conspiracist'. (Was this already a cliche in 2001? Probably not, and what we have here is a Potus problem for later audiences.)

The big shock, though, comes from Charles – the kindly roommate with his adorable niece. Why is Charles here, at the psychiatric hospital, looking distressed at the doctor's questions? Because he, too, is a fiction. He is a projection of Nash's beautiful, broken mind. Even Alicia struggles to believe that Charles isn't real. 'Charles isn't imaginary,' she says. 'He and John have been best friends since Princeton.' The psychiatrist gently asks if she has ever met Charles, or spoken to him – and why didn't Charles come to their wedding? 'I believe John's world is laced with delusions,' he says. 'Like dreams walking through his waking life.'

A Beautiful Mind won four Oscars, and its success partly comes from making Nash's mathematical achievements legible to a mass audience – for a few moments, even the most innumerate viewer can believe they understand his brilliance. But the film also accomplishes a successful feint. Even those viewers who suspect that the spy stuff is a delusion might miss the fact that homely, normal, non-sinister Charles is *also* a product of Nash's imagination. For a moment, we get an insight into the terrifying disorientation of schizophrenia – where fiction feels as solid as fact. When doctors talk about schizophrenics 'hearing voices', they mean that those voices sound as natural and normal as your spouse calling you from the next room.

Both *A Beautiful Mind* and the book by Sylvia Nasar on which it is based also make an explicit link between Nash's madness and his mathematical brilliance. Once, when asked why he believed that aliens were sending him messages through newspapers, the real Nash replied: 'Because the ideas I had about supernatural beings came to me the same way that my mathematical ideas did. So I took them seriously.' One of the reasons that his colleagues took so long to realise that he was in the grip of paranoid delusions was that . . . well, he was always kind of odd. And he was the kind of odd that high-level mathematicians often are. In the film, Nash goes off his medication, and begins to see patterns again: secret messages in the newspapers. He regains his ability to formulate equations, after months slumped in his chair at home.

One of the most extraordinary facets of Nash's story is that he came off anti-psychotic drugs in 1970 and still managed to keep his delusions at bay. In the film, this is represented by the moment he realises that Charles' niece Marcee does not age; after that, he simply refuses to acknowledge them both. (The film fudges the real Nash's refusal to take medication; he suspected that the studio didn't want to encourage other schizophrenics to copy him.)

This stereotype of the mad genius is not pure myth. Studies of personality suggest that many creative people may score highly for mental openness – which, when taken to extremes, can mean a mind that cannot distinguish truth from delusion. 'How near is madness to genius,' wrote the French philosopher Denis Diderot.

There's something else which made *A Beautiful Mind* so

appealing to audiences, though, and it's the idea that Nash suffered for his brilliance. In the ledger-book of life, he got one huge credit – rare mathematical ability – and in some cosmic way he had to pay for it. Something about this idea appeals to us deeply. It feels *right*. It feels *just*. Think how many stories of genius have to do with their flaws: Beethoven, the great composer, went deaf; Milton, the poet, went blind; Mozart was a prodigy who couldn't deal with the adult world; Leonardo da Vinci was tormented by endless inspiration, and was so overwhelmed he never achieved his potential. Even Picasso's parasitism can be seen this way: the great masculine artist who needed women's blood to paint his masterpieces. So many of our stories of genius are really about a person who has something wrong with them: oddness is transformed into specialness by the alchemical quality of genius. A simple, boring story of success would be dull; we crave the bittersweet. There is heroism in overcoming.

Biopics have been around since the early days of Hollywood, but their popularity has grown steadily since the turn of the millennium. Putting a famous name in a film title is a way of getting a midsized project off the ground, in an era of superhero franchises and blockbuster IP. Plus, a juicy lead role – particularly one that seems like Oscar bait – can get you a star on board, too.

Those forces have made biopics into our biggest exponent of the genius myth – because most of these biopics are dedicated to burnishing legends rather than destroying them. Baz Luhrmann's *Elvis*, for example, 'is uncritical of Presley's appropriation of black music or the fact that his future wife Priscilla was 14 years old to his 24 when they began dating'.[1] *Bohemian Rhapsody* is extremely heavy handed in claiming that no one really believed in Queen's decision to release a six-minute single full of nonsense about Galileo and fandangos, but the band stayed true to their artistic vision. (They are shown as single-minded rebels, like Ignaz Semmelweis.) Authorised biopics of living people are particularly prone to hagiography: *King Richard*, about the father of tennis players Venus and Serena Williams, cannot come to any conclusion other than that his hard-driving ambition was responsible for his daughters' success.

Why are these distortions inevitable? Because biopics only work when they use the facts of a life in service of a dramatic theme. My favourite example of the genre is the film adaptation of Peter Shaffer's *Amadeus*, which explores the idea of envy by telling the story of Mozart through his contemporary Salieri, a composer who was simply not as good, despite trying a lot harder. (How does that experience feel? Very bad, it turns out.) For many successful biopics – *Schindler's List*, *Braveheart*, *Gandhi* – the theme is resistance, and at minimum a biopic needs to contain an element of struggle. As a medium, film is more sparse and shallow than novels, and so single protagonist stories, of a lone rebel against an uncaring regime, work particularly well.

Biopics make an implicit claim for their subject's importance – and that *this* life tells us something profound about America, or maternal love, or sporting success, or the human condition itself. Without this motor underneath, the action falls flat. (Sometimes I like to remember the comedian Denis Leary's verdict on Oliver Stone's biopic of Jim Morrison and the Doors: 'Let me tell you something. We need a two-and-a-half-hour movie about the Doors? Folks, no we don't. I can sum it up for you in five seconds, OK. I'm drunk. I'm nobody. I'm drunk. I'm famous. I'm drunk. I'm fucking dead. There's the whole movie, OK!? Big fat dead guy in a bath tub, there's your title for you.')[2] Biopics are also political: it matters whose stories get told. Under pressure from activists and actors themselves, Hollywood has made a real effort to expand its range of biopic subjects, from *Milk* (the assassinated gay rights campaigner Harvey Milk) to *Hidden Figures* (black female NASA scientists in the 1960s). Biopics struggle to take the focus off the individual and acknowledge the importance of *scenius*. Christopher Nolan's film *Oppenheimer* was a rare example that attempted to show a charismatic leader acting as a force multiplier on the talent around him: J. Robert Oppenheimer is not the most talented physicist at Los Alamos; his genius is organisational. Audiences can find such films messy and distracting. Whose story is this, anyway?

Hollywood has developed a template for biopics about geniuses: the deficit model. The great man, misunderstood by the world, overcomes challenges and breaks free of normality to achieve something extraordinary. He suffers for it – for every credit, there is a debit. But most of all, he is the sun at the centre of the picture, with everyone and everything else orbiting around him. This is how stories work, but it is no longer how science works – remember the Large Hadron Collider at CERN, with its hundreds of scientists and dozens of nationalities? Or the terrible arguments about who deserves a Nobel Prize in the scientific categories, which are limited to three recipients, when so many breakthroughs are shared between entire teams?

Once you notice this model, you'll start seeing it everywhere. Look at *The Social Network*, where Mark Zuckerberg creates Facebook because he can't make human connections. In *My Left Foot*, a paralysed man learns to paint with his only working limb and eventually writes his memoir. In *Good Will Hunting*, a janitor turns out to be a mathematical wizard. In *Rain Man*, Dustin Hoffman's character lives in a mental institution and must keep to rigid routines, but is also a savant who can do calculations in his head. In *Shine*, a gifted pianist must overcome the trauma of his father's abuse. We love these kinds of stories. The strapline for the (flop) 2004 film *Raising Genius*, about a boy raised by obsessive-compulsive parents, gives an idea of the general vibe: 'He's seriously gifted. And totally twisted.'

Thinking about it, this could also be the strapline for *A Beautiful Mind*.

The deficit model of genius is so powerful that it warps real lives around its contours. The biopic format cannot handle reality. Take *The Theory of Everything*, for which Eddie Redmayne won a Best Actor Oscar for his portrayal of the physicist Stephen Hawking. At the beginning, when we are in 1960s Cambridge, Redmayne looks less like Hawking and more like Austin Powers – there's a bowtie, a bowl haircut and a jacket that looks suspiciously like velvet. The social awkwardness of this Stephen Hawking is restrained, which is appropriate since he's playing a man who was charming enough to seduce his second wife from a motorised wheelchair. In fact, one of the refreshing choices of *The Theory of Everything* is its refusal to turn a disabled man into a suffering saint. This Hawking is horny. (The real-life version liked to go to Stringfellows and watch the strippers.) He is also funny, and free from self-pity, except for a brief moment of despair when he first receives his diagnosis of motor neurone disease.

This is all charming and well-judged. What bothers me is that the film skates over the idiosyncrasies of the real Hawking much more freely than Ron Howard's film does with John Nash. His first wife fell in love with someone else but stayed with her husband; Hawking then fell in love with his nurse, Elaine Mason, who became his second wife. (The film makes no mention of the subsequent accusations that Mason was abusive to him.) *The Theory of Everything* also struggles to convey Hawking's achievements in physics: radiation from black holes does not lend itself to film visuals. But the real sticking point, in dramatic terms, is that Hawking did his best work *before* his physical deterioration.

THE DEFICIT MODEL

The two are not connected in the way the film's narrative yearns for them to be.

That's a problem because Hawking's bestseller, *A Brief History of Time*, was famously a much-unread book. People bought it to look smart, but they also bought it because of the ideal it represented – a brilliant brain in a broken body. The deficit model of genius. Without motor neurone disease, Stephen Hawking would have still been a truly significant physicist, but he would not have become a pop-culture icon: immortalised as a character in *The Simpsons*, making headlines for taking a plane trip at zero gravity, solicited for his thoughts about God. After all, his collaborator Roger Penrose is barely known outside of the academy, despite his equally impressive achievements – a superb theorist of geometry, Penrose inspired two works by M. C. Escher with his imaginary shapes, and he also wrote on consciousness. (Penrose lived long enough to win a Nobel in physics in 2020 for his work on black holes; Hawking died in 2018, without one.)

Hawking's disability boosted his fame, placing him in the same realm as Albert Einstein – everyone's go-to example of a Big Brain. The mythology of Hawking made him more than a scientist. He became a symbol. Although that inspired future physicists, others in his field still wonder if his fame was an entirely positive thing. 'The elevation of tenuous "Theories of Everything" – validated through celebrity rather than by empirical facts – over the vast, open-ended enterprise of engaging the physical world scientifically was, and is, deeply corrosive,' wrote the Nobel-winning physicist Frank Wilczek.[3] 'His status as an idol was also, I think, hard on Stephen. He knew better. Less would have been more.'

Recently, the computer pioneer Alan Turing has also received this treatment. Benedict Cumberbatch has never looked more like a beautiful robot made of porcelain than he does in *The*

Imitation Game, the biopic about Turing and his work breaking Nazi codes at Bletchley Park. The film's refrain, repeated three times, is: 'It's the people no one imagines anything of that do things no one can imagine.'

This is a classic underdog story, even if that involves massaging the facts somewhat. When Turing arrived at Bletchley Park, in his late twenties, he was already a Fellow at a Cambridge college, and had already written several important research papers. The film's Turing is unable to understand jokes, although he can solve crossword puzzles in minutes. He can't make friends – at his (public) school, his only companion was another boy called Christopher. At Bletchley, he alienates the team leader, Hugh Alexander – another maths prodigy – and can't even understand that 'we are going for a sandwich' is itself a type of code: an invitation to join the others for lunch. This is all the deficit model of genius. You get mathematical brilliance, but the cost is social skills. The story has another echo of *A Beautiful Mind*, because Turing also gets put on medication that neuters him – literally. After being convicted of homosexuality, he is chemically castrated, and finds that he can't even do a crossword puzzle. The world has tried to make him 'normal', but extinguished his brilliance in the process.

The deficit model of genius is a compelling myth but also a dangerous one. Because – just like *Yesterday* and *Cover Version* – there is a shadow version of *A Beautiful Mind*, one that was never made into a film. It is called *The Laws of Madness*.

'The monkeys are eating my brain,' screamed Michael Laudor the day he was accepted to Yale Law School. He suffered from schizophrenia, and saw his life as a contest between warring television channels in his brain: the 'Suicide Channel' that told him to kill himself, and the 'Calm Channel' where everything was peaceful.

After Laudor emerged from eight months in a mental health facility as a teenager, his father advised him to try for Yale, in the hope it would encourage his son's brilliance and support his mental struggles. He was right. Laudor became editor of the *Yale Law Review*, graduated with high marks and took a postgraduate degree. He also decided to reveal his disorder publicly in the hope of helping others.

In 1995, the *New York Times* ran a profile of Laudor that described him as '32, and by all accounts a genius'.[4] Read it now and you can see all the beats of the deficit model: he can quote the *Aeneid* with ease; he skipped classes at school but scored high grades anyway; he felt he was talking to the interviewer 'through walls of cotton and gauze'; he was dedicating 70 per cent of his brain to staying in touch with reality. 'Brilliance was the fulcrum of the story, the point at which Michael was lifted above the stereotypes of schizophrenia, much as intelligence had elevated him above ordinary expectations before he got sick,' his childhood friend Jonathan Rosen wrote later.[5] Rosen felt the article downplayed the true extent of Laudor's illness: he was given space to dismiss a question about whether he was violent as a 'stereotype', even though by this point he had threatened his parents with a knife because he was convinced they were Nazis.

The appealing portrait of the article – of Laudor as Prometheus, struggling every day to overcome (a sanitised version of) his illness – led to a bidding war for his memoir, to be titled *The Laws of Madness*. The winning offer was more than $600,000 – and on top of that came $1.5 million for the film rights from Ron Howard, the director of *A Beautiful Mind*. Brad Pitt was attached to star.

Later, *Time* reported that working on the memoir became a source of stress to Laudor, who was a perfectionist. Friends started to worry about him.[6] He was the 'most famous schizophrenic in

America,' Rosen wrote, 'a perverse designation, though strangely in tune with the aura of specialness that had characterized so much of his life, and that had shaped the expectations we'd grown up with'.[7] When Laudor pitched the adaptation of his memoir in Hollywood, he told executives that he managed his delusions by imagining them on television screens. 'The movie people found his method of controlling his hallucinations a perfect cinematic conceit.'

Unfortunately, that's exactly what it was – a fictional conceit. On 17 June 1988, Michael Laudor was found wandering the Cornell University campus in Ithaca, New York, covered in blood. He quickly confessed to killing his girlfriend Caroline – and officers found her body, covered in stab wounds, at their shared home 200 miles away. He had thought she was an imposter, an alien sent to torment him, or perhaps a robot or a doll. He had stopped taking his meds. He had not wanted to go to a secure hospital for treatment for his paranoid delusions. 'Michael's friends and family and his supporters at Yale had thought intelligence could save him, allow him to transcend the terrible disease that was causing his mind to detach from reality,' wrote Rosen. They could not.

And so *The Laws of Madness* was never completed; the film version was never made. In 1998, Michael Laudor was ruled unfit to stand trial and committed to a secure hospital surrounded by razor wire. Three years later, *A Beautiful Mind* was released.

PART THREE

The Birth of the Modern Genius

Disruptors

'Move fast and break things.'
Early Facebook motto

If I asked you where you thought the most geniuses could be found on the planet today, what would you say? In the early modern era, the answer might have been one of the great universities, or a royal court. In the 1700s, it might have been a meeting of the Royal Society in London. In the 1900s, it might have been that photographer's studio in Paris where the first Impressionist exhibition was held. But today, new paintings rarely cause a national scandal, poetry is a niche pursuit and the sciences have become so highly specialised (and so collaborative) that towering figures emerge less often. Instead, since the late twentieth century, the place in the Western world most readily identified with genius is that curving strip of Northern California just below the Golden Gate Bridge; an area that takes in San Francisco, Oakland, Palo Alto, Mountain View and Cupertino.

Silicon Valley.

The myth of this part of California started before the Second World War, when Stanford graduates Bill Hewlett and Dave Packard founded their electronics company, Hewlett-Packard. (Even earlier than that, Lee de Forest perfected the vacuum tube in Palo Alto.) The eastern states had non-compete clauses in employment contracts, which allowed bosses to sue their workers for defecting to a rival. But California did not, so its companies benefited from a constant exchange of skills as the best engineers moved around more freely. The existence of Stanford University was also crucial: its graduates founded many of the early Silicon Valley firms. And so was the presence of the military: in the US, the Department of Defense is one of the biggest investors in scientific research. The development of GPS was funded by the U.S. Naval Research Laboratory in the 1960s, and the early internet was funded by DARPA, the Defense Advanced Research Projects Agency. In the years after the Second World War, America was much richer than bombed-out, ration-struck Europe, which meant that the US could attract the best foreign scientists and academics. (The US also attracted some of the *worst* foreign scientists – the Nazis who had experimented on prisoners or collaborated with the regime – reasoning that their research was simply too valuable to waste.) All these factors turned the Valley into a site of *scenius* – somewhere that began to attract the brightest, hungriest young minds. William Shockley might have lucked into a career in California, but many other pioneering scientists of his generation migrated there specifically. It was the place to be.

I've mentioned Stanford and the defence industry because, although the Valley was funded and nurtured by public institutions and tax dollars, it has since developed a mythology that leans heavily towards Great Man theory, rugged individualism and the ideology of 'disruption'. The last of those is a theory developed by Harvard Business School professor Clayton Christensen in the mid 1990s, where he tried to explain how established businesses serving the top end of the market are dislodged by cheaper, scrappier rivals. The theory of disruption implied a kind of Darwinism in markets, where the fittest companies survived – and where natural justice would dethrone incumbents who had grown too bloated and comfortable.

Unfortunately, that is not always the case. The giants can afford to hire lobbyists to convince politicians to shape laws and policies that are favourable to them, for a start. America no longer has strong anti-monopoly laws, and so incumbents can also buy up smaller rivals and potential competitors. (In the course of two years in the early 2010s, Facebook bought thirty companies, including the photo-sharing service Instagram, the facial-recognition software Face.com, the bookmarking tool Spool, the advertising platform Atlas, the virtual reality company Oculus and the messaging service WhatsApp.) As for the great men, the history of Silicon Valley has plenty of those – people who are attached to heroic mythologies and see themselves as unusually prescient, insightful, *special* people. Mark Zuckerberg is now, unbelievably, one of the most normal-seeming of his generation of millennial boy-kings, and he is so obsessed with the challenges of absolute power that he has called his three daughters after Roman emperors (Maxima, August and Aurelia). The early Facebook investor Peter Thiel has become one of the right's leading thinkers – a libertarian who champions monopolies and has grown rich on government defence contracts. Steve Huffman, the co-founder of Reddit, had laser eye surgery in 2015 in case civilisation ends and he can no longer obtain glasses.[1] Sam Altman of OpenAI is a doomsday prepper, once telling friends that he keeps gold, guns and potassium iodide (for radiation exposure) on hand in case of the apocalypse.[2]

The generation above these men also had its share of mythmakers. 'Steve Jobs and Steve Wozniak have become archetypes: the Genius Entrepreneur and the Genius Engineer,' writes Adam Fisher in his oral history of the Valley.[3] You could add another epithet for Jobs – the 'genius asshole', an archetype that has now proliferated across our culture. He screwed his friends and collaborators out of money they were due, parked in handicapped spots, didn't have a number plate on his Mercedes, frequently told people 'this is shit' and washed his feet in the toilet. At the same time, he wore black roll-necks, cultivated a personal intensity and inserted lines into computer adverts about how Apple's products 'pushed the world forwards'. (He also oversaw the creation of some truly excellent consumer technology – I am a Mac and iPhone stan – and the creation of a studio that makes beautiful, tear-jerking animated films.) What Jobs did, like Pablo Picasso before him, was successfully convince everyone around him that the assholeness was indivisible from the genius. His early collaborator Steve Wozniak once told Jobs' biographer Walter Isaacson that if he had run Apple, it would have been a nicer place to work. Then he added: 'But if I had run Apple, we may never have made the Macintosh.'[4] (By this point, you will probably be asking the same question that I am – is that actually true? And if so, was the trade-off worth it?)

As the 2020s dawned, however, the shine started to rub off Silicon Valley. When I read Kara Swisher's memoir *Burn Book* in early 2024, I was struck by how much she had turned on the boy-kings of Silicon Valley, whose legends she had once burnished through columns in the *Washington Post* and *Wall Street Journal*. 'While my actual son filled me with pride,' she writes, 'an increasing number of these once fresh-faced wunderkinds I had mostly rooted for now made me feel like a parent whose progeny had turned into, well, assholes.'[5] Everywhere she looked, these masters of the universe were complaining about their grievances, obsessing over their status or trading on past glories.

To me, Swisher's memoir felt like a bellwether – a repudiation of the tech genius mythology from a woman who once relished being a myth-maker. But she is not alone. In 2010, the *New*

Yorker's Malcolm Gladwell was considered a Luddite for arguing, in the middle of the Arab Spring, that 'the revolution will not be tweeted'. Those days are gone. Today, the prevailing mood among tech commentators is cynicism. Cryptocurrencies haven't set banking free – they have allowed people to be conned out of their life savings. The crypto billionaire Sam Bankman-Fried wasn't another wild-haired boy-king with a dream to remake the world; he was a common crook, and is now in jail. NFTs – non-fungible tokens – weren't the future of the art industry; they were, as their critics said, fundamentally worthless digital certificates. Social networks didn't so much connect the world as pump raw sewage into the information water-system. Even generative artificial intelligence, the most hyped technology of the age – and the recipient of billions of venture-capital funding – leaves me ambivalent. (I love my automatic AI transcription service, and AI-generated images and movie clips are now *astonishing* in their ability to mimic reality, but . . . then what?) Twenty years ago, OpenAI's Sam Altman would have been uncritically hailed as a wonder-maker, a magician and a sage. Today, most journalists I know regard him as the man whose product might destroy thousands of jobs – copywriters, translators, animators, voice-over artists. The obsession with the 'future' that began in the late nineteenth century has corroded into knee-jerk cynicism about the grand claims of progress made by today's genius elite. Progress for whom, exactly?

Let's finish, then, with the dominant genius myth of our age – as its power begins to wane. We'll start with Thomas Edison. He didn't work in California – but his base, Menlo Park in New Jersey, gave its name to a town in Silicon Valley. In his undoubted achievements, but also his taste for showmanship, Edison has an echo today: Elon Musk. Here is a man who *did* disrupt the space industry but who also seems to revel in being an asshole.

This is partly a debate about values but also about geopolitics. The deification of Silicon Valley was a reflection of the power of America during the twentieth century: this was the land of opportunity, the home of innovation, the owner of the future. But the US is no longer the world's undisputed superpower. With India and China rising, debates about the future-gazing tech geniuses of Silicon Valley are also debates about the importance of America itself. Just as Shakespeare became the argument for the pre-eminence of the English language, Elon Musk – and Sam Altman, Peter Thiel and the rest – are living arguments that America still leads the world. No wonder they are such reliable generators of debate and discussion. To understand why that is, come with me to a small town on the train line south from New York, and prepare to meet the American Prometheus.

Thomas Edison:
The Lightbulb Moment

'The man who invented cats' eyes got the idea when he saw the eyes of a cat in his headlights. If the cat had been going the other way, he would have invented the pencil sharpener.'

Ken Dodd

Thomas Alva Edison worked at Menlo Park for less than a decade, but it has become central to his legend – both for what this period produced, and for the work style he adopted while he was there. If you want to look anywhere for the moment when the Romantic idea of genius – the tubercular poet communing with nature – yielded to the modern one – of a workaholic tech bro harnessing the white heat of technological innovation – look to this New Jersey hamlet in the late 1870s.

In December 1875, Edison chose to move to Menlo Park because the rent was cheap, he could live near to his workshop and the countryside was quiet. The hamlet also had the advantage of being on a train line to the city of New York. This would become important as fleets of gawkers, journalists and the actress Sarah Bernhardt all made the pilgrimage there to see Edison at work. (Bernhardt recorded a speech from *Phèdre* in French for him, and the surviving minute shows her to have been an extraordinary ham.)

Menlo Park is where Edison made his greatest invention on

18 July 1877: the phonograph. For the first time, this device allowed users to record and play back speech and music. But that wasn't the problem that Edison and his team of engineers and tinkerers were trying to solve. They were looking for new diaphragms – vibrating membranes – to improve telephone receivers. In their search for materials, they considered everything from silk sheets to a pig's bladder, testing the devices by using a finger to pick up the vibrations. This process gave Edison an idea. He turned to one of his assistants, Charles Batchelor, and said: 'Batch, if we had a point on this we could make a record on some material which we could afterwards pull under the point, and it would give us the speech back.'[1] The team rigged up the contraption, and Edison spoke the first words ever recorded by a human: 'Mary had a little lamb.' His engineers played it back. The recording wasn't perfect, but the concept worked.

The phonograph now seems primitive – it initially required a single-use wax cylinder – but it was Edison's most genuine conceptual innovation. (No, not the lightbulb, to which we'll return later.) The assembled crowd at Menlo Park didn't really grasp its importance at the time. The note in Edison's laboratory logbook was very casual, sandwiched among entries on the telephone, and it was also signed by Batchelor and fellow assistant James Adams: 'the spkg vibrations are indented nicely & theres [sic] no doubt that I shall be able to store up & reproduce automatically at any future time the human voice perfectly'.

The entire lab ignored the phonograph for six months while they continued to work on improvements to the telephone. They didn't even settle on what to call this new device for some time; alternative names included the 'glottophone', 'didaskophone' and 'klangophone'. In time, these complicating details would be airbrushed out of the story, while other details would become more prominent. Edison's brainwave came during the lab's midnight dinner break – when a porter would bring up food and the engineers would eat together before resuming work through the night. You can take one of two contradictory lessons from this fact: the first is that collaboration and personal relationships are vital to creative success and conceptual breakthroughs. The alternative is that you have to stay up past midnight to achieve anything great.

In November, *Scientific American* published a breathless letter by a business associate of Edison's, Edward Johnson, describing the phonograph in precise detail – complete with illustrations. He was concerned that a rival French team might get there first and wanted to make sure Edison received the proper credit. (The French method turned out to involve watching the throat and lips move, and was therefore a bust.) A month later, Edison and his assistant took a prototype of the phonograph into the offices of the magazine and set it on the table. 'How do you do?' it asked the onlookers. The journalists were as shocked as their modern counterparts encountering ChatGPT a century and a half later. Here was a machine with a ghost inside.

In a classic case of the Potus problem, it's hard now to understand the awe that the phonograph inspired. Even in its imperfect form, the machine dazzled crowds in New York and Pennsylvania. To contemporary onlookers, Edison had manipulated time itself – you could hear an orchestra from the past perform again for you right now. Your own voice might now survive a hundred years. The editors of *Scientific American* were overwhelmed by the prospect of hearing the voices of the dead – an everyday miracle we now take for granted. One newspaper imagined a world where the wealthy would capture voices and keep them in a 'well-stocked oratorical cellar'. (Instead, we got podcasts.) All the publicity gave Edison new ideas for how to use his machine. He had imagined the phonograph as a vehicle for speech, but now he understood the possibility for musical recordings, children's toys and speaking clocks.

The phonograph was invented at a time when the invisible world was yielding to scientific enquiry, but also a time that spawned charlatans and showmen who claimed they could manipulate unseen forces. This was the age of radiation – and ectoplasm. This was an age when a legitimate scientist like Marie Curie could attend seances, and when the creator of the ultra-rational Sherlock Holmes, Arthur Conan Doyle, could believe in fairies at the bottom of the garden. To outsiders, it was hard to tell who was the Isaac Newton of gravity and who was the Isaac Newton of alchemy. One thing was certain, however. This was exciting. Perhaps humans could master the world in a way never before imagined. The future was coming, and Thomas Edison was one of those ushering it in. 'He invented the profession of inventing,' writes his biographer Wyn Wachhorst.[2]

That eerie demonstration of the phonograph for *Scientific American* launched what you might call Edison mania, establishing him as a template for genius. The original Prometheus had stolen fire from the gods; the 'American Prometheus' had done something almost as inexplicable, by capturing something as insubstantial as sound. Those who championed Edison were also making an argument for America – here was the New World, full of pioneer spirit, not burdened by the past like stuffy old Europe.

Other aspects of Edison's mythology have changed over time, just as the story of Gauss' precocious mathematical ability twisted and turned to find its perfect form. Initially, Edison was 'the Wizard of Menlo Park', a man fizzing with ideas; a practical man with dirt on his hands, pulling sixty-hour sleepless marathons to accomplish the impossible. His deafness, which was probably congenital and grew worse over time, was reimagined as a superpower, in the way contemporary activists sometimes now talk about dyslexia or autism. Edison wasn't distracted from his thoughts by the chatter of the world.

He was also used as an argument against the bureaucracy and rigidity of the schooling system – a halfway house between Rousseau's idea of natural gifts untainted by formal education, and the modern Silicon Valley disdain for rote learning and credentialed experts. The story went that Edison's teachers had never seen his potential, so he picked up everything he needed to know from books. In early biographies, his middle-class family was downgraded to poverty to make his success better fit the American ideal of just deserts. He was implicitly compared with the literary character Tom Sawyer, a cheeky American boy, through depictions of young 'Tom Edison' – even though his family and friends called him 'Al', for Alva. His Protestant work ethic was offered as further proof that anyone could make it in America with enough grit and pluck. He was a bootstrapping entrepreneur, a rugged capitalist.

The real story is more complicated and more interesting. After the initial publicity for the phonograph died down, it became obvious that its single-use cylinders limited its commercial potential. Attempts to embed phonographs in children's toys failed because the devices were both clunky and prone to break. But the Edison myth was unstoppable – as were the frequent attempts to debunk his overhyped pronouncements. 'Ironically, the public set up an image which Edison could not help but believe to some degree,' writes Wachhorst. 'As a result the unreality of the image seems to have involved him in chronic frustration and, as the years wore on, defeat.'[3]

The way the myth-making process worked was this. Favoured reporters, such as Amos Cummings of the *New York Sun*, were given exclusive access to Edison. They would travel to Menlo Park, and during the course of their conversation Edison would mention, with fake casualness, some other great breakthrough he believed was imminent. Very few of these inventions would actually appear, although the ones that did were impressive enough to hold off the naysayers for a little longer. Either way, the reporters had their story, and Edison had his publicity.

By the late 1870s, he was famous enough to receive eighty letters a day seeking his wisdom (and, quite often, his money). Photographic portraits of him went on sale – one shows him tired from a long night inventing the phonograph, slumped at a desk. His work habits were, to use a phrase from more than a century later, 'extremely hardcore'.

It's funny that we have come to use the phrase 'lightbulb moment' to describe a momentary flash of inspiration, because the birth of the lightbulb was slow, incremental and highly contested. Although Edison holds U.S. Patent No. 223898 for the 'electric lamp', it's not really fair to call him its inventor. Between 1802 and 1809, Humphry Davy demonstrated the principle of incandescence through a series of experiments in London. In 1838, the Belgian Marcellin Jobard heated a carbon rod inside a vacuum, passed an electric current through it and observed the glow it produced. By 1860, the Englishman Joseph Swan had created a working prototype of the lightbulb, using carbonised paper filaments, but it quickly burned out.

The problem that Edison and his Menlo Park team faced in the late 1870s was not conceptual. The basic elements of the incandescent bulb were already established. The challenge was to create a better vacuum, a longer-lasting filament and a reliable supply of electricity. Only then could 'glow bulbs' replace the other available options: the gas lamps fitted in upper-class homes, and the giant, smelly carbon arc lamps used outdoors.

As usual, once Edison became interested in the subject of the lightbulb, he could not resist boasting to the press about how easy a solution would be; so simple that a bootblack might understand it. He skipped meetings with potential investors, telling them that he was working through the night because the solution was so tantalisingly close. He invited reporters to Menlo Park to witness his prototype. What he didn't tell the journalists was that the platinum filament he was using, far from lasting 'for ever', would burn out if the demonstration lasted more than a few minutes.[4] His enthusiasm made him a dilettante. He set aside the work he had been doing on the phonograph; after its initial burst of popularity, the invention would languish for a decade while Edison was consumed by other projects. Like Elon Musk taking on the established car manufacturers, Edison and his lightbulbs presented a threat to an established industry. Gas lamps were smelly and dirty, and the suppliers were widely held to be charging too much. Edison's electric lights were the future – cleaner, hopefully cheaper; a great American engineering triumph. If he could make them work.

After several months, it became apparent that nothing of value was emerging from Menlo Park. A planned demonstration was cancelled. Visitors were barred from the laboratory. Journalists responded by laying on thick flattery to maintain their access to the great man; one writer called Edison 'my esteemed manipulator of the fiery lightning', which even the most crawling modern tech writers would find a bit ripe. (In January 1879, that same writer, Edwin Fox of the *New York Herald*, received eight shares in the newly formed Edison Electric Light Company as a gift.)[5] Doesn't all this seem curiously modern? A genius was created by an admiring group who had a commercial (and personal) interest in his continued veneration. For as long as Edison's legend sold newspapers, being the writer with the inside track on Edison was a prestigious position. And the man himself helped out: in a blaze of publicity, he sent explorers around the world to search for the perfect material for the filament. One of the explorers claimed not to have changed his clothes for ninety-eight days as he 'penetrated the wilderness of the Amazon'.

Luckily for writers like Edwin Fox, their subject eventually realised that platinum filaments were unworkable. The lab began to try alternatives, and on 21 October 1879, Charles Batchelor created a bulb with a carbonised sewing thread, which glowed for more than forty hours before Edison ended the experiment by turning up the voltage until it burned out. Soon after, the lab discovered that carbonised paper was even better. A new Sprengel pump made the vacuum better. Edison devised a mains system, complete with meters to measure how much electricity each house consumed. All these improved elements combined to make a viable electric bulb. To my mind, the power grid was Edison's most underrated innovation. By demonstrating, as he did in New York, that homes could be supplied with electricity through a meter system, he created the Electric Age.

That moment should have been Edison's greatest triumph. But what came next was a soul-sapping gauntlet of lawsuits, patent battles and mergers. If Edison was hungry to take the credit for inventing the lightbulb, it was partly because his investors demanded it. They wanted to protect their patents – and they knew how powerful Edison was as a brand name. We can see many of the faults of modern Silicon Valley in action during this period: the hype cycle, the lionisation of the founder or frontman, the attempt to create a monopoly by driving competitors out of business. Rinse and repeat.

The final insult was when Edison lost the 'current war' to fellow entrepreneur George Westinghouse, whose alternating current beat his direct version as the industry standard. Even Edison Electric eventually adopted alternating current, and

Edison was pushed out. The company merged with another supplier and then became General Electric in 1892.

Like the Beatles, then, Edison had *it* – that indefinable quality – and then he didn't. You could say the same about Einstein, who died a global celebrity but out of fashion with his fellow physicists.[6] Or Picasso, who grew more famous and less respected as he approached old age. In the last decade of the nineteenth century, writes Wyn Wachhorst, 'growing ever older, less energetic and more disillusioned, Edison increasingly talked more and invented less'. His collaborators moved on, drifted away or died. An ore-milling project took years and produced nothing of worth. He was tied up in litigation over his inventions. He claimed to have invented the movie camera but one of his employees was revealed as the true brain behind it. His grand new laboratory in West Orange burned down in 1914. He spent years convinced that a sufficiently powerful battery would make an electric car possible – and then Ford produced the Model N and Model T, which ran perfectly well on gas, killing off the idea for nearly a century. Edison's interviews became less about his inventions and more about his pronouncements on the state of the nation. (He did not go full Shockley, but certainly demonstrated the same willingness to air his thoughts on subjects outside his expertise.) By the 1900s, he had been swallowed by his public image: 'Edison seemed more willing to rest on his laurels, pretending always to be maintaining the old pace.'[7]

Why did Edison's great gift ebb away? There are many potential answers. One is that there was a change in the *scenius*: he was the last dabbler who could compete with the new industrial scale of chemistry and engineering. In the 1870s, a small lab like the one at Menlo Park could find conceptual innovations and knock-up prototypes to explore them. By the end of the century, that had become almost impossible. Another possibility is that

Edison was a conceptual innovator and he peaked early. As he became older, he calcified into the assumptions of the field – assumptions that he had helped to create. Just like Einstein lived long enough to be puzzled by quantum mechanics, Edison survived to see the radio boom, but could never grasp its commercial potential.

As his ability to generate breakthroughs diminished, his mythology only grew. In old age, Edison became the great sage, full of homespun wisdom and supernatural insights into the cosmos. His interviews were a reliable source of headlines, as he offered his opinion on women (obstinate), Turks (smelly) and the soul (non-existent). The recruitment questionnaire he used for his companies – the 'Edison Test' – leaked in 1921. Questions included 'Who was Paul Revere?', 'How is sulphuric acid made?' and, somewhat bleakly, 'What was the approximate population of England, France, Germany and Russia before the war?' Einstein reportedly took this test and flunked it – something that was presented as a triumph for the self-taught tinkerer over the ivory-tower academic.

That archetype became the most popular form of the Edison mythology. In 1932, the year after Edison died at the age of eighty-four, *Harper's Monthly* ran an article by a former assistant. This depicted the inventor spitting on the floor and declaring, in Midwestern dialect: 'Hell! There ain't no rules around here! We are trying to accomplish somep'n.'[8] (A preview of Silicon Valley's taste for 'disruption' and creative destruction.) Seven years after his death, his name was invoked to oppose the New Deal, a massive public works programme and expansion of the welfare state, by his former secretary A. O. Tate, who called the deal a threat to 'individual initiative'.

Those close to him – the ones who weren't cashing in themselves, at least – noticed that the myth was replacing the man. His employee Mary Nerney criticised the authorised biographies for making him 'a conventional figure . . . a great name, a bust in time for the Hall of Fame, but not Edison'. There was no longer any need to debunk him or question whether his inventions would actually arrive: in death, he passed into a new role as a national symbol.

There is no doubt that he was a selfish genius. The ferociously talented Nikola Tesla lasted only a year at Edison's laboratory and left after winning a bet with Edison (which the latter then claimed was a joke). Tesla later refused the Nobel when it was offered to him jointly with Edison. True, the American inventor pushed his lab workers forward by the strength of his enthusiasms, but he held them back when he lost interest or careered off down another rabbit hole.* More recent biographies 'have brought to light an introverted, antisocial egomaniac to whom close personal relationships meant almost nothing, including those within his own family'.[9] He neglected his first wife almost completely, leaving her at home alone while he had all those midnight dinners at the laboratory. His eldest son Thomas Jr was a classic failson – unable to live up to his father's stature, he became a wastrel. He was eventually convinced to put his famous last name to a piece of quack machinery called the 'Magno-Electric Vitalizer'.

The myth-making blotted out Edison the manager, celebrated for his mastery of complex systems and his ability to run a laboratory, and boiled him down to the sole inventor of the phonograph and the lightbulb. He became a parable for children. Since the Second World War, Wachhorst notes, 'the ratio of juvenile

---

* Edison Electric hired one of the very few black engineers working at the time, Lewis Latimer, but it was only to use Latimer's knowledge of other electric companies as opposition research during one of Edison's many patent fights.

to adult Edison literature has steadily increased, and the average age level of readers has dropped'. Today, he is a morality tale for children: *work hard, and you can achieve anything.* Interest in Edison as a man has fallen away, and what remains is the American Adam, the Prometheus, the Wizard of Menlo Park.

Elon Musk: Extremely Hardcore

'The true artist will let his wife starve, his children go barefoot, his mother drudge for his living at seventy, sooner than work at anything but his art.'

George Bernard Shaw

In November 2022, Elon Musk sent an email to the staff at Twitter, the social network he had bought seven months earlier for $44 billion. 'Going forward, to build a breakthrough Twitter 2.0 and succeed in an increasingly competitive world, we will need to be extremely hardcore,' he wrote. 'This will mean working long hours at high intensity. Only exceptional performance will constitute a passing grade.' Anyone who declined was promised three months' severance pay.

In buying Twitter, Musk turned himself into the network's most visible user – and one of the most famous people in the world. In return for his billions, he acquired huge influence, a thousand fanboys and about as many demolitions in the liberal media. Whenever he made an apparently silly decision – scrambling the site's verification mechanic, for example, which allowed a random prankster to claim to be a pharmaceutical company offering cheap insulin – onlookers were invited to read it through the prism of his genius. After all, this was the man behind PayPal, Tesla and SpaceX, as well as the less-known Neuralink and Boring Company. He was Tony Stark in *Iron Man* – capricious, yes, but therefore an iconoclast, which is exactly what had made him successful. He had taken on the established, fossil-fuel addicted auto industry and won. He had challenged the government's grip on space travel, and triumphed. The qualities that allowed him to do this were his phenomenal work rate, his wide reading and perhaps even his self-confessed neurodivergence. Whatever he was, he wasn't *normal* – the one thing that a genius cannot be. 'No one normal could have done that,' Joan told Alan Turing in *The Imitation Game*. 'The world is an infinitely better place precisely because you weren't.'

Because of these qualities, Musk's institutional and private backers calculated, he could remake the struggling social network, turning it from a niche product beloved by journalists and nerds into a profitable business with global reach. Twitter would now be the world's 'town square' and the home of unfettered free speech.

Of course, that didn't happen. Since buying Twitter, Musk has rebranded the service as 'X', a name he has loved since his first days in California. He has also relaunched himself. His political committee donated more than $100 million to the Republicans ahead of the 2024 US presidential election, and soon after Donald Trump's win, he began to refer to himself as the 'first buddy'. Throughout the campaign, he joked about a 'department of government efficiency', or DOGE, named after a decade-old internet meme about a cute dog. On stage at a rally in Madison Square Garden, New York, he suggested cutting $2 trillion out of the US federal budget – a third of its value. The implication was that because he ran successful private companies, he could run a government better than a bunch of bureaucrats. He was duly appointed to Trump's governing team as an advisor.

Musk's political interventions have created a fierce giant-killing instinct. *Who does this guy think he is?* To me, his trajectory seems like a tragic example of someone being radicalised by social media – Musk made the drug dealer's mistake of getting high on his own supply. Throughout 2024, he posted dozens of times a day on X – stealing memes, replying to conspiracy theorists and generally basking in attention. A whole gang of (mostly) men vied for his attention by saying the kind of things he liked to hear. The woke mind virus was killing America! Britain was a free-speech hellhole! The 'mainstream media' was lying and biased, and only X could bring truth to the masses! At the same time, active user numbers fell, the 'For You' feed filled up with flagrant racism and videos of random violence, and advertisers abandoned the platform. In January 2024, disclosure filings revealed that one of Musk's backers, Fidelity Holdings, had marked down the value of their investment by 71 per cent. The company, which he bought for $44 billion, was now deemed to be worth just $10 billion.

The schadenfreude was loud and unconfined. This alleged genius had taken a buzzy company, many liberals argued, and nosedived it straight into the ground. Even Musk took to saying that it was worth the financial loss to protect free speech (by which he meant the conservative and pro-Trump speech that he liked). After years of being covered in the press like a visionary, Musk was now treated as an idiot. The harder thing to accept, however, is that the same person can be both. Musk is still the man who drove down the cost of space travel with reusable rockets, and who made buying an electric car seem cool rather than an act of penance. But he is also the man who keeps falling for badly photoshopped news headlines. His detractors can't accept this, and neither can he, because they both believe in the genius myth – that you're either an all-round special person, or you're not. How can the same person succeed so brilliantly at SpaceX and Tesla, and then go on to slash Twitter's value by three-quarters? Simple: Elon Musk is good at some things, and not at others. To understand that, we need to stop thinking of genius as a transferable skill. 'At its core, SpaceX was a physics problem,' wrote Ryan Mac and Kate Conger. 'Tesla was a manufacturing problem. But Twitter was a social and psychological problem.'[1]

One cloudless day in the autumn of 2022, I found myself at Cape Canaveral, on Florida's space coast. I had been on a work trip in the state, but my return home was delayed by a small hurricane. Once the rain stopped, I had two more days until the next available flight, and so I got in my SUV and drove east from Orlando to the Kennedy Space Center. This is more than a glorified warehouse for old rockets and space station capsules. The space centre is a temple to human – and specifically American – achievement. You start your journey with some rather dry exhibits about the early days of Florida as a settlement, before crossing to a hall dedicated to the astronauts of the American space programme.

I was idly wandering round, contemplating a visit to the IMAX theatre, wondering why the bus tours of the launch centre were suspended, when I realised that the crowd of tourists was moving as a herd. Where were they going? As it happened, they were heading out of the back, to a viewing area with a big screen. In fifteen minutes' time, a rocket would blast off from the launchpad five miles away, delivering a satellite into orbit. I followed them, took a seat and was rewarded with one of the most humbling sights that the modern world has to offer – the sight of something made by humans leaving the only home we've ever known. Watching that orange streak burn through the bright blue sky, I became swept up in the romance, the ambition, the sheer *unlikeliness* of it all. A species that didn't have electric lights or recorded sound four lifetimes ago could now head for the stars.

What also struck me was the intense co-ordination needed for space exploration. Dozens of engineers and technicians were involved, and if any one of them made a small mistake, it could send the rocket spiralling out of control, lost in a flash of flame. Space travel is the ultimate collective endeavour; a manufacturing miracle as much as a conceptual one. If we burn enough fuel, we can generate enough thrust to propel an object fast enough and high enough to escape earth's gravity. OK, then. What kind of fuel? How much? And what kind of object?

Space travel is expensive, risky and dangerous. In 1986 and 2003, NASA suffered two shuttle explosions that killed everyone on board. In both cases, the programme was halted for months afterwards to investigate. In 2011, it was suspended entirely, and for a while American astronauts had to hitch a ride with the Russians on a Soyuz capsule, at a cost of $86 million a seat. That changed in 2020, when SpaceX successfully flew one of its Dragon crew capsules to the International Space Station with two astronauts on board. Elon Musk now had a power held only by nations.

The launch I watched went off perfectly. It's always strange to see something in real life that you've seen a dozen times in movies: the 'T minus 10' countdown, mission control calling the stage separations and that deep, deep *growl* of the engines. Watching the rocket streak across the sky, I felt every bit as overawed as those first Victorians listening to the disembodied voice of the phonograph. This was *magic*. And therefore perfect territory for the flourishing of the genius myth: anyone who could make this happen must, surely, be a superior type of human.

Elon Musk fascinates me – and I'm far from alone. His public image reflects both the persistence of the genius myth, and the persistent attempts to demolish it. I'm tempted to argue that the referendum on Musk will be won by the debunkers, simply because *we know too much about him*. How can you maintain an air of intellectual mystique while pumping out brain farts every five minutes? But then I remember that the sociologist Herbert Spencer tried to debunk the Great Man theory of history more than a century ago, and yet it persists. *Yesterday* was a more commercial film than *Cover Version* would have been. (Sorry to Jack Barth, but may I plead the Coen brothers' *Inside Llewyn Davis* in evidence? A beautifully made film about a failed musician, which did not set the box office on fire.) YouTube is full of quacks and charlatans insisting that they, like Galileo, are standing up to the scientific consensus by promoting chem trails, or 9/11 conspiracies, or vaccine denialism. In hindsight, the mythology of genius is so powerful that it might well smother the memory of how Musk arrived at Twitter headquarters after his acquisition, carrying a sink – purely so he could tweet 'Let that sink in.'

The Musk mythology begins with his childhood in the tough, masculine culture of white Afrikaners in Pretoria, South Africa. By all accounts, he was a brilliant, odd, bullied child. He was writing code for computer games at twelve. Like the young Edison, Elon was a compulsive reader, memorising encyclopedia entries and regurgitating them to his unimpressed classmates. He was once beaten up so badly – kicked in the head and pushed down a flight of stairs – that he later had a nose job to deal with the after-effects. His father Errol was volatile, an alpha male with a harsh temper and old-fashioned ideas about most things (he now has two children with his former stepdaughter). Yet when his parents divorced, Elon choose to live with Errol for a time. According to his first biographer Ashlee Vance, the young Elon would drift off into reveries, which isolated him from the outside world as surely as Thomas Edison's deafness did. (In fact, Musk's mother Maye took him for hearing checks, and had his adenoids removed as a result. The reveries continued.)

Once he had moved to America, Elon Musk then benefited from *scenius*. He ended up in Silicon Valley after studying at Queen's University in Ontario and the University of Pennsylvania. (He withdrew from a planned postgraduate course at Stanford.) His first company – the online directory Zip2 – was founded in the San Francisco Bay Area. Elon created Zip2 with his younger brother Kimbal and a $28,000 gift from their father Errol.[2] (Another unacknowledged leg-up.) He absorbed the 'grind' mentality of Silicon Valley start-ups – the legacy of Edison's all-night inventing sessions. 'Musk never seemed to leave the office,' writes Vance. 'He slept, not unlike a dog, on a beanbag next to his desk.' The young entrepreneur told a venture capitalist that he was like a samurai: 'I would rather commit seppuku than fail.' After pissing off many of his coders by redoing their work, and having fistfights with Kimbal in the office, he sold Zip2 to Compaq for $307 million in cash.

Around this time, he married his college sweetheart Justine. She later wrote an essay in *Marie Claire* about being Musk's 'starter wife', which claimed he was obsessed with making her dye her hair ever more blonde. He told her at their wedding: 'I'm the Alpha.' They had six children – one boy who died of sudden infant death syndrome, then twins and triplets.[3]

Musk ploughed his share of the Zip2 money into his next business, X.com, from which he was pushed out by a boardroom coup. Still, he made $180 million from the sale. During that period, he became a staple of the dotcom gossip blog Valleywag, because he couldn't stop himself counter-attacking whenever the site was mean about him. He wanted to be seen and heard – but only on his terms. In his memoir, the screenwriter William Goldman writes about the difference between mere actors and movie stars. The stars, he says, share one quality in common, aside from talent. *They want it.* You can say the same about Musk (or Thomas Edison). They didn't just want to achieve great things. They were also happy to play a genius in public. Musk encourages a view of himself as a workaholic with a perpetually burning brain – even his hobbies are framed as being extremely hardcore. In the autumn of 2024, he told the podcaster Joe Rogan that he was in the top twenty players in the world for a stretch of the video-game *Diablo 4*.

Now consider some other figures regularly described as 'tech geniuses' and 'visionaries'. The Twitter co-founder Jack Dorsey reportedly eats only seven meals a week, and the Israeli historian Yuval Noah Harari undertakes silent meditation retreats lasting up to sixty days. Other notables in Silicon Valley eat only liquid food, or sleep a few hours a night, or go to Burning Man and find themselves while taking shrooms in the desert. The venture capitalist Bryan Johnson is trying to live for ever through various chemical means, including blood transfusions from his teenage son. (He stopped when he felt no benefit.) This is a clique of people in love with their own extraordinariness, and with the money and resources to pursue their wildest fantasies.

Then there's autism. In adulthood, Musk has suggested that he might have the developmental disorder, making it hard for him to read emotional cues. We know that people with autistic traits are over-represented in Silicon Valley and in technical professions, although insufficient research has been done on why that might be. In an influential *Wired* article in 2001, the journalist Steve Silberman described autism as 'geek syndrome', particularly in its milder manifestation, then known as Asperger's. 'It's a familiar joke in the industry that many of the hardcore programmers in IT strongholds like Intel, Adobe, and Silicon Graphics – coming to work early, leaving late, sucking down Big

Gulps in their cubicles while they code for hours – are residing somewhere in Asperger's domain,' Silberman wrote.[4] 'Though no one has tried to convince the Valley's best and brightest to sign up for batteries of tests, the culture of the area has subtly evolved to meet the social needs of adults in high-functioning regions of the spectrum. In the geek warrens of engineering and R&D, social graces are beside the point. You can be as off-the-wall as you want to be, but if your code is bulletproof, no one's going to point out that you've been wearing the same shirt for two weeks.'[5]

The mythology here would be offensive to some people with autism, and so it is not always articulated out loud: *perhaps the best people to work with computers are somehow like computers themselves.* But others consider the condition to be a badge of honour. One of the most active Musk fan accounts on X is called Autism Capital. In some online spaces, being 'an autist' or 'having the tism' is seen as a sign of intellectual nonconformity. In September 2024, Musk commented, 'interesting observation', as he shared a post by Autism Capital which claimed that autism was a superpower. 'People who can't defend themselves physically (women and low T men) parse information through a consensus filter as a safety mechanism,' the post read. 'They literally do not ask "is this true," they ask, "will others be OK with me thinking this is true."' The post continued: 'Only high T alpha males and aneurotypical people (hey autists!) are actually free to parse new information with an objective "is this true?" filter. That's why a Republic of high-status males is best for decision-making. Democracy, but a democracy only for those who are free to think.'

Truly, the ideas of Francis Galton will never die – which is why this book traces a line from his views to the cultural energy of today's online right. Never mind that this line of thinking collapses after a moment's thought – there were plenty of big butch lads who enthusiastically supported Nazi Germany, for example. Not great decision-making, or respect for democracy, on their part. Meanwhile, some of the bravest resisters, such as the priest Dietrich Bonhoeffer or the student protester Sophie Scholl, were either 'low T' men or women.* To me, that Autism Capital post is intended to flatter its target audience in the same way that Mensa flattered the high IQ low achievers a century before. Never mind what you have to show for your life, know that you are a special sort of person, of the *type* who should rule the world.

Now, it shouldn't be surprising that a dominant group in a society might try to claim that their success is merely the result of natural justice. (White Europeans did it throughout the nineteenth century, after all.) The most avid propagandists in history are people explaining why they have risen to the top.

Today, the mythology of the genius as a human computer has translated into a fetish for the 'hard sciences' – physics, chemistry and engineering – reminiscent of the idolisation of high IQ a century earlier. (No coincidence that these are some of the few academic disciplines still dominated by men.) And it has created the cult of the brilliant engineer, who must be freed from outside interference or responsibility. This is the only true type of achievement – and, the implication goes, the only thing necessary for great innovation to happen. Everything else is just middle management (snore), menial work (lowly) or HR (for girls). But those SpaceX rockets wouldn't get off the ground without a whole support structure, right down to the person who lets the

---

* Bonhoeffer was hanged in a concentration camp in April 1945, while Scholl was guillotined in 1943, along with her friends in the White Rose movement. She and her brother had been turned in by the university maintenance man, who looks from the photos like someone who was able to 'defend himself physically'.

extremely hardcore people into the office on Sundays and public holidays.

Look around Silicon Valley and it becomes more and more obvious that the geeks are not the only important workers. When Google began to expand, its founders brought in Eric Schmidt – a regular businessman – to be the 'grown up' in the room. Mark Zuckerberg made a similar decision when he hired Sheryl Sandberg as chief operating officer at Facebook in 2008. When the Google engineer James Damore wrote his famous memo in 2017 – suggesting that Google's attempts to recruit more female engineers were doomed, because women 'have a stronger interest in people rather than things' – a more senior ex-Googler replied.* 'People who haven't done engineering, or people who have done just the basics, sometimes think that what engineering looks like is sitting at your computer and hyper-optimizing an inner loop, or cleaning up a class API,' wrote Yonatan Zunger on Medium.[6] He disagreed with that idea.

> Essentially, engineering is all about cooperation, collaboration, and empathy for both your colleagues and your customers. If someone told you that engineering was a field where you could get away with not dealing with people or feelings, then I'm very sorry to tell you that you have been lied to. Solitary work is something that only happens at the most junior levels, and even then it's only possible because someone senior to you – most likely your manager – has been putting in long hours to build up the social structures in your group that let you focus on code.

---

* Damore was fired after the memo leaked, and wrote an update to it that began: 'I value diversity and inclusion, am not denying that sexism exists, and don't endorse using stereotypes.' He told an interviewer that perhaps his autism had led him to underestimate how controversial the memo would be.

A technology company cannot succeed without brilliant engineers. But it also could not succeed if it employed *only* brilliant engineers. Even a queen bee needs workers.

This cultural baggage of the modern tech genius lifts them from 'people who work in IT' into a special class who are presumed to have great insights into the future. Oddness is rewritten as specialness. This dynamic reminds me of how traditional societies viewed shamans, as members of the tribe with a connection to the gods, and the strange ascetic lifestyles – dieting, taking hallucinogens, trances – to match. Shamans 'have undergone transformative experiences and emerged with new abilities: They alone can see spirits,' writes the anthropologist Manvir Singh.[7] 'Convinced that shamans diverge from normal people, communities accept that they have superhuman abilities. Like Superman's alien origins and the X-Men's genetic mutations, shamans' transformations assure people that they deviate from normal humanness, making their claims of supernatural engagement more believable.' Compare that description of strangeness and specialness with the treatment of Mark Zuckerberg in *The Social Network*. A young man who can't make friends develops Facebook, a directory of billions of social connections. It has the quality of a fable, because it is a genius myth: the real Zuckerberg was already dating his future wife Priscilla during the events depicted in the film, so he clearly wasn't *that* much of an antisocial weirdo.

This aesthetic of the hardcore, isolated and pure man feeds the genius myth. In Musk's worldview, private companies are nimble and cost-effective, and governments are slow and boring. But his two most famous businesses, Tesla and SpaceX, only exist because of government support – American taxpayers kept them afloat. (SpaceX was rescued from the brink of going broke by a $1.6 billion NASA contract to resupply the International Space

Station in December 2008, while some Tesla buyers benefited from $7,500 in tax credits from the US government, a scheme designed to encourage the transition to electric vehicles.) The various biographies of Musk make clear that his employees (the ones who stuck around, anyway) took pride in his extreme work habits. They wanted to work for someone who slept under his desk sometimes, who shouted at engineers, who demanded the impossible, who seemed to absorb information like a human computer. It made the sacrifices demanded of them bearable and proved that they were doing something beyond the reach of normies.

Having worked in a daily newspaper one-tenth as demanding as Musk's universe, I recognise this impulse. Among my senior colleagues, slogging on past 9 p.m., I saw a kind of Stockholm syndrome: a feeling that if they were this miserable, stressed and overworked, there *must* be a higher purpose. I remember feeling when I left that I had failed. I couldn't hack it. I wasn't extremely hardcore. Then I remembered that one of my last jobs had been writing captions on pictures of animals dressed as Harry Potter characters. If a genius is often a sadist, then many of the rest of us are secret masochists.

The aura of genius that surrounds Musk has fed an equally strong impulse to debunk him. The aura of genius that surrounds Musk has fed an equally strong impulse to debunk him. The most notorious example might be the one I mentioned all the way back at the beginning – the 2022 sequel to the film *Knives Out*, which depicts a tech billionaire called Miles Bron. This Musk-like figure invites his friends to a private island to solve a murder. The big reveal is not the killer's identity, but that Bron is an idiot who stole his big idea from his business partner – and the idea is terrible anyway, an alternative fuel that is too dangerous to be used. (In the years before the film's release, several Teslas burst into flames when the batteries overheated.)

Many Silicon Valley observers now slot Musk into the Miles Bron template rather than the Thomas Edison one. Musk has helped these people by not only giving them ammunition, but loading the gun. He is addicted to publicity: there are wives – so many wives! – children – so many children! – and ever more absurd and inflammatory statements. When he tried to back out of buying Twitter, he was sued in a Delaware court that demanded access to his text messages. These are unedifying in the extreme – so many sycophants! – but also deeply naive about the ability of a man with a background in engineering and logistics to solve intrinsically human problems like content moderation and speech norms. One text from a potential investor proposed a '#gameplan' for Twitter which began with equally abundant punctuation and self-confidence: '1.),, Solve Free Speech.' 'For this crew, the early success of their past companies or careers is usually prologue, and their skills will, of course, transfer to any area they choose to conquer (including magically *solving free speech*),' wrote The Atlantic's Charlie Warzel.[8] 'But what they are actually doing is *winging it*.'

After his acquisition of Twitter, Musk appeared to make it his mission to annoy as many journalists as possible. What had been a combative relationship became intensely toxic. But just like in his early Silicon Valley days, that only made him *more* appealing as a subject. He is now one of the most famous people in the world – the top of everyone's mental list of potential geniuses. But has he passed decisively across the Edison horizon, transforming from talented innovator to inveterate bloviator? (Or in his case, innovator to shitposter.)

I wonder if Musk has another act left in his career. The second half of which might follow the same arc as Edison's, coasting downwards on the fumes of publicity – another brilliant mind lost to Galaxy Brain syndrome. At the time of writing, SpaceX is developing rockets for a manned Mars mission, which looks promising. The company has already succeeded in catching a reusable rocket – the size of a skyscraper – on a landing pad using metal 'chopsticks'. Donald Trump will surely ease the regulatory burdens on SpaceX, which might either lead to a triumphant journey to the red planet, or a repeat of the *Challenger* disaster. And with Trump in the White House, Musk's many legal challenges – such as the lawsuit over his refusal to honour the severance agreements of the ousted Twitter executives – are less pressing.

When elections are over, everything the winning campaign did is often treated as inspired, and everything the losing campaign did as a costly mistake. This applies even when the margin of victory is a few thousand votes. The same is true of Elon Musk's genius – the judgement will be delivered in retrospect, only when we know whether his compulsive risk-taking has paid off.

A more fair assessment is the one I gave at the start: that his work at Tesla and SpaceX shows flashes of genius, but he has succumbed to the idea that he is therefore a special person. In 2023, he posted a list that showed software companies now dominated global 'unicorns' – billion-dollar tech companies. He was scathing. 'Major misallocation of capital imo. Most on this list won't make it,' he tweeted. (Incidentally, this was a few months after buying a software company himself.) 'Not enough talent in manufacturing & heavy industries.'

'Interesting point, but an example might make it clearer,' tweeted back the tech investor Paul Graham.[9] 'Can you think of a prominent person who's currently wasting his talents in software when he could be working on manufacturing and heavy industries?'

Musk appeared not to get the joke.

Musk's other companies have survived – and in some cases, prospered – under his chaotic but driven management. Why has his tenure at X, by contrast, seemed so cursed? Perhaps Musk, like many geniuses who fancy themselves solitary achievers, has shed the support structures which once moderated his impulses.

There's a character in Ashlee Vance's biography who hovers at its margins: Mary Beth Brown, or MB, Musk's executive assistant. She is described as working twenty-hour days, just like him, juggling his family life and work commitments, the 'only bridge between Musk and all of his interests'.[10] At SpaceX, her desk was in front of his, allowing her to not only act as a praetorian guard – protecting him from unwelcome distractions – but also give guidance to workers on when was the best time to approach their mercurial boss. Anyone who has worked in a large, bureaucratic institution will recognise the importance of figures like MB: someone who knows where the paperclips are kept and where the bodies are buried. But their very unassuming nature and supportive role – the opposite of a selfish genius – makes them easy to underestimate.

And sure enough, in 2014 Musk dispensed with the services of Mary Beth Brown after twelve years. She had, according to Vance, asked to be paid a salary comparable to the executives of SpaceX. Instead, she was let go. (Musk claims this anecdote is 'total nonsense' and that the company's growth meant that he needed multiple specialist assistants. Vance stood by his reporting, saying it was 'well sourced'.)

To me, Brown sounds a little like a 'work wife', someone who juggled his diary and (presumably) snatched the video-game controller out of his hands when it was time to concentrate. By the time of the Twitter takeover, she had been replaced by Jehn Balajadia, whose title was operations co-ordinator for the Boring Company, but who 'was treated as a glorified assistant'.[11] During that turbulent time, she reportedly told Twitter executive Esther Crawford, another young woman, that 'Elon is special in this world. It is our job to protect him and make sure what he wants to have happen, happens. We need to protect the mission.'[12] Initially, Crawford agreed. She even posted a photograph of her in the San Francisco offices, napping in a sleeping bag – extremely hardcore. Later, though, she began to be reminded of the Christian cult in which she grew up in Oklahoma: 'But instead of a prophet, Balajadia had Musk.'*

Maybe this is something that everyone who is hailed as a genius manages to do – create their own secular cult. And that's why Elon Musk is so controversial, because you are either a believer or a heretic. Is Musk the man who defeated Detroit's fossil fuel addiction and smashed the stranglehold of bloated aerospace companies – a once-in-a-generation innovator who should be granted great latitude to do and say weird things? Or is Musk a narcissistic man-child who burns through staff and allies with unseemly haste, whose success was a fluke and whose triumphs depended on taxpayer cash anyway? Does a Musk need a Mary Beth Brown – where MB stands in for all of the rest of us? Should we all just get out of his way and let him do what the hell he wants, in return for a mission to Mars?

The cultural argument that Musk represents is that he can be an asshole as long as he's a visionary. 'When Musk sets unrealistic goals, verbally abuses employees, and works them to the bone, it's understood to be – on some level – part of the Mars agenda,' writes Vance.[13] 'Some employees love him for this. Others loathe him but remain oddly loyal out of respect for his drive and mission . . . Where Mark Zuckerberg wants to help you share

---

* Crawford was laid off three months after posting the photograph.

baby photos, Musk wants to . . . well . . . save the human race from self-imposed or accidental annihilation.'

In 2023, Walter Isaacson – the biographer of Albert Einstein and Leonardo da Vinci – published his biography of Elon Musk. Among other scoops, the book revealed that Musk and his then-partner Grimes had a previously unknown child, who was born to a surrogate. (The baby is called Techno Mechanicus, which probably ensures he will grow up to live a blameless life as a quantity surveyor and rename himself Steve.) That brought Musk's known children to twelve: six with his first wife, three with Grimes and three with an executive at one of his companies, Shivon Zilis. More have followed since. He regularly posts about how 'population collapse due to low birth rates is a much bigger risk to civilization than global warming' and he's certainly doing his bit to stave off the apocalypse – although he is a mere amateur compared with Telegram founder Pavel Durov, who claims to have fathered a hundred children through sperm donation.

At the same time, he has become obsessed with the 'woke mind virus', which he says caused one of his children to transition their gender. He blamed air crashes on underqualified minority candidates, posting: 'It will take an airplane crashing and killing hundreds of people for them to change this crazy policy of DIE',[14] a play on DEI, or diversity, equity and inclusion. (This from someone who was raised in apartheid South Africa, and should therefore have some insight into the structural barriers faced by minorities.) He appears to spend hours every day reading and passing on memes that a teenage boy would find unsophisticated. He is one of the clearest examples of how the mythology of genius – the sense of being a special sort of person – can warp someone's outlook. Racial differences, IQ, the importance of clever people having children . . . what an irony that the seductive power of the genius myth has led Elon Musk into the same intellectual space as Francis Galton.

Conclusion: An Idea That Won't Stay Dead

'I am, somehow, less interested in the weight and convolutions of Einstein's brain than in the near certainty that people of equal talent have lived and died in cotton fields and sweatshops.'

Stephen Jay Gould, *The Panda's Thumb*

For the Greeks and Romans, genius was something by which you were possessed; the animating spirit of art and science which acted through men. The Romantics saw the genius as a secular holy man, a cousin of the mad saints who lived up poles. The Victorians tried to boil down genius to a number, and add it to the great project of classifying the world. Today, we look for the roots of genius in ever more granular data, still refusing to accept its random, unpredictable nature. 'One way of thinking about these transformations in both science and genius is to regard them as aspects of the long-term secularisation of society,' writes Newton's biographer Patricia Fara.[1] 'Genius resembles sanctity, both words being impossible attempts to pin down an ineffable quality.' In other words, we used to have God. Now we have geniuses.

But there is simply no way to line up historical figures and assign value to them in a scientific fashion. Francis Galton tried to do it, and fell into the trap of assuming that the world was well-ordered and fair. His heirs tried something else: they invented the idea of 'IQ' and assumed that general intelligence explained why some people succeeded and others did not. The best of these researchers, like Lewis Terman, tried to find evidence for their assumption – and came away humbled.

At its worst, IQ was a false god, and a self-fulfilling prophecy. For Hans Eysenck, the study of genius made him into a niche kind of celebrity. He was what a clever person looked like – maybe even, he might have thought to himself with one of his characteristic exclamation marks, a little bit of a genius! His wife certainly thought so. His students seemed to think so. And a genius can't be expected to play by the rules which apply to other people. Yet the proof that high intelligence is not the same as genius – and that it can be experienced as a curse – comes from the high IQ societies, with their oddball officers and petty squabbles. Perhaps the founders of Mensa and other clubs show us something else, too: *why* the mythology of genius came about in the first place. Society must have a mechanism for allowing the weird to prosper, because those strange people might have insights or talents that are also out of the ordinary. We need, too, a mechanism for dealing with envy – and the idea of a separate class of geniuses is helpful here. (We are all Gauss' classmates, unable to complete the maths problem that seems so obvious to a superior brain.) And we need to reconcile ourselves to monstrosity and selfishness, when they come hand in hand with incredible achievements.

Maybe there is even a sneaking admiration for the genius – the person who gets away with it. Look at Picasso, described as a 'cannibal' and a 'vampire' by those close to him. We shouldn't see his selfishness in opposition to his genius – but as something that fed its mythology. He was a pure id, an aspirational ideal to lower-status men trapped in bourgeois domesticity and wage slavery. His unexpected analogue is perhaps Donald Trump, a figure who seemed to his supporters to be able to do whatever he wanted.

CONCLUSION: AN IDEA THAT WON'T STAY DEAD

This is a powerful dream for all kinds of people. In 'The Life with a Hole in It', Philip Larkin's narrator imagines his perfect life, as 'the shit in the shuttered chateau / Who does his five hundred words / Then parts out the rest of the day / Between bathing and booze and birds'.

Picasso isn't revered in spite of his selfishness and arrogance, his destruction of the lives around him, his childlike insistence on being the centre of attention, his teenage lust and his adult neediness. He is revered *because of them*. He made himself the sun around which everyone else had to orbit. What a fantasy. What freedom. Who wouldn't dream of that from their dead-end job and their nagging life of personal responsibility? He is a phoenix – beautiful, as long as you don't stand too close to the flame.

Some people are so monstrously indulged that their demands scorch everything around them. Others are given so little support that the flame of their talent is extinguished. It is depressing to contemplate the limitless talents we have wasted by excluding certain categories of people from 'greatness' – whether legally, in the form of marriage bars or racial segregation, or culturally, as we award the label of *genius* according to predetermined ideas of intellect and talent. 'You must admit that the genesis of a great man depends on the long series of complex influences which has produced the race in which he appears, and the social state into which that race has slowly grown,' wrote Herbert Spencer in 1873.[2] 'Before he can remake his society, his society must make him.'

Spencer was writing in response to the Victorian essayist Thomas Carlyle's argument for what we now call Great Man theory – although Carlyle himself described his proposed academic discipline as hero worship.[3]

Today, no historian would describe their work like this – most would prefer to emphasise social and material conditions over the actions of individuals. Nonetheless, Great Man theory – genius studies by another name – is an idea that will not die, because it produces much more exciting stories than any other approach, with protagonists and antagonists, moments of revelation, high-stakes decisions and emotional investment. In the Renaissance, Giorgio Vasari found that his audience loved gossip more than high-minded arts criticism. Biopics continue to be safe bets for Oscar nominations even now. And while science has never been more collaborative – think of CERN, or the race to find a coronavirus vaccine – the relevant Nobel Prizes are still limited to three recipients each. The stories we understand have protagonists, even though modern science relies on teams.

We also have artificial intelligence. The enormous strides forward made by large language models and image generators mean that one type of genius ought to be under particular threat: the artist. Thanks to AI, it has never been easier to be creative. If you want a portrait of yourself in the style of van Gogh, a song about cheese in the voice of Bob Dylan, or even a poem summarising the contents of this book in the meter of a Petrarchan sonnet – that's all available, about three clicks away. But AI in its current form suffers from a debilitating lack of originality. It is a prediction machine, working out from all the examples in its database what word or pixel should belong next to the one before. Many of the greatest works of genius, meanwhile, are unpredictable – wholly original; profoundly wrong according to the previous rules of the genre. Even if a computer could accomplish a paradigm shift, I have a hunch that we wouldn't care: without a mind behind it, we would find the breakthrough somehow meaningless. The critic James Baldwin described reading literature as experiencing a connection with another consciousness across space and time. 'Art has to be a kind of

CONCLUSION: AN IDEA THAT WON'T STAY DEAD

confession,' he told an interviewer in 1961.[4] 'The effort it seems to me, is: if you can examine and face your life, you can discover the terms with which you are connected to other lives, and they can discover them, too – the terms with which they are connected to other people. This has happened to every one of us, I'm sure. You read something which you thought only happened to you, and you discovered it happened 100 years ago to Dostoevsky.' Substitute ChatGPT for Dostoevsky and the magic is gone. We need myths, and myths need people.

Where does genius go now? Honestly, I am surprised the concept has been so durable, given that we live in a time when the private lives (and opinions) of the talented and famous are so accessible to us. (Every time I express admiration for someone online, I fear an onlooker popping up, like Clippy the Microsoft Office assistant, to ask if I'm aware of their shortcomings.) We have moved from hero worship to impossible standards.

Despite this, the myths of genius stagger on: the lone rebel, the brilliant asshole, the child prodigy, the great man. Yuval Noah Harari's insights into humanity are boosted by tales of his silent retreats and vegan diet. We love a sporting rivalry, pitting two greats against each other – Chris Evert and Martina Navratilova, or Joe Frazier and Muhammad Ali. (One last apology for the lack of sports in this book.) We use Taylor Swift to argue about female empowerment and 'childless cat ladies'. We want our lives to have a mythic dimension.

So after all this, you might be wondering: should anyone be called a genius? I'll tell you what I think – it doesn't matter what I think. We *need* the idea of genius – the demigod, the superhero, the shaman. We need stories to make sense of the world. But I wish that we would move back to the ancient idea of genius, something that is found in particular actions, or specific works.

To me, it makes more sense to call, say, a particular painting *genius* than pin the label on the person who created it. The invention of the transistor was a moment of genius. William Shockley was not. *War and Peace* is an act of genius. Lev Tolstoy was a demanding aristocrat who went very peculiar indeed.

Talking like that moves us away from the idea of a special class of people – an idea that has poisoned too many of those who believed it. But it acknowledges that we will always yearn for the transcendent, the extraordinary, the feathers of the phoenix. We can find that instead in moments of alchemy, brief and serendipitous collisions, the beautiful texture of interwoven lives. We should not be opposed to celebrating talent, or ambition, or achievement. But we should be humble about where those qualities can be found, and whether they are always properly recognised. There are many seeds of genius in the world. We must nurture as many as we can.

Acknowledgements

In some ways, *The Genius Myth* is a continuation of my first book, *Difficult Women*, which argued that feminist revolutionaries were often ornery and obsessive. Well-behaved women don't make history, and self-deprecating normies don't get called geniuses. I knew from the start this was a risky project to take on – basically a history of Western thought, capering across science and the arts, attempting to distil centuries of research into readable prose. I would like to thank Andrew Gordon at David Higham for trusting that I could tackle it, and my editor at Vintage, Bea Hemming, for investing in it (and me). Thank you to my agent Sarah Chalfant and to Emma Smith for their advice, skill and moral support. Huge thanks must also go to the staff at the London Library, which offered a blessed relief from my own company, and to Gladstone's Library in Wales. The team at Penguin have been a delight to work with: thanks to copy editor James Nightingale for fastidiously changing all my double quotation marks to singles (and picking up all kinds of other horrors); Alison Davies on publicity for stopping me saying 'Yes' too much; Mairéad Zielinski on marketing; and Louise Navarro-Cann on editorial support. Thanks also to Peter McNamara and Ross Anderson for fact-checking the knottier sections. For Thesis in the US, I'm grateful to Niki Papadopoulos for seeing this book's potential and taking a chance on it and to Leila Sandlin for guiding me expertly through the production process. Working for

ACKNOWLEDGEMENTS

The Atlantic has also made me a better writer; thank you to El Jefe, Jeffrey Goldberg, and my editor Dante Ramos in particular.

I'm not sure if there's a version of *scenius* for jobbing hacks, but I've been very lucky to have so many brilliant friends and acquaintances to call on when I needed specialist advice. Adam Rutherford, whose own outstanding book *Control* deals with the history of eugenics, was a cheering presence; who else could I talk to about Francis Galton? Stuart Ritchie kindly helped me understand some of the key bits of intelligence research. Chris Morris explained Prince's musical magic and told me about Galton's cake trick. Cordelia Fine sent me useful links on sex differences and intelligence. Chris Kavanagh was a sounding board on the subject of charismatic charlatans. Craig Brown not only talked to me about the Beatles, but offered me an excellent lunch at his house in Aldeburgh (though I was sad not to play him at ping-pong; apparently, he's a demon). Janice Turner let me stay in her house by the seaside at a particularly low point; Laura McInerney's energising hatred of productivity gurus was a regular delight. Ian Leslie's work on influence and creativity, and his love of the Beatles, unlocked so many doors for me; as did Henry Oliver's writing on late bloomers. Richard Morris and Gwyn Davies, the producers of my BBC series *Great Wives*, pushed me to look at Sofia Tolstaya and a host of other women who lived with the dark side of genius; I've borrowed from those scripts for the chapter. The intellectual salon no longer exists, so instead Gia, Tracy, Caroline, Becca, Hadley, Janice and Sarah gave me constant support and inspiration on its replacement, WhatsApp.

I would also like to thank all my interviewees, particularly those who shared personal memories of Chris Goode, speaking honestly and empathetically about a difficult period in their lives. The fundamental decency shown by Simon Stephens will always

ACKNOWLEDGEMENTS

stay with me. Jack Barth was generous with his time talking about an incident I'm sure he would rather forget. So many authors have already mapped out the terrain I have covered, and I owe them all a huge debt: this entire book stands on the shoulders of giants. And a couple of frauds.

Robert Icke pushed me to pick this topic, out of all the topics in the world, and Alex Garland argued with me about the status of Jane Austen. Watching both of them work has opened my eyes to the collision of creativity, commerce and sheer luck involved in making great art. The book is dedicated to them.

Finally, to the one person who makes everything possible: Jonathan. I promise I won't write another book. Unless I have a really, really good idea. No! I promise. Probably.

References

INTRODUCTION

1. Sam Harris, 'The Trouble with Elon', *Sam Harris* (Substack), 15 January 2025.
2. Charlotte Klein, 'Walter Isaacson: Elon Musk Is a Genius When It Comes to Engineering, Not Human Emotion', *Vanity Fair*, 19 December 2023, https://www.vanityfair.com/news/elon-musk-walter-isaacson-human-emotion
3. Wallace E. Williams and Douglas Emory Wilson (eds.), *Collected Works of Ralph Waldo Emerson*, vol. IV (Belknap Press, Cambridge, Mass., 1987).

AVONIAN WILLY

1. Ian Hamilton, *Keepers of the Flame: Literary Estates and the Rise of Biography* (Hutchinson, London, 1992), p. 20.
2. Ibid., p. 21.
3. Andrew McConnell Stott, *What Blest Genius? The Jubilee That Made Shakespeare* (W. W. Norton, London, 2019), p. 130.
4. Quoted by McConnell Stott, p. 181.
5. Marina Picasso, *Picasso: My Grandfather* (Chatto & Windus, London, 2001), p. 121.
6. Tim Berners-Lee, interviewed in 2007. Retrieved from https://achievement.org/achiever/sir-timothy-berners-lee/#interview

REFERENCES

SECULAR SAINTS

1. Ingrid Rowland and Noah Charney, *Collector of Lives: Giorgio Vasari and the Invention of Art* (W. W. Norton, New York, 2017).
2. Giorgio Vasari, *The Lives of the Most Excellent Painters, Sculptors, and Architects*, vol. I. This modern translation was based on the second edition (Everyman's Library, Dutton, New York, 1983), p. 280.
3. Vasari, vol. IV, p. 110. This edition spells his name 'Michelagnolo', which I have changed for consistency.
4. Ibid., p. 126.
5. Vasari, vol. II, p. 156.
6. Ibid., p. 159.
7. Ibid., p. 167.
8. Brian Hayes, 'Gauss's Day of Reckoning', *American Scientist*, May–June 2006, https://www.americanscientist.org/article/gausss-day-of-reckoning
9. Eric Bell, *Men of Mathematics: The Lives and Achievements of the Great Mathematicians from Zeno to Poincaré* (Simon & Schuster, New York, 1937).
10. Darrin McMahon, *Divine Fury: A History of Genius* (Basic Books, New York, 2013), p. 77.
11. Rebecca Solnit, 'Mysteries of Thoreau, Unsolved', *Orion*, June 2013. Reprinted here: https://www.dreamythology.com/uploads/1/7/2/1/17214690/mysteries-thoreau-unsolved.pdf
12. Laura Dassow Walls, *Henry David Thoreau: A Life* (Chicago University Press, Chicago, 2017), p. 195.
13. Kay Redfield Jamison, *Touched with Fire: Manic Depressive Illness and the Artistic Temperament* (Free Press, New York, 1996).
14. Susan Sontag, *Illness As Metaphor* (Allen Lane, London, 1979), p. 13.
15. Christine Battersby, *Gender and Genius: Towards a Feminist Aesthetics* (The Women's Press, London, 1989), p. 3.

REFERENCES

GALTON'S GOOD BREEDING

1. Quoted in Michael Bulmer, *Francis Galton: Pioneer of Heredity and Biometry* (Johns Hopkins University Press, Baltimore, 2003), p. 4.
2. Charles Darwin's letter to his sister Catherine, dated 22 May 1833. Available at https://www.darwinproject.ac.uk/letter?docId=letters/DCP-LETT-206.xml
3. Oliver Sacks, 'An Anthropologist on Mars', *New Yorker*, 27 December 1993.
4. Francis Galton, 'Co-relations and Their Measurement, Chiefly from Anthropometric Data', *Proceedings of the Royal Society of London*, vol. 45 (1888), pp. 135–145.
5. Lyndsay Andrew Farall, *The Origins and Growth of the English Eugenics Movement, 1965–1925* (Garland, New York, 1985), pp. 23–24.
6. Nicholas Wright Gillham, *A Life of Sir Francis Galton* (Oxford University Press, Oxford, 2001), p. 353.

TERMAN'S TERMITES

1. James Flynn, interview with *The Guardian*, 2007, https://www.theguardian.com/technology/2012/sep/23/james-flynn-iq-scores-environment
2. Lewis Terman, *Autobiography of Lewis M. Terman*, first published in Carl Murchison (ed.), *History of Psychology in Autobiography* (Clark University Press, Worcester, 1930). Retrieved at psychclassics.yorku.ca/Terman/murchison.htm
3. 'A Dangerous Man: Lewis Terman and George Stoddard, Their Debates on Intelligence Testing and the Legacy of the Iowa Child Welfare Station,' *Annals of Iowa*, vol. 72, no. 1 (Winter 2013).
4. Lewis Terman, *Genetic Studies of Genius*, vol. I (Stanford University Press, Redwood City, 1926), p. 249.

5. Lewis M. Terman and Melita H. Oden, *The Gifted Child Grows Up*, vol. IV of *Genetic Studies of Genius* (Stanford University Press, Stanford, 1947), p. 370.
6. Joel N. Shurkin, *Terman's Kids: The Groundbreaking Study of How the Gifted Grow Up* (Little Brown, Boston, 1992).
7. Terman, in a speech to Sigma Xi at Stanford, 1941. Quoted in Shurkin, p. 69.
8. Shurkin, p. 139.

CYRIL AND HANS: TWIN FLAMES

1. Quoted from Leslie Hearnshaw, *Cyril Burt: Psychologist* (Hodder & Stoughton, London, 1979), p. 235.
2. Ibid, p. 17.
3. Victor Serebriakoff, *IQ: A Mensa Analysis and History* (Hutchinson, London, 1966), p. 11.
4. Quoted in Hearnshaw, p. 152.
5. Arthur Jensen, in Neil Mackintosh (ed.), *Cyril Burt: Fraud or Framed?* (Oxford University Press, Oxford, 1995), p. 102.
6. Hearnshaw, p. 148.
7. From the foreword to Serebriakoff, p. 15.
8. Hans Eysenck, in Mackintosh, p. 126.
9. Hans J. Eysenck, *Genius: The Natural History of Creativity* (Cambridge University Press, Cambridge, 1995), p. 155.
10. Ibid., p. 127.
11. Anthony J. Pelosi and Louis Appleby, 'Psychological Influences on Cancer and Ischaemic Heart Disease', *British Medical Journal*, vol. 304 (1992), pp. 1295–1298. Anthony J. Pelosi and Louis Appleby, 'Personality and Fatal Diseases', *British Medical Journal*, vol. 304 (1993), p. 1295.
12. Anthony J. Pelosi, 'Personality and Fatal Diseases: Revisiting a Scientific Scandal', *Journal of Health Psychology* (2019).

13. As recorded on Google Scholar, accessed at https://scholar.google.com/scholar?hl=en&q=A+revised+version+of+the+psychoticism+scale&btnG=&as_sdt=1%2C5
14. Roderick D. Buchanan, *Playing with Fire: The Controversial Career of Hans Eysenck* (Oxford University Press, Oxford, 2010), p. 324.
15. Philip Corr, 'In Defence of the Twitter Pariah', *Times Higher Education*, 31 March 2016, https://www.timeshighereducation.com/features/in-defence-of-the-twitter-pariah
16. Retrieved from https://www.grossarth-maticek.de/information-fu%cc%88r-frau-buss-und-byrne-kings-college-london

WILLIAM SHOCKLEY AND THE GENIUS SPERM BANK

1. Joel N. Shurkin, *Broken Genius: The Rise and Fall of William Shockley, Creator of the Electronic Age* (Macmillan, London, 2006), p. 13.
2. Edward Boyer, 'Controversial Nobel Laureate Shockley Dies', *Los Angeles Times*, 14 August 1989. Retrieved from https://www.latimes.com/archives/la-xpm-1989-08-14-mn-369-story.html
3. Paul Graham, 'Taste for Makers', 2002, https://paulgraham.com/taste.html
4. Shurkin, pp. 16–17.
5. Frederick Seitz, *On the Frontier* (American Institute of Physics, New York, 1994). Quoted by Shurkin.
6. Quoted by Shurkin.
7. Kathryn Paige Harden, 'Some Personal Reflections on the Genetics of Intelligence', 16 January 2018, now available at https://kph3k.medium.com/some-personal-reflections-on-the-genetics-of-intelligence-9be61458a9f3
8. Quoted by Shurkin. The full interview is by Syl Jones, 'Playboy Interview: William Shockley', *Playboy*, August 1980, pp. 69–102,

REFERENCES

https://www.playboy.com/magazine/articles/1980/08/playboy-interview-william-shockley

9. Sam Friedman and Aaron Reeves, *Born to Rule: The Making and Remaking of the British Elite* (Harvard University Press, Cambridge, 2024). Quoted here from their Substack post 'Common People', at https://samf.substack.com/p/common-people
10. David Plotz, *The Genius Factory: The Curious History of the Nobel Prize Sperm Bank* (Random House, New York, 2005), p. 36.
11. Quoted in Plotz, p. 97.
12. 'Sperm Bank's First Mother Once Served Time For Fraud', *New York Times*, 14 July 1982.

MARILYN AND ME

1. 'Love Stories We Love', *Parade*, 6 February 2015, https://parade.com/373247/parade/love-stories-we-love
2. Ellen Wulfhorst, 'Artificial Heart Inventor, IQ Genius Wed', UPI, 24 August 1987, https://www.upi.com/Archives/1987/08/24/Artificial-heart-inventor-IQ-genius-wed/1810556776000/
3. Mega Society Judgment, March 2003, https://megasociety.org/judgment.html
4. Christopher Langan, Facebook, posted on 27 February 2019, www.facebook.com/groups/ctmurealitytheory/permalink/10156990902072486
5. Irene Gardner Keeney, 'Troy Man Has a Lot on His Mind', *Albany Times Union*, 26 June 1988, https://www.timesunion.com/7dayarchive/article/Troy-man-has-a-lot-on-his-mind-15640272.php
6. Darryl Miyaguchi, 'A Short (and Bloody) History of the High I.Q. Societies', last updated 19 January 2000, http://miyaguchi.4sigma.org/BloodyHistory/history.html#Mega
7. Grady M. Towers, 'The Outsiders', last updated 24 September 2012,

archived at https://web.archive.org/web/20121005072129/http://prometheussociety.org/cms/articles/the-outsiders

8. Quoted in Justin Ward, 'More Smarter', *Baffler*, 2019, https://thebaffler.com/latest/more-smarter-ward

SO YOU WANT TO BE A GENIUS?

1. Sarah Lyall, 'They Can't Get Enough of "The West Wing" Right Now', *New York Times*, 29 December 2019, https://www.nytimes.com/2019/12/29/us/politics/west-wing-politics.html
2. E. T. Bell, *Men of Mathematics* (Victor Gollancz, London, 1937), p. 29.
3. Thomas Kuhn, *The Structure of Scientific Revolutions* (University of Chicago Press, Chicago, 1968), p. 2.
4. William F. Ogburn and Dorothy Thomas, 'Are Inventions Inevitable? A Note on Social Evolution', *Political Science Quarterly*, vol. 37, no. 1 (March 1922), pp. 83–89.
5. Arthur I. Miller, *Einstein, Picasso: Space, Time, and the Beauty That Causes Havoc* (Basic Books, New York, 2001).
6. Robert K. Merton, 'The Matthew Effect in Science', *Science*, vol. 159 (January 1968).
7. Harriet Zuckerman, 'Nobel Laureates in Science: Patterns of Productivity, Collaboration, and Authorship', *American Sociological Review*, vol. 32, no. 3 (June 1967), pp. 391–403.
8. Arthur Koestler, *The Act of Creation* (Macmillan, New York, 1964), p. 705.
9. Isaiah Berlin, 'The Hedgehog and the Fox' (Weidenfeld & Nicolson, London, 1953).
10. Manny Farber, 'White Elephant Art vs Termite Art', *Film Culture*, no. 27 (Winter 1962–1963).
11. René Dubos, *Louis Pasteur: Free Lance of Science* (Scribner, New York, 1950).

REFERENCES

THE REBEL

1. Heather Heying, 'What If We're Wrong?', *Areo*, 19 May 2021, originally published at https://www. areomagazine.com/2021/05/19/what-if-were-wrong
2. Jack M. Lawrence et al., 'The Lesson of Ivermectin: Meta-analyses Based on Summary Data Alone Are Inherently Inreliable', *Nature*, vol. 27 (2021), pp. 1853–1854, https://www.nature.com/articles/s41591-021-01535-y
3. 'Uniforms and Workwear: Guidance for NHS Employers', NHS, 2 April 2020, https://www.england.nhs.uk/wp-content/uploads/2020/04/Uniforms-and-Workwear-Guidance-2-April-2020.pdf
4. Josh Glancy, 'Mark Rylance: My Evening with the Quack-Loving, but Delightful Moonbat', *Sunday Times*, 23 June 2024.
5. Sue Roe, *The Private Lives of the Impressionists* (Vintage, London, 2007), pp. 127–129.
6. As translated by Mario Livio, 'Did Galileo Truly Say "And Yet It Moves"? A Modern Detective Story', *Scientific American*, 6 May 2020.
7. David Wootton, *Galileo: Watcher of the Skies* (Yale University Press, New Haven, 2010), p. 190.
8. Freeman Dyson, *The Scientist as Rebel* (New York Review of Books, New York, 2006).
9. Quoted in Nicholas Dawidoff, 'The Civil Heretic', *New York Times*, 25 March 2009.

MONSTERS AND TORTURED ARTISTS

1. Xavier de Sousa, 'Silence Is Not an Option', *Deliq.*, 7 October 2022, https://statesofdeliquescence.blogspot.com/2022/10/silence-is-not-option.html
2. David Levesley, 'Ponyboy Curtis: How a Cult Theatre Director Disguised Abuse as Art', *Face*, 13 October 2022, https://theface.com/society/

REFERENCES

ponyboy-curtis-how-a-cult-theatre-director-disguised-abuse-as-art-chris-goode
3. Megan Vaughan, *Synonyms for Churlish*, 19 May 2015, https://synonymsforchurlish.tumblr.com/post/119361897188/in-what-distant-deeps-or-skies-burnt-the-fire
4. Lucy Ellinson, 'Act on Concerns', *Deliq.*, 7 October 2022, https://statesofdeliquescence.blogspot.com/2022/10/act-on-concerns.html
5. Claire Dederer, 'What Do We Do With the Art of Monstrous Men?' *Paris Review*, 20 November 2017.
6. Roger Ebert, 'Tess', *RogerEbert.com*, 1 January 1980, https://www.rogerebert.com/reviews/tess-1980
7. Hadley Freeman, 'What Does Hollywood's Reverence for Child Rapist Roman Polanski Tell Us?' *Guardian*, 30 January 2018, https://www.theguardian.com/film/2018/jan/30/hollywood-reverence-child-rapist-roman-polanski-convicted-40-years-on-run
8. Published on synonymsforchurlish.com, 11 March 2018. The site has since been deleted, but the original text is aggregated here: https://www.tumgik.com/insecttribe-blog
9. Paul Paschal, 'On Working With, and After, Chris Goode', *Deliq.*, 7 October 2022, https://statesofdeliquescence.blogspot.com/2022/10/on-working-with-and-after-chris-goode.html

GREAT WIVES

1. Translation by Cathy Porter, in Porter (ed.), *The Diaries of Sofia Tolstoy* (Alma Books, London, 2017). I have used Sofia's formal name – her family would have called her 'Sonya' – and the feminine form of 'Tolstoy' to distinguish her from her husband.
2. A. N. Wilson, *Tolstoy* (Hamish Hamilton, 1988; updated edition, Atlantic Books, 2015).
3. Alexandra Popoff, *Sophia Tolstoy: A Biography* (Free Press, New York, 2010), p. 44.

REFERENCES

4. Ibid., p. 85.
5. James Meek, 'Rereading Anna Karenina', *Guardian*, 31 August 2012.
6. Sofia Tolstoy, *My Life*, trans. Alexandra Popoff, and quoted in her biography of Tolstaya.
7. Alexandra Popoff, *Tolstoy's False Disciple* (Pegasus, New York, 2014), p. xviii.
8. Jennifer Schaffer, 'The Wife Glitch', *Baffler*, April 2020, https://thebaffler.com/outbursts/the-wife-glitch-schaffer
9. Gertrude Stein, 'The Autobiography of Alice B. Toklas', *Atlantic*, May 1933, https://www.theatlantic.com/magazine/archive/1933/05/autobiography-of-alice-b-toklas-i/650491
10. Holsinger discussed his search on the podcast of the *Sociological Review*, available here: thesociologicalreview.org/podcasts/thanks-for-typing/thanks-to-my-wife-gender-and-politics-in-the-academy

KEEPERS OF THE FLAME

1. Sarah Boxer, 'The Last Irascible', *New York Review of Books*, 23 December 2010.
2. Andrea Gabor, *Einstein's Wife: Work and Marriage in The Lives of Five Great Twentieth-Century Women* (Penguin, London, 1996), p. 42.
3. Quoted by Gabor.
4. Ian Hamilton, *Keepers of the Flame* (Hutchinson, London, 1992).
5. Evelyn Toynton, *Jackson Pollock* (Yale University Press, New Haven, 2012), p. 105.
6. Ibid., p. 107.
7. Hans Luijten, *Jo van Gogh-Bonger: The Woman Who Made Vincent Famous*, trans. Lynne Richards (Bloomsbury, London, 2023), p. 3.
8. Russell Shorto, 'The Woman Who Made Van Gogh', *New York Times Magazine*, 14 April 2021.
9. Toynton, p. 115.

REFERENCES

A COVER VERSION

1. Vince Mancini, 'How One "Yesterday" Screenwriter's Dream Became Something of a Nightmare', *Uproxx*, 21 May 2020, https://www.uproxx.com/movies/jack-barth-interview-yesterday-writer-richard-curtis
2. Ibid.

ALCHEMY

1. Craig Brown, *One Two Three Four: The Beatles in Time* (Fourth Estate, London, 2020).
2. Ibid., p. 9.
3. Dean Keith Simonton, *Greatness: Who Makes History and Why* (Guilford, New York, 1994), p. 183.
4. David Galenson, *Old Masters and Young Geniuses: The Two Life Cycles of Artistic Creativity* (Princeton University Press, Princeton, 2006).
5. F. Scott Fitzgerald, *The Crack-Up* (1945). Quoted in Galenson, p. 165.
6. Simonton, p. 213.
7. Ian Leslie, '64 Reasons to Celebrate Paul McCartney', *Ruffian*, 8 December 2020, https://ianleslie.substack.com/p/64-reasons-to-celebrate-paul-mccartney

THE DEFICIT MODEL

1. William Kohler, 'How the Biopic Became the New Must-have IP for Film Studies', *Little White Lies*, 20 February 2023, https://lwlies.com/articles/how-the-biopic-became-the-new-must-have-ip-for-film-studios
2. Denis Leary, 'More Drugs', from the album *No Cure for Cancer* (1992).
3. Frank Wilczek, 'Revisiting the Unusual Celebrity of Stephen Hawking', *New York Times*, 18 April 2021, https://www.nytimes.com/2021/04/18/books/review/hawking-hawking-charles-seife.html

REFERENCES

4. Lisa W. Foderaro, 'A Voyage to Bedlam and Part the Way Back', *New York Times*, 9 November 1995.
5. Jonathan Rosen, 'American Madness', *Atlantic*, 11 April 2023, https://www.theatlantic.com/magazine/archive/2023/05/american-madness-schizophrenia-mental-illness/673490
6. Howard Chua-Boan, 'A Precarious Genius', *Time*, 29 June 1998, https://time.com/archive/6733023/a-precarious-genius
7. Rosen.

DISRUPTERS

1. Evan Osnos, 'Doomsday Prep for the Super Rich', *New Yorker*, 22 January 2017.
2. Tad Friend, 'Sam Altman's Manifest Destiny', *New Yorker*, 3 October 2016.
3. Adam Fisher, *Valley of Genius: The Uncensored History of Silicon Valley* (Hachette, New York, 2018), p. 12.
4. Walter Isaacson, *Elon Musk* (Simon & Schuster, London, 2023), p. 7.
5. Kara Swisher, *Burn Book: A Tech Love Story* (Piatkus, London, 2024), p. 2.

THOMAS EDISON: THE LIGHTBULB MOMENT

1. Randall E. Stross, *The Wizard of Menlo Park: How Thomas Alva Edison Invented the Modern World* (Crown, New York, 2007), p. 29.
2. Wyn Wachhorst, *Thomas Alva Edison: An American Myth* (MIT, Cambridge, 1981), p. 13.
3. Wachhorst, p. 98.
4. Stross, p. 97.
5. Ibid., p. 106.
6. See David Bodanis, *Einstein's Greatest Mistake: The Life of a Flawed Genius* (Little Brown, London, 2016).

7. Wachhorst, p. 90.
8. Cited by Wachhorst, p. 180.
9. Ibid., p. 209.

ELON MUSK: EXTREMELY HARDCORE

1. Kate Conger and Ryan Mac, *Character Limit: How Elon Musk Destroyed Twitter* (Cornerstone Press, London, 2024), p. 324.
2. Ashlee Vance, *Elon Musk: How the Billionaire CEO of SpaceX and Tesla Is Shaping Our Future* (Virgin Books, London, 2015), p. 62.
3. Justine Musk, 'I Was a Starter Wife', *Marie Claire*, 10 September 2010, https://www.marieclaire.com/sex-love/a5380/millionaire-starter-wife
4. Steve Silberman, 'The Geek Syndrome', *Wired*, December 2001.
5. Silberman later expanded his work in *Neurotribes: The Legacy of Autism and How to Think Smarter About People Who Think Differently* (Allen & Unwin, London, 2015).
6. Yonatan Zunger, 'So, About This Googler's Manifesto,' *Medium*, 6 August 2017, https://medium.com/@yonatanzunger/so-about-this-googlers-manifesto-1e3773ed1788
7. Manvir Singh, 'Modern Shamans', *Conversation*, 2 May 2019, https://theconversation.com/modern-shamans-financial-managers-political-pundits-and-others-who-help-tame-lifes-uncertainty-113302
8. Charlie Warzel, 'Elon Musk's Texts Shatter the Myth of the Tech Genius,' *Atlantic*, https://www.theatlantic.com/technology/archive/2022/09/elon-musk-texts-twitter-trial-jack-dorsey/671619
9. Paul Graham (@paulg), Twitter (now X), posted 9 April 2023, https://twitter.com/paulg/status/1645107536616357888?s=20
10. Vance, p. 119.
11. Conger and Mac, p. 314.
12. Ibid.

13. Vance, p. 17.
14. Elon Musk (@elonmusk), X, posted 9 January 2024, https://x.com/elonmusk/status/1744821656990675184

CONCLUSION: AN IDEA THAT WON'T STAY DEAD

1. Patricia Fara, *Newton: The Making of a Genius* (Macmillan, London, 2002), p. 16.
2. Herbert Spencer, *The Study of Sociology* (Henry S. King & Co, London, 1873), p. 35.
3. Thomas Carlyle, *On Heroes, Hero-Worship, and the Heroic in History* (London, 1840). Found at https://www.gutenberg.org/files/1091/1091-h/1091-h.htm
4. James Baldwin, radio interview with Studs Terkel, 1961. Available at https://studsterkel.wfmt.com/programs/james-baldwin-discusses-his-book-nobody-knows-my-name-more-notes-native-son

Sources and Further Reading

BOOKS

Battersby, Christine, *Gender and Genius: Towards a Feminist Aesthetics* (The Women's Press, London, 1989)

Bell, E. T., *Men of Mathematics* (Victor Gollancz, London, 1937)

Berlin, Isaiah, *The Hedgehog and the Fox* (Weidenfeld & Nicolson, London, 1953)

Bodanis, David, *Einstein's Greatest Mistake: The Life of a Flawed Genius* (Little Brown, London, 2016)

Brown, Craig, *One Two Three Four: The Beatles in Time* (Fourth Estate, London, 2020)

Buchanan, Roderick D., *Playing with Fire: The Controversial Career of Hans Eysenck* (Oxford University Press, Oxford, 2010)

Bulmer, Michael, *Francis Galton: Pioneer of Heredity and Biometry* (Johns Hopkins University Press, Baltimore, 2003)

Claridge, Gordon et al., *Sounds From the Bell Jar: Ten Psychotic Authors* (Malor Books, San Jose, 2021)

Conger, Kate and Ryan Mac, *Character Limit: How Elon Musk Destroyed Twitter* (Cornerstone Press, London, 2024)

Drake, Stillman, *Galileo: Pioneer Scientist* (University of Toronto Press, Toronto, 1990)

Dubos, René, *Louis Pasteur: Free Lance of Science* (Scribner, New York, 1950)

Dyson, Freeman, *The Scientist as Rebel* (New York Review of Books, New York, 2006)

Ellis, Havelock, *Man and Woman: A Study of Human Secondary Sexual Characters* (Walter Scott, London, 1894)

Epstein, David, *Range: How Generalists Triumph in a Specialised World* (Macmillan, London, 2019)

Eysenck, Hans J., *Genius: The Natural History of Creativity* (Cambridge University Press, Cambridge, 1995)

Fara, Patricia, *Newton: The Making of a Genius* (Macmillan, London, 2002)

Farral, Lyndsay Andrew, *The Origins and Growth of the English Eugenics Movement, 1865–1925* (Garland, New York, 1985)

Fisher, Adam, *Valley of Genius: The Uncensored History of Silicon Valley* (Hachette, New York, 2018)

Forrest, Derek, *Francis Galton: The Life and Work of a Victorian Genius* (HarperCollins, London, 1974)

Friedman, Sam and Aaron Reeves, *Born to Rule: The Making and Remaking of the British Elite* (Harvard University Press, Cambridge, 2024)

Gabor, Andrea, *Einstein's Wife: Work and Marriage in the Lives of Five Great Twentieth-Century Women* (Penguin, London, 1996)

Galenson, David, *Old Masters and Young Geniuses: The Two Life Cycles of Artistic Creativity* (Princeton University Press, Princeton, 2006)

Galton, Francis, *Memories of My Life* (Methuen, London, 1908)

Gessen, Masha, *Perfect Rigour: A Genius and the Mathematical Breakthrough of the Century* (Icon Books, London, 2011)

Goldman, William, *Adventures in the Screen Trade* (Grand Central Publishing, New York, 2012)

Goldsmith, Barbara, *Obsessive Genius: The Inner World of Marie Curie* (W. W. Norton, New York, 2006)

Gould, Stephen Jay, *The Mismeasure of Man* (Penguin, London, 1981)

Greer, Germaine, *The Obstacle Race* (Farrar, Straus & Giroux, New York, 1979)

Hamilton, Ian, *Keepers of the Flame: Literary Estates and the Rise of Biography* (Hutchinson, London, 1992)

Hearnshaw, Leslie, *Cyril Burt: Psychologist* (Hodder & Stoughton, London, 1979)

Isaacson, Walter, *Elon Musk* (Simon & Schuster, London, 2023)

Jamison, Kay Redfield, *Touched with Fire: Manic-Depressive Illness and the Artistic Temperament* (Free Press, New York, 1996); *An Unquiet Mind: A Memoir of Moods and Madness* (Vintage, London, 1997)

Kanigel, Robert, *The Man Who Knew Infinity: A Life of the Genius Ramanujan* (C. Scribner's, New York, 1991)

Kaufman, Scott Barry (ed.), *The Complexity of Greatness: Beyond Talent or Practice* (Oxford University Press, Oxford, 2013)

Keynes, Milo (ed.), *Sir Francis Galton, FRS: The Legacy of His Ideas* (Macmillan, London, 1993)

Koestler, Arthur, *The Act of Creation* (Macmillan, New York, 1964)

Kuhn, Thomas, *The Structure of Scientific Revolutions* (University of Chicago Press, Chicago, 1968)

Luijten, Hans, *Jo van Gogh-Bonger: The Woman Who Made Vincent Famous*, trans. Lynne Richards (Bloomsbury, London, 2023)

Mackintosh, Neil (ed.), *Cyril Burt: Fraud or Framed?* (Oxford University Press, Oxford, 1995)

McConnell Stott, Andrew, *What Blest Genius?: The Jubilee That Made Shakespeare* (W. W. Norton, London, 2019)

McMahon, Darrin, *Divine Fury: A History of Genius* (Basic Books, New York, 2013)

Miller, Arthur I., *Einstein, Picasso: Space, Time, and the Beauty That Causes Havoc* (Basic Books, New York, 2001)

Murchison, Carl (ed.), *History of Psychology in Autobiography* (Clark University Press, Worcester, 1930)

Paige Harden, Kathryn, *The Genetic Lottery: Why DNA Matters for Social Equality* (Princeton University Press, Princeton, 2021)

Picasso, Marina, *Picasso: My Grandfather* (Chatto & Windus, London, 2001)

Plotz, David, *The Genius Factory: The Curious History of the Nobel Prize Sperm Bank* (Random House, New York, 2005)

Popoff, Alexandra, *Sophia Tolstoy: A Biography* (Free Press, New York, 2010)

Ritchie, Stuart, *Intelligence: All That Matters* (John Murray, London, 2015)

Roe, Sue, *The Private Lives of the Impressionists* (Vintage, London, 2007)

Rowland, Ingrid and Noah Charney, *Collector of Lives: Giorgio Vasari and the Invention of Art* (W. W. Norton, New York, 2017)

Serebriakoff, Victor, *IQ: A Mensa Analysis and History* (Hutchinson, London, 1966)

Shurkin, Joel N., *Broken Genius: The Rise and Fall of William Shockley, Creator of the Electronic Age* (Macmillan, London, 2006); *Terman's Kids: The Groundbreaking Study of How the Gifted Grow Up* (Little Brown, Boston, 1992)

Simonton, Dean Keith, *Greatness: Who Makes History and Why* (Guilford, New York, 1994)

Sontag, Susan, *Illness As Metaphor* (Allen Lane, London, 1979)

Steptoe, Andrew (ed.), *Genius and the Mind: Studies of Creativity and Temperament* (Oxford University Press, Oxford, 1998)

Stillinger, Jack, *Multiple Authorship and the Myth of the Solitary Genius* (Oxford University Press, Oxford, 1991)

Stross, Randall E., *The Wizard of Menlo Park: How Thomas Alva Edison Invented the Modern World* (Crown, New York, 2007)

Sulloway, Frank J., *Born to Rebel: Birth Order, Family Dynamics, and Creative Lives* (Abacus, London, 1996)

Swisher, Kara, *Burn Book: A Tech Love Story* (Piatkus, London, 2024)

Terman, Lewis, *Genetic Studies of Genius* (Stanford University Press, Redwood City, 1926)

Tolstoy, Sofia, *The Diaries of Sofia Tolstoy*, ed. Cathy Porter (Alma Books, London, 2017)

Toynton, Evelyn, *Jackson Pollock* (Yale University Press, New Haven, 2012)

van Gogh-Bonger, Jo, *A Memoir of Vincent Van Gogh* (Pallas Athene, London, 2023)

Vance, Ashlee, *Elon Musk: How the Billionaire CEO of SpaceX and Tesla Is Shaping Our Future* (Virgin Books, London, 2015)

Vasari, Giorgio, *The Lives of the Most Excellent Painters, Sculptors, and Architects* (1550, 1558; English modern translated edition: Everyman, New York, 1996)

Vickers, Julia, *Lou Von Salomé: A Biography of the Woman Who Inspired Freud, Nietzsche and Rilke* (McFarland, Jefferson, 2008)

Wachhorst, Wyn, *Thomas Alva Edison: An American Myth* (MIT, Cambridge, 1981)

Wilson, A. N., *Tolstoy* (Hamish Hamilton, London, 1988; updated edition, Atlantic Books, London, 2015)

Wootton, David, *Galileo: Watcher of the Skies* (Yale University Press, New Haven, 2010)

Wright Gilham, Nicholas, *A Life of Sir Francis Galton* (Oxford University Press, Oxford, 2001)

ARTICLES

Farber, Manny, 'White Elephant Art vs Termite Art', *Film Culture*, no. 27, (Winter 1962–1963), p. 196

Galton, Francis, 'Co-relations and Their Measurement, Chiefly from Anthropometric Data', *Proceedings of the Royal Society of London*, vol. 45 (1888), pp. 135–145

Hilmer, Michael J., Michael R. Ransom and Christina E. Wilmer, 'Fame and the Fortune of Academic Economists: How the Market Rewards Influential Research in Economics', *Southern Economic Journal*, vol. 82, no. 2 (October 2015)

Kleon, Austin, 'Further Notes on Scenius', 12 May 2017, https://www.austinkleon.com/2017/05/12/scenius

Leslie, Ian, '64 Reasons to Celebrate Paul McCartney', *The Ruffian*, 8 December 2020, https://ianleslie.substack.com/p/64-reasons-to-celebrate-paul-mccartney

Livio, Mario, 'Did Galileo Truly Say "And Yet It Moves"? A Modern Detective Story', *Scientific American*, 6 May 2020

McNutt, Steve, 'A Dangerous Man: Lewis Terman and George Stoddard, Their Debates on Intelligence Testing, and the Legacy of the Iowa Child Welfare Research Station', *The Annals of Iowa*, vol. 72 (2013), pp. 1–30

Merton, Robert K., 'The Matthew Effect in Science', *Science*, vol. 159 (January 1968)

Ogburn, William F., and Dorothy Thomas, 'Are Inventions Inevitable? A Note on Social Evolution', *Political Science Quarterly*, vol. 37, no. 1 (March 1922)

Pelosi, Anthony J., 'Personality and Fatal Diseases: Revisiting a Scientific Scandal', *Journal of Health Psychology* (2019)

Runciman, David, 'Competition Is for Losers', *London Review of Books*, 23 September 2021, https://www.lrb.co.uk/the-paper/v43/n18/david-runciman/competition-is-for-losers

Schaffer, Jennifer, 'The Wife Glitch', *The Baffler*, April 2020, https://www.thebaffler.com/outbursts/the-wife-glitch-schaffer

Silberman, Steve, 'The Geek Syndrome', *Wired*, December 2001, https://www.wired.com/2001/12/aspergers

Shorto, Russell, 'The Woman Who Made Van Gogh', *The New York Times Magazine*, 14 April 2021

Ward, Justin, 'More Smarter', *The Baffler*, 2019, https://www.thebaffler.com/latest/more-smarter-ward

Zunger, Yonatan, 'So, About This Googler's Manifesto', Medium, 6 August 2017, https://medium.com/@yonatanzunger/so-about-this-googlers-manifesto-1e3773ed1788